Mobile Ad-Hoc Networks: Applications

Mobile Ad-Hoc Networks: Applications

Editor

Zheng Yun Man

scitus academics

Mobile Ad-Hoc Networks: Applications
Edited by **Zheng Yun Man**

ISBN: 978-1-68117-506-5
Library of Congress Control Number: 2016943022

SCITUS Academics LLC,
www.scitusacademics.com
Box No. 4766, 616 Corporate Way,
Suite 2, Valley Cottage,
NY 10989

Printed in United States of America on Acid Free Paper

Preface

In the next generation of wireless communication systems, there will be a need for the rapid deployment of independent mobile users. Recent trends in compact computing and wireless technologies are expansion of ad hoc network. Ad hoc network consists of versatile flat forms which are free to move expeditiously. Ad hoc networks are multi-hop network that use wireless communication for transmission without any fixed infrastructure. The networks are form and deform on-the-fly without the need for any system. Ad hoc structure does not require an access point, it is easy to setup, especially in a small or temporary network. Each node in the network forwards the packet without the need of central administration. In ad hoc network, node acts as a router to send and receive the data. An advantage of the system is robustness, flexibility and mobility. Significant examples include establishing survivable, efficient, dynamic communication for emergency/rescue operations, disaster relief efforts, and military networks. Such network scenarios cannot rely on centralized and organized connectivity, and can be conceived as applications of Mobile Ad Hoc Networks. A Mobile Ad Hoc Network is an autonomous collection of mobile users that communicate over relatively bandwidth constrained wireless links. Since the nodes are mobile, the network topology may change rapidly and unpredictably over time. The network is decentralized, where all network activity including discovering the topology and delivering messages must be executed by the nodes they, i.e., routing functionality will be incorporated into mobile nodes. Being infrastructure-less and without central administration control, wireless ad-hoc networking is imparting a more and more significant role in spreading the coverage of traditional wireless infrastructure. The book Mobile Ad-Hoc Networks: Applications presents state-of the-art practices and resolutions for wireless ad-hoc networks. It emphasizes on the coverage of ad-hoc networks: vehicular ad-hoc networks, security and caching, TCP in ad-hoc networks and evolving applications.

Table of Contents

CHAPTER 1

A Multimedia Data Visualization Based on *Ad Hoc* Communication Networks and Its Application to Disaster Management

Youhei Kawamura [1,*], Markus Wagner [2], Hyongdoo Jang [3], Hajime Nobuhara [1], Takeshi Shibuya [1], Itaru Kitahara [1], Ashraf M Dewan [4] and Bert Veenendaal [4]

[1]Faculty of Engineering, Science and Information Systems, University of Tsukuba, Ibaraki Prefecture 305-8573, Japan

[2]School of Computer Science, University of Adelaide, Adelaide, SA 5005, Australia

[3]Department of Mining Engineering and Metallurgical Engineering, Curtin University, Perth, WA 6433, Australia

[4]Department of Spatial Sciences, Curtin University, Perth, WA 6433, Australia

ABSTRACT

After massive earthquakes and other large-scale disasters, existing communication infrastructure may become unavailable and, therefore, it can be quite difficult for relief organizations to fully grasp the impact of the disaster on the affected region. Consequently, this will be the cause of delays to offer the strategic assistance, and to provide water and food, *etc.* In order to solve the problem of re-establishing communication infrastructure to allow for information gathering, we developed an *ad hoc* mobile communications network for disaster-struck areas using ZigBee. As the communication speed of ZigBee is low, we propose a problem-specific image compression method for the multimedia data visualization. By using the proposed method combined with GPS information, it is possible to quickly grasp the damage situation in the region. Through our communication experiments in Tsukuba City, Japan we confirm the effectiveness of our system as a disaster information gathering and management system.

KEYWORDS

disaster; communications system; control of information

1. INTRODUCTION

When large-scale disasters strike, a quick damage assessment is very important. Especially in the early stages, because of an allocation limitation of available manpower, it will be a key task to rapidly develop a rescue strategy according to precise information. For example, immediately after the Great East Japan Earthquake in 2011, people could not use communication systems, such as mobile phones and the Internet, in disaster-struck areas. With this lack of communication systems, the decision-making process of aid allocation and appropriate rescue operation was delayed [1,2,3,4]. As a result, emergency provisions were not adequately delivered to some evacuation centers.

In this series of research, a disaster management system has been proposed by Ishii and Kawamura [5], which collects and manages disaster information in an integrated fashion at control centers *via ad hoc* networks in order to support rescue efforts, distributions of relief goods, and so on. Concretely, in case of the disaster, investigators or volunteers install ZigBee terminals (see Figure 1 for an example) that have been stored in the evacuation centers or at other safe storage places in areas with interrupted communications infrastructure immediately after the occurrence of a major disaster. After installation, an *ad hoc* network is constructed automatically. The locations of these terminals are determined by the radio wave propagation analysis and optimal placement method that was developed by Ishii and Kawamura [5]. Investigators who are investigating the damages with the help of PCs or PDAs can gather information and transfer these data to the control center via the created ZigBee network. Additionally, it is possible that affected members of the public join the efforts of the professional relief organizations and share their information using their own PCs or PDAs.

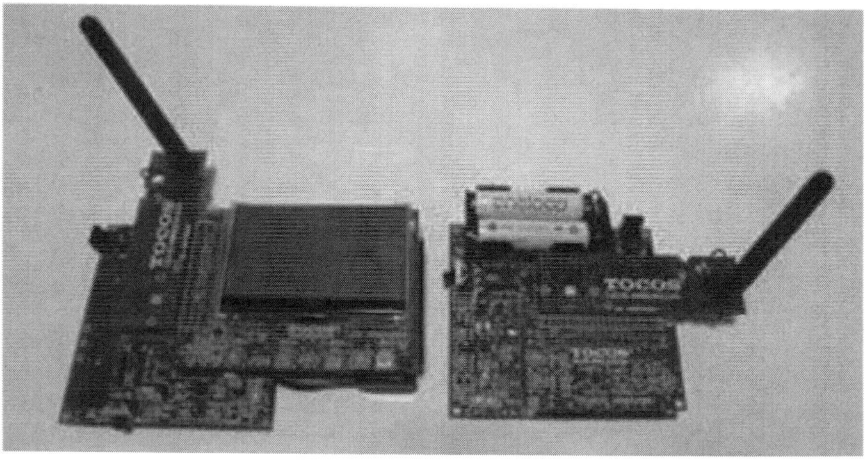

Figure 1. ZigBee module used in this study.

Through this long-term research project, a disaster information management system will be developed and the communication speed, its availability, and the terminal installation time between the control center and evacuation centers will be assessed. As the ZigBee communication network standard is not suitable for the transmission of large volumes of data such as image data due to its low transmission rate (256 kbps), we propose a new transmission method that is the combination of GPS information and improved PIC format compression that focuses on spatial information. In a real-world experiment, we assess the effectiveness and the compression ratios by using our proposed disaster information management system.

The structure of this article is as follows. In Chapter 2, we provide an overview of the whole proposed disaster information management system. Then, we propose our method of transmitting and receiving maps in low-speed communication systems in Chapter 3. Finally, we describe in Chapter 4 our experiments of sending and receiving data in Tsukuba City, Japan.

2. DISASTER INFORMATION MANAGEMENT SYSTEMS

2.1. Current Status of Disaster Information Management

Currently, Multi-Channel Access (MCA) wireless communication systems and Ushahidi are put into effect as disaster information management systems after disasters.

Ushahidi (Figure 2, Watanabe *et al.* [6,7]) is the system that was used when the riots occurred during the elections in Kenya (2008). This open source web service was created to share information where such incidents occurred. Concretely, users can send information, such as "There is a riot in the area A" or "There is crime in the area B" via email, which will then appear on top of Google Maps. It has also been used to help collect situational information about military actions in the Gaza Strip (2009), Haiti (2010), after the earthquake and tsunami in Japan (2011), to monitor the elections in India and Mexico (2009), and in other cases. When the Great East Japan Earthquake occurred, the disaster information managing system named "sinsai.info", which is based on Ushahidi, was not only used to grasp the situation of the disaster area, but also to collect and share information about water supplies, official announcements, notices, news, and evacuation calls. It was quickly available and lots of people could understand the situation with the help of the online information visualization. *Via* email, posts on websites, and *via* the information sharing service Twitter it was possible to collect information continuously.

In contrast to the web service Ushahidi, MCA (Multi-Channel Access System) is a commercial wireless communication system (Figure 3). It supports a large number of system users and can use a variety of radio channels. This system consists of a "control station" that the operating body installs and manages, and of "command" and "mobile stations" that the users install and manage in order to achieve radio communication between the units. For example, this system can be used by local governments to share information with fire-fighters and emergency personnel, even if both teams use different wireless communication technology.

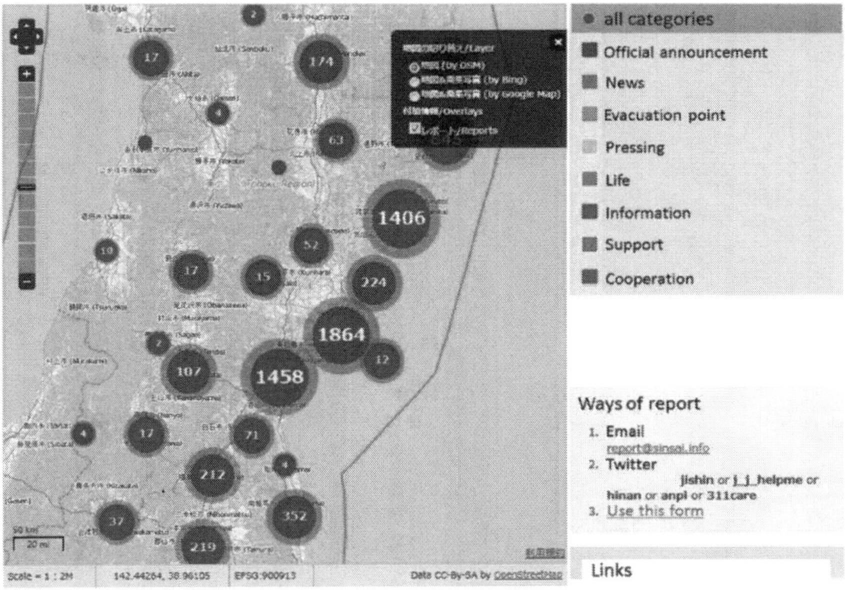

Figure 2. One example of a system based on Ushahidi.

2.2. Overview of the Proposed Zigbee Disaster Control System

When a large-scale disaster such as the Great East Japan Earthquake occurs, the damage can be severe enough to take out MCA control stations, as well as fixed-line telephones, mobile phone stations, *etc.* Consequently, it can become difficult to use any of the two above-described disaster information management systems. We consider it an essential requirement for disaster control systems that wireless communication system can work even in such situations where hardly any previously existing infrastructure is available.

In this long-term research project, we develop a disaster information management system that uses the ZigBee communication standard (http://www.zigbee.org/). Figure 4 shows the overall flow of the proposed system. The disaster information management system is installed on PCs located in the control center and in the evacuation centers. This system contains the GIS data (*i.e.*, the geographical map data). The following is the organizational flow of the proposed system:

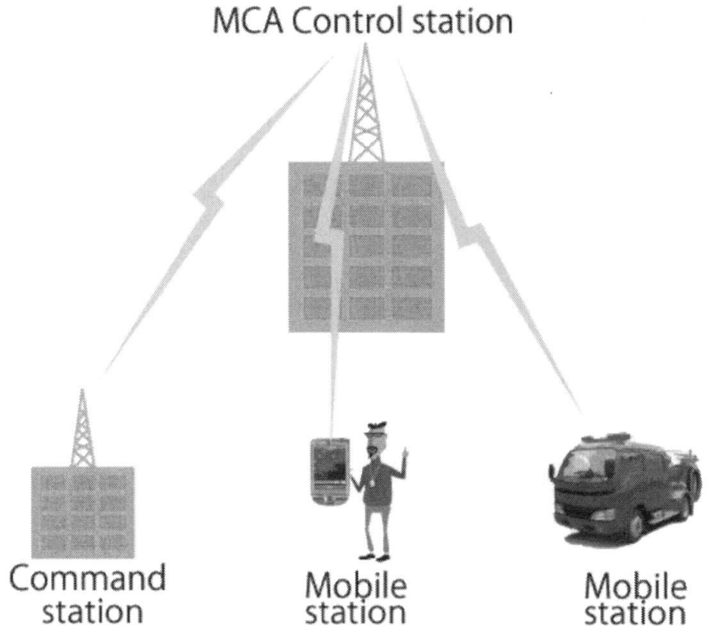

Figure 3. One example of a system based on the Multi-Channel Access System.

[Step ①] Immediately after the disaster (Corresponding to ① in Figure 4), the optimal allocation of ZigBee terminals between the control center and evacuation centers is calculated by using the PC in the control center.

[Step ②] The maps are updated with the of Step ① (Corresponding to ② in Figure 4).

[Step ③] Figure 5 illustrates a "ZigBee positioning situation". The communication terminal equipment carried by the investigators has a ZigBee communication module and a GPS module (corresponding to the red square in Figure 5); it must also display the coverage map using a PC or PDA (corresponding to ② in Figure 4). ZigBee terminals (assumed to have been stockpiled in the city hall or in evacuation centers within hours after the disaster) are placed along the way according to the computed optimal arrangement (Corresponding to ③ in Figure 4).

[Step ④] After the deployment of the ZigBee terminals, data transfers across the ZigBee network are available within the ranges that are visualized on the digital map (Corresponding to ④ of Figure 4). After this installation, this system will continue to work until the batteries run out after several months, or until the terminal are collected again.

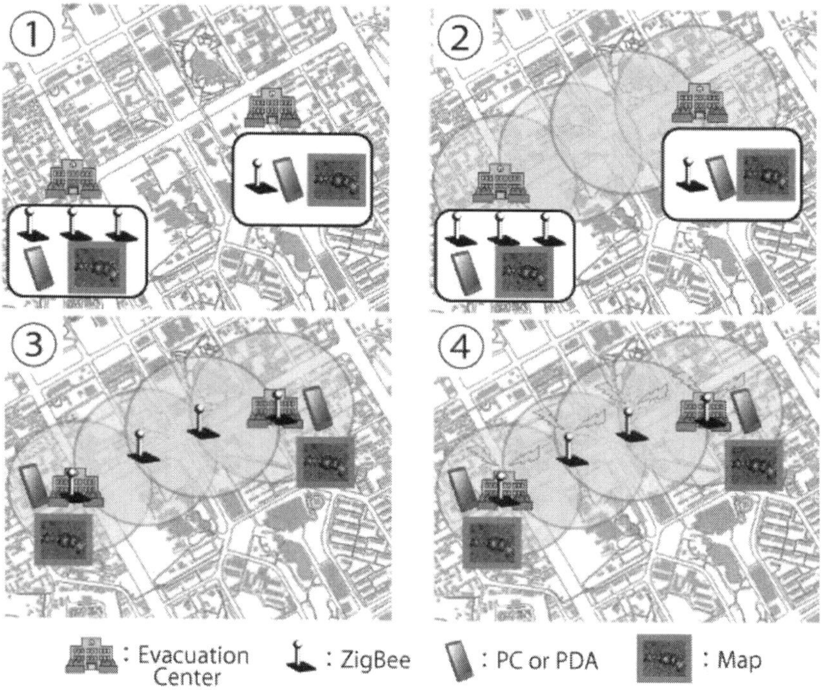

Figure 4. The process of establishing connections between centers: when the evacuation centers are established ①, the ZigBee network is planned ②, then the ZigBee nodes are located ③, and the network can be used ④.

Disaster information is information on a variety of materials, such as water supply information, official announcements, notices, news, and location of evacuation centers. In our case, disaster information consists of GPS data and text data, which is displayed on a map as a blue square. In our system, these texts (information) are displayed on the right of the map in chronological order, and once they are selected the corresponding information is highlighted. Additionally, GPS information is highlighted as a color change from blue to green (corresponding to the green of Figure 5), and the relevant text comes up to the first line (corresponding to the yellow of Figure 5). If the PDA or PC have been newly added to this system, or that system is re-connected after a temporary cut of the connection to the network, it is possible to acquire missing information by using the "request update function".

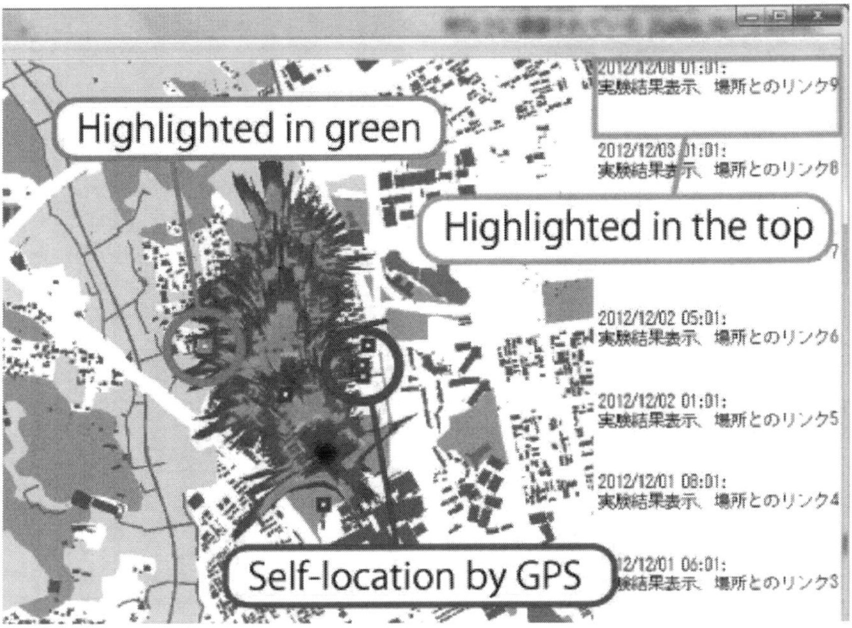

Figure 5. Screen of the proposed system.

2.2.1. ZigBee Network

ZigBee is one of the communication standards for wireless sensor networks, and it has mainly been used in instrumentation control (see, for example, Kawamura *et al.* [2]).

Table 1 is a comparison of ZigBee with other typical wireless communication standards. Due to its characteristics, ZigBee is suitable, for example, for building automation, industrial automation, and home automation. Furthermore, ZigBee is also used in automatic meter reading, in security systems, and in remote control.

Table 1. Comparison of different communication standards.

Name	ZigBee	Wi-Fi	Bluetooth
Communication distance	10–3000 m	100 m	10 m
Communication speed	250 kbps	11 Mbps	1 Mbps
Network capacity	65,536 nodes	32 nodes	7 nodes
Life-time on battery	several months	several hours	several days
Application	instrumentation control	wireless LAN	wireless accessories

ZigBee has the following four advantages for our scenario:

- Support of a large network

As up to 65,635 terminals ("ZigBees") can be configured to form one wireless network, and the configuration can happen independently of location and time.

- *Ad hoc* network

It is easy to build an *ad hoc* network, and more stable communication can be realized by providing a higher density of terminals along the intended transfer paths.

- Low electric power consumption

Maintaining a long-term battery-powered network is possible.

- Low cost

The costs of the ZigBee terminals are low, so it is possible to configure a wide area network by using a large number of them.

With the recent introduction of Bluetooth Low Energy (BLE) a competitor to ZigBee has been developed. While the energy consumption of BLE is significantly below that of Bluetooth, other features still make it unsuitable for our purposes (see for example, Mohan *et al.* [8] and Baker [9]). First, BLE is designed for small, local area networks and it is typically set up in star topologies or in one-to-one connections. ZigBee on the other hand is typically run in wider area networks and in mesh topologies that are significantly more robust when individual nodes fail. This is why we decided to build our disaster information management system based on ZigBee.

Despite these desirable advantages, ZigBee has the disadvantage of providing a relatively low communication speed. In practice this means that it is possible to send and receive data, such as text data of some kilobytes, however, it is difficult to transmit and receive multimedia data of some megabytes. To compensate for this problem, we are using a lightweight text-based communication in the present system. For the transmission of map data, we require significantly compressed data.

2.2.2. Optimized Arrangement Method and Radio Wave Propagation Analysis

It is necessary to construct the network as quickly as possible immediately after the disaster. In order to establish communication between the control center and all evacuation centers, we must decide on the installation locations of the ZigBee terminals. While deciding, we must consider the locations of woodland and water, because these influence the signal attenuation. There is also a need to respond flexibly to changes in the map information, as structures can collapse, and tsunamis and earthquakes can uproot forests. It is necessary to invest a small amount of computation time for estimating the radio wave propagation.

A radio wave propagation analysis method that was developed by Kawamura *et al.* is used in this system. This method uses a sequential tracking method that considers the transmission along the line-of-sight only (no transmission through obstacles, reflections, and diffractions) to reduce the computational complexity. The radio attenuation is estimated for different types of vegetation, and digital maps created based on GIS (Geographic Information System) to get the geographic information in the affected area (Ishii and Kawamura [5]). This method is then used by an iterated ray-launching method that greedily connects the control center with the evacuation sites; the eventual terminal locations are then determined along the paths of the simulated connections. The same algorithms are used by Moridi *et al.* [10] in a mine monitoring and communication system.

3. TRANSMITTING AND RECEIVING MAP-DATA IN LOW-SPEED COMMUNICATION

It can be expected that severe disasters change the geographical information, for example, the vegetation is changed, as are man-made structures. Nevertheless, it is necessary that members of the public and of relief organizations can communicate, even when the variations happen. In order to deal with such alterations, our system predicts the radio wave propagation and computes the optimal arrangement using the new map that is obtained and sent to each evacuation center after the disaster. Figure 6 shows the proposed map data transmission method. New map data based on satellite images can be available a few hours after a disaster. This, then, allows us to optimally arrange the terminals based on the situation at hand. Investigators, who have PCs or PDAs to collect disaster related information, need the map of the area and also a visualization of the available range of the radio communication. Therefore, an operator at an evacuation center needs to send updated geographical information (bit-mapped image, ① in Figure 6 shows in the red square the map as updated by a person who is present at the site) based on updated GPS information that is obtained via PCs and PDAs. All information will be combined for the modified map (② in Figure 6 shows the original map, ③ in Figure 6 shows the new map).

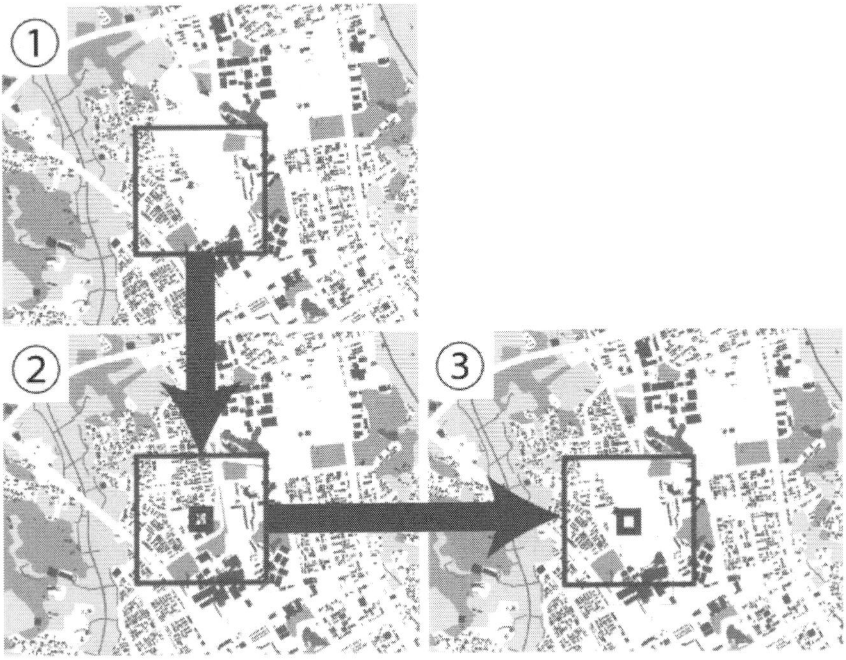

Figure 6. Map data update method.

Initially, this map image would be a bitmap and its image size would be too large to send across low-speed communication networks, such as a ZigBee network; therefore, image-compression is necessary. In this chapter, we propose a new problem-specific image-compression method.

3.1. Existing Image-Compression Methods

The PIC image format can be used for images that have continuous large areas of same colors, such as maps showing geographical information. Our method adopts PIC's run-length encoding method to longitudinal (vertical) direction and it has the characteristic of invertible transformation; for an in-depth description, see Carlson [11].

Figure 7 shows the image-compression method by PIC. Figure 7a shows the original state of the image. First of all, the picture is explored for each pixel from upper left to lower right line-by-line. If the color of an exploring pixel is same as some of the next pixel, the color information of the next one is deleted. If the color of the exploring pixel is different from some of the next pixel, the color information of next one is kept. This process is repeated until the lower right corner of the image is reached in order to find all the points where the color changes. Afterwards, all such points form "chains" from the top to the bottom of the image (Figure 7, ■ and ▲). In the actual compression step, the distances between the points where the colors change is recorded, as is the color itself, and also the direction of the chain and the offset.

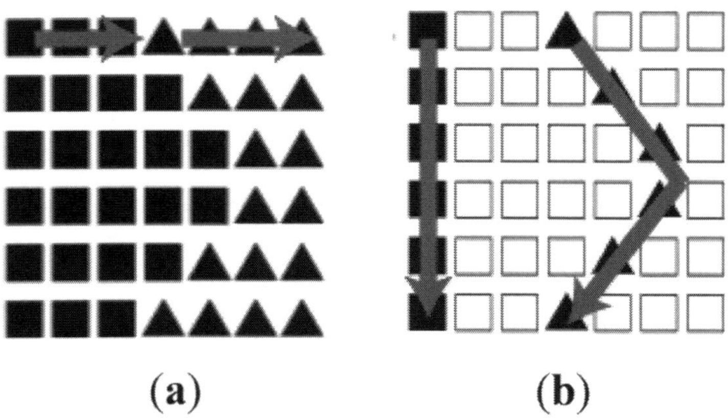

Figure 7. PIC format. (**a**) shows the original picture, (**b**) the right outlines the compression technique.

3.2. Proposed Image-Compression Method

The proposed method is an adaption of the PIC method to improve the compression for disaster-related information management systems. Images of maps have few colors because the colors represent just a small number of geographical information categories. The correspondences of geographical information and colors are stored in a database. Since this database does not change, the control center, the evacuation centers, and the investigators can share it in advance. In the database, geographical information and colors are encoded using three bits, e.g., “000 = road, 001 = water area, *etc.*”. We call this suggested compression method GIM-format (Geographical Information Image). In case further data compression is necessary, we will limit the GIM images to only the sector around the current investigators (suggested image data size is 400 × 400 pixels). We will call this method GIMS-format (GIM Sector).

3.3. Comparison of Image-Compression Methods

Figure 8 shows map images that have four different levels of detail. First, we compress each image with GIM, GIMS, PIC, GIF, PNG, and JPEG using Adobe Illustrator; then we compare the resulting data-sizes. The original image data size is 28,473 kB (3006 × 2622 pixels, bitmap format). Note that, in the case of the GIMS-format, we report the mean of nine 400 × 400 pixels cut-outs from the original image.

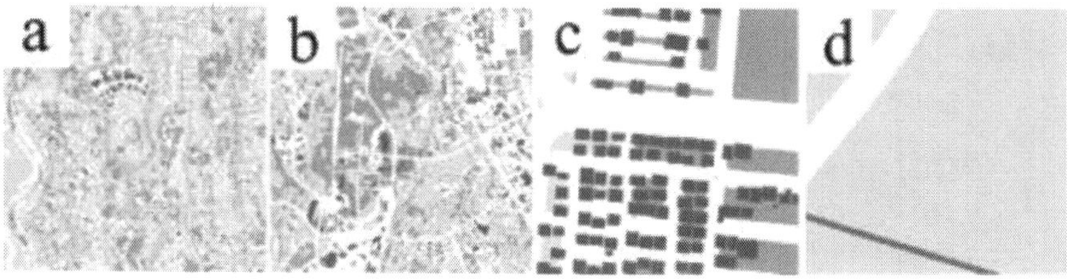

Figure 8. Image data used. The four figures (**a**–**d**) show shows map sections at four different levels of detail.

The results of the compressions are shown in Table 2. The GIM- and GIMS-format are the most effective compression methods. The resulting size of the GIM-format is approximately half of the others format images (except PIC-format) and is about 0.6 times the size of the PIC-format. In particular, the more large areas of the same colors are in the images, the more effective the compression is. PIC is more effective for images that have many small areas of same colors. This complements the effectiveness of the GIM-format for images that have many areas of same color.

Table 2. Comparison of compression methods, number are file sizes in KB.

	a	**b**	**c**	**d**
GIMS	3.62	3.43	0.43	0.14
GIM	252	161	21	6
PIC	355	226	26	8
GIF	567	350	79	20
PNG	615	444	66	50
JPG	980	824	268	187

It is shown that all images can be compressed to 4k bytes or less by cutting out the important sections; thus, dividing the images makes it possible to transmit only necessary map information via the low-speed ZigBee network.

4. EVALUATION EXPERIMENT FOR THE PROPOSED SYSTEM

4.1. Outline of the Evaluation Experiment

We conducted three experiments to evaluate the proposed disaster control system.

1) Following the system flow, the time is measured for the calculation of the optimal locations of four ZigBee terminals.

2) The experimenters transmit and receive disaster related information at 20 different spots. On each spot, the communication speed and the communication quality were measured.

3) Then, the experimenters obtain new map information about their vicinity from a control center using GPS information and update it. After that, the new range of the radio communication is calculated and visualized.

The investigated area for the installation of the ZigBee terminals is 800 × 500 meters around Kasuga 4-chome of Tsukuba City, Japan. Figure 9 shows the calculated optimal arrangement of ZigBee terminals. In the first experiment, four ZigBee terminals were placed; the time was measured while an experimenter placed the terminals.

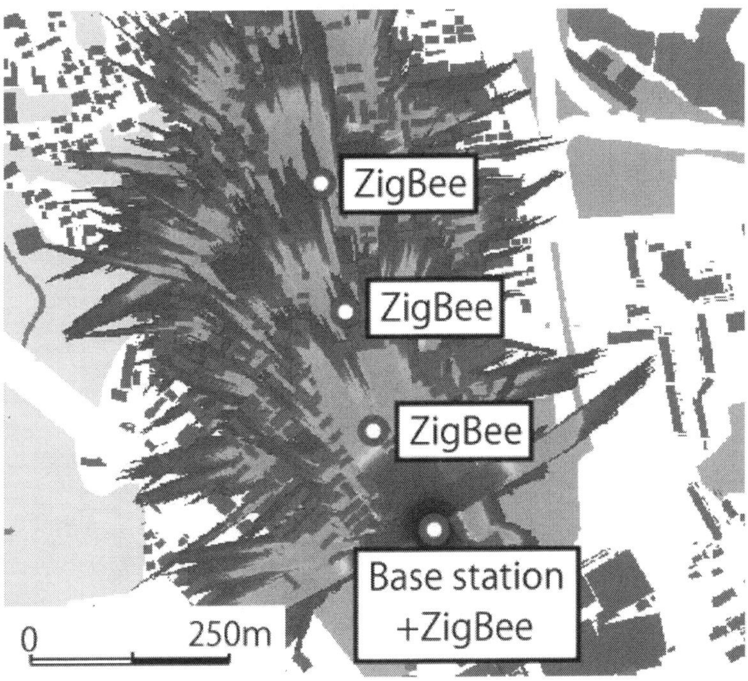

Figure 9. Figure of placement plan.

In the second experiment, the data transmitted and received consists of GPS data and "a communication experiment spot + the number of spot". The data was transmitted from a PC at an evacuation center to a PC on a control center through the ZigBee network. Additionally, the time required to send text data was measured using synchronized clocks on both PCs. By comparing the time-stamps of the messages with the receiving PC's time, we could calculate the transmission times. In addition, we consider a special (and likely) scenario in this second experiment: in one of the 20 measurements, an investigator leaves the area with ZigBee network coverage while investigating (either accidentally or on purpose) and then returns back into the ZigBee covered area. For this scenario, we have implemented a "request update function" to fetch data from the evacuation center was not received due to the missing signal.

In the third experiment, the map image only around an investigator (experimenter) was cut out and the map data was compressed at the evacuation center. The compressed image was sent to the control center and uncompressed. This process was conducted five times at different spots. As in Section 3, the original image size was 3006 × 2622 pixels, while the images were cut out into the size of 400 × 400 pixels for the GIMS-format.

4.2. Results of the Evaluation Experiment

In this section, we describe the results of our study in Tsukuba City, Japan. In this study, we measured the setup time needed, we measured the availability and speed of our ZigBee network, and we updated the geographical information locally and centrally.

4.2.1. Installation and Preparation Time

The experiment's starting time was 13:40 and system installation and preparation was completed at 14:12. In these roughly 30 min four ZigBee terminals (including the control center) were placed according to optimal arrangement calculated with a PC in an evacuation center. Based on results of a previous experiment in this area, it was assumed that one person can cover (investigate) 0.4 km^2 area in 30 min. We can use these numbers to estimate the resources needed in a real large-scale disaster: if the residential area of Tsukuba City (241.07 km^2) would be struck by a disaster, only 100 people (with 24 ZigBees each) would be needed to establish complete coverage with our proposed system within three hours.

4.2.2. Communication Availability

Figure 10 shows the results of transmitting and receiving the multimedia data at 20 spots. 19 spots were located inside of coverage of ZigBee communication and one was located "out of range" as described above. At 13 spots (Figure 10, numbers on white background) out of the 19 spots, data reception was possible. At the six others spots (Figure 10, numbers on red background), communication failed. There are buildings or elevated areas between these spots (Figure 10, numbers 8, 10, 12, 14, 16). The reasons of these failures are probably diffractions of the radio waves. As reflection, diffraction, and permeation of radio waves were not considered when the radio wave attenuation was estimated, the estimation error will be large in case there are a lot of buildings at that moment. Data obtained by an experimenter at spot 15 (Figure 10, yellow square) was stored when it was observed, and it was sent after the experimenter came inside the coverage of the ZigBee network. Subsequently, the stored data was received at the control center. This was a successful proof of the concept that an investigator can collect data while being out of the communication range and then share this data when coming into the communication range again.

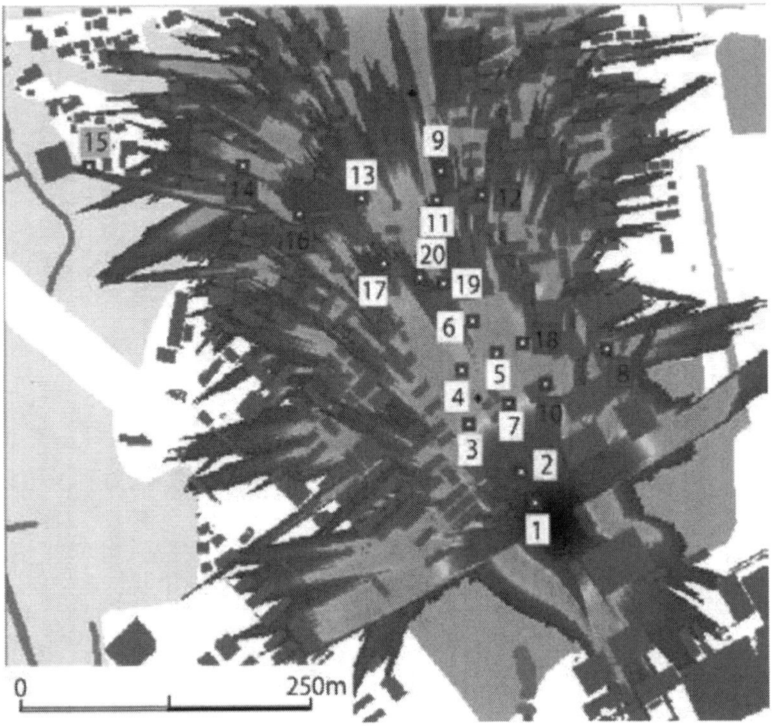

Figure 10. Experimental results of communication situation.

4.2.3. Communication Speed

Figure 11 shows the communication speed at each spot. Communication speeds were measured while the data was transmitted from an evacuation center to a control center at each spots. The images were transmitted and received at 300 ms intervals to prevent one image from splitting into two data sets. Many results concentrated around 300 ms regardless of the distance between the measured spot and the control center, and regardless of how many terminals the data went through. Interestingly, at three spots (Figure 11, numbers 5, 11, 17), results are around 700 ms. This means that first transmission or recipient failed, so the data was transmitted a second time. Thus, the resulting communication time increased to approximately 300 × 2 (ms).

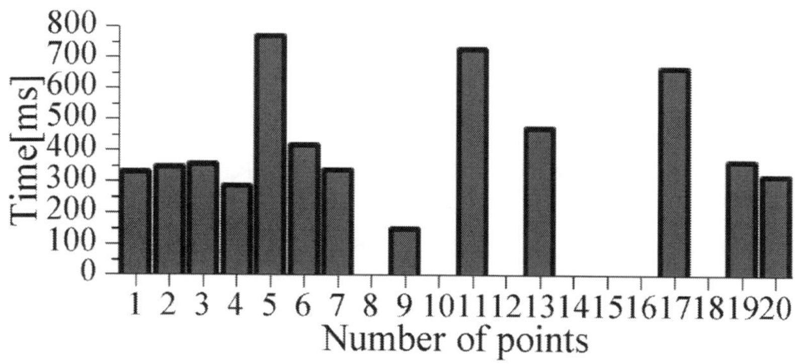

Figure 11. Experimental results of the communication speed tests.

4.2.4. Sending and Receiving Geographical Data Updates

Figure 12 shows the process of a geographical information update (image update) with a PC in an evacuation center. ① inFigure 12 is sent by an investigator to the control center after a disaster, and ② in Figure 12 is a stored image obtained before a disaster at an evacuation center. ③ in Figure 12 in the evacuation center is update from ② to ① only around the investigators GPS location. ④ in Figure 12 shows the result of prediction of radio wave propagation based on the old pre-disaster map and ⑤ in Figure 12 shows the result of it based on the updated post-disaster map. Using only the geographical information around an investigator significantly reduces the size of the transmitted data; moreover, the investigators know where to go to communicate based on the updated coverage prediction, so they can easily receive and transmit disaster-related information.

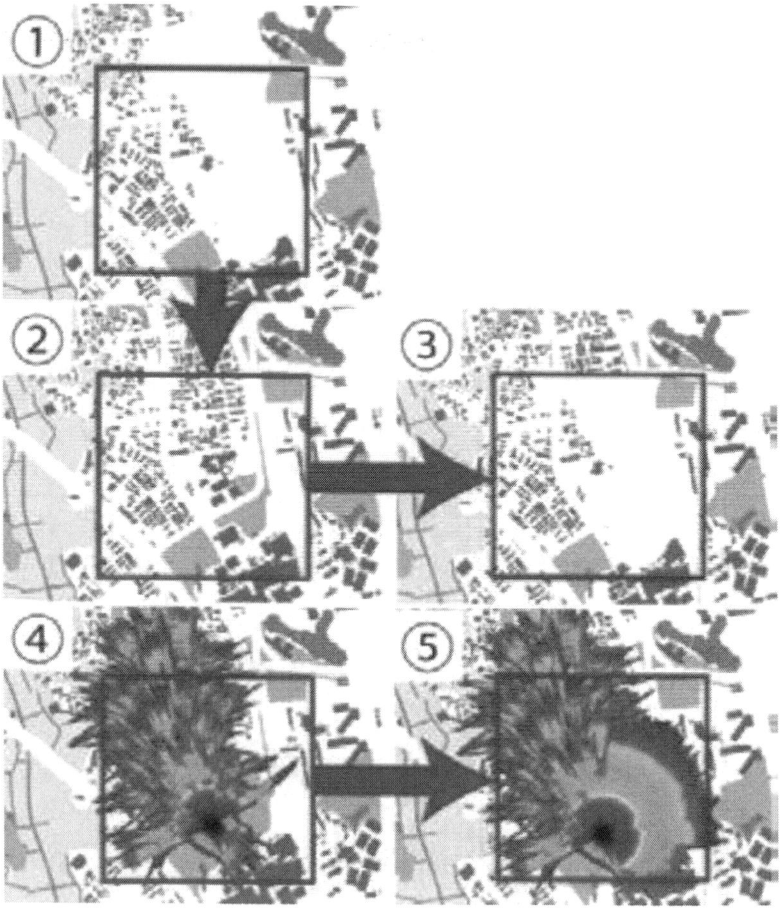

Figure 12. Experimental results of sending and receiving geographical data updates.

5. CONCLUSIONS

In this article, we described and evaluated a ZigBee wireless communication system that can be used to quickly gather information and to coordinate efforts when existing communication networks are become unavailable.

We proposed the GIM-format for geographical information and compared it with other image-compression methods. The size of GIM-format compressed images is approximately half of those generated by the other formats (except for the PIC-format). In particular, when the images have many large areas of identical colors (as it is the case of geographical data), the compression is very effective. In addition, we showed that the file size can be reduced further by limiting the image dimensions to the area of interest around the investigator's GPS location.

Through extensive experiments in Tsukuba City, we confirmed that our proposed disaster communication system can be used to gather disaster-related information and to send that data to the control center, which can then update the map for all investigators.

In addition, the experiment of transmitting and receiving map-data proved that the method is effective for the low-speed communication network of ZigBee terminals.

To conclude, the proposed disaster control system can be an alternative communication infrastructure when existing infrastructure is damaged by a major disaster. The system is easy to use even for laypeople, which enables the affected people to assist the professional organizations in their emergency relief efforts.

ACKNOWLEDGMENTS

The authors would like to thank the reviewers and the editors for their comprehensive feedback, which helped to improve the quality of the article.

AUTHOR CONTRIBUTIONS

All authors collaborated on this article in different ways that range from the inception of the idea, to the implementation of the tool, the conduct of the study, and the editing of the article. All authors contributed enough to warrant their coauthorship.

CONFLICTS OF INTEREST

The authors declare no conflict of interest.

REFERENCES

1. Sugit, H.; Fukuta, T.; Tamura, T.; Yokoi, T.; Hara, T.; Kashima, T.; Azuhata, T.; Shibasaki, B.; Yagi, Y. IISEE-NET: Information network for earthquake disaster mitigation of developing countries. In *Bulletin of the International Institute of Seismology and Earthquake Engineering*; Building Research Institute: Ibaraki, Japan, 2003; pp. 137–143.

2. Kawamura, Y.; Dewan, A.; Veenendaal, B.; Shibuya, T.; Hayashi, M.; Kitahara, I.; Nobuhara, H.; Ishii, K. Using GIS to develop a mobile communications network for disaster-damaged areas. *Int. J. Digit. Earth* **2014**, *7*, 279–293.

3. Kawamura, Y.; Ishii, K.; Jang, H.; Wagner, M.; Nobuhara, H.; Dewan, A.; Veenendaal, B.; Kitahara, I. Analysis of radio wave propagation in an urban environment and its application to initial disaster response support. *J. Dis. Res.* **2015**,*10*, 655–666.

4. Nakahata, Y.; Kawamura, Y. Development of the landslide observation system using ZigBee. In Proceedings of the 2010 Society of Instrument and Control Engineers Annual Conference (SICE), Taipei, Taiwan, 18–21 August 2010; pp. 1191–1194.

5. Ishii, K.; Kawamura, Y. Analysis of radio wave propagation in an urban environment and its application to initial disaster response support. In Proceedings of the 2010 Society of Instrument and Control Engineers Annual Conference (SICE), Taipei, Taiwan, 18–21 August 2010; pp. 1195–1198.

6. Watanabe, N.; Uno, K. Utilization of sensor Web and spatial information platform as a supportive measure for field work monitoring. *Rep. Inst. Sci. Tech. Res.* **2011**, *23*, 62–66.

7. Watanabe, K.; Ichikawa, T. A study of the information exchanging system for a person requiring care at the time of earthquake disaster. *SIG Tech. Rep.* **2006**, *92*, 25–29.

8. Mohan, M.; George, N.; Davis, D. ZigBee technology for data communication—A comparative study with other wireless technologies. *Int. J. Adv. Res. Comput. Sci.* **2014**, *5*, 261–265.

9. Baker, N. ZigBee and Bluetooth strengths and weaknesses for industrial applications. *Comput. Contr. Engin. J.* **2005**, *16*, 20–25.

10. Moridi, M.A.; Kawamura, Y.; Sharifzadeh, M.; Chanda, E.K.; Wagner, M.; Jang, H.; Okawa, H. Development of underground mine monitoring

and communication system integrated ZigBee and GIS. *Int. J. Min. Sci. Technol.* **2015**. in press.

11. Carlson, W.E. A Survey of Computer Graphics Image Encoding and Storage Formats. *Comput. Graph.* **1991**, *25*, 67–75.

CHAPTER 2

Efficient Location Services Using Hierarchical Topology of Mobile Ad Hoc Networks

Prasad Naik Hamsavath, G. V. Singh

School of Computer and Systems Science, Jawaharlal Nehru University, New Delhi, India.

ABSTRACT

The thesis work was carried out in two phases. Firstly, we have designed the Cluster-Based Object Location Services (CBOLS) for finding the object location in a cluster based network topology. Secondly, to take the advantages of clustering architecture of Mobile Ad hoc Networks, we have especially designed Object Location Clusters Algorithm (OLCA) for efficient Object Location management in MANET. Our comparison of simulation analysis shows that the CBOLS is more efficient and accurate in location information services and more robust than GLS and HRLS. In addition, we believe that our comparative study with the various location services schemes was facilitated accurate results in ad hoc networks. we are portioned our network area by designing a new clustering algorithm called OLCA (Object Location Clusters Algorithm) for efficient object location in Mobile Ad hoc Networks. Simulation results and comparative analysis shows the performance and effectiveness of CBOLS and OLC.

KEYWORDS

Location; Clusters; Objects; Nodes; MANET

1. INTRODUCTION

Location information has recently been applied to MANET [1]. There are three types of Location Services are available with the Mobile Ad hoc Networks. Such are Proactive, Reactive and Hybrid as explained at **Figure 1**.

In order to provide end-to-end communication throughout the network, mobile nodes must cooperate in handling network topology functions. It is very challenging issue in order to maintain the location information of the mobile hosts due to absence of centralized/dedicated servers in Mobile ad-hoc networks. Therefore location management becomes an important issue.

2. LITERATURE REVIEW

Routing protocols [2-6] are studied as a part of our research and an important subject. A variety of location based routing protocols [7-12] are exist and these protocols are of good scalability, and less overhead. These protocols usually assume that its part of the algorithm for obtaining location's information with the help of a global position system (GPS) [13]. Though these protocols seem to offer better location services, but they increase the routing delay time due to updation of location services as part of its algorithm. So, it is necessary to design an efficient algorithm for better location updates and searches. Clustering for efficient location services in MANET by utilizing the benefits of clusters for achieving the better throughput and performance.

After study of literature review, we have exclusively proposed a cluster based location services protocol called Cluster Based Object Location Services (CBOLS) for efficient location updates and searches.

3. CBOL ALGORITHM

1) Initialize LOCN packet;[1]

2) Initialize LACK packet;

3) Initialize LREQ packet;

4) Initialize LREP packet;

5) int Location Registration() {

6) broadcast LOCN to its neighbors;

7) Acknowledge LACK who receive LOCN;

8) for (LOCN=0; LOCN ≤ its neighbors; LOCN++) do;

9) if (LOCN received = true) do;

10) send LACK;

11) return LACK;

12) else

13) repeat step 8; }

14) call Location Query();

15) int Location Query(){

16) do

17) broadcast LREQ to its destination node via its Clusterheads;

18) record its field in Location_table before sending LREQ;

19) if (CH received LREQ = true) do

20) record its LREQ field in its Location_table;

21) if (check LREQ field seen previously = true) do

22) discard LREQ packet;

23) 23) else if (LREQ field & CH Location_table field = true) do {

24) send LREP packet;

25) return LREP;

26) Terminate(); }

27) else if (LREQ field & CH Location_table field ! = true) do

28) send LREQ packet to its nearest CH via Gateway;

29) check if (two Gate exists = true) do

30) Find the shortest path using CH routing table entries;

31) Send LREQ packet to its nearest Gateway having highest weight;

32) if (GW received LREQ = true) do

33) record its LREQ field in its Location_table;

34) if (check LREQ field seen previously = true) do

35) discard LREQ packet;

36) else if (LREQ field & GW Location_table field = true) do {

37) send LREP packet;

38) return LREP;

39) Terminate(); }

40) else if (LREQ field & GW Location_table field ! = true) do

41) send LREQ to its nearest CH;

42) if (CH received LREQ = true) do

43) record its LREQ field in Location_table;

44) if (check LREQ field seen previously = true) do

45) discard LREQ packet;

46) else if (LREQ field & CH Location_table field = true) do {

47) send LREP packet;

48) return LREP;

49) 59) Terminate(); }

50) else

51) repeat step 23 - 49; }

52) void Terminate();{

53) Exit Application(); }

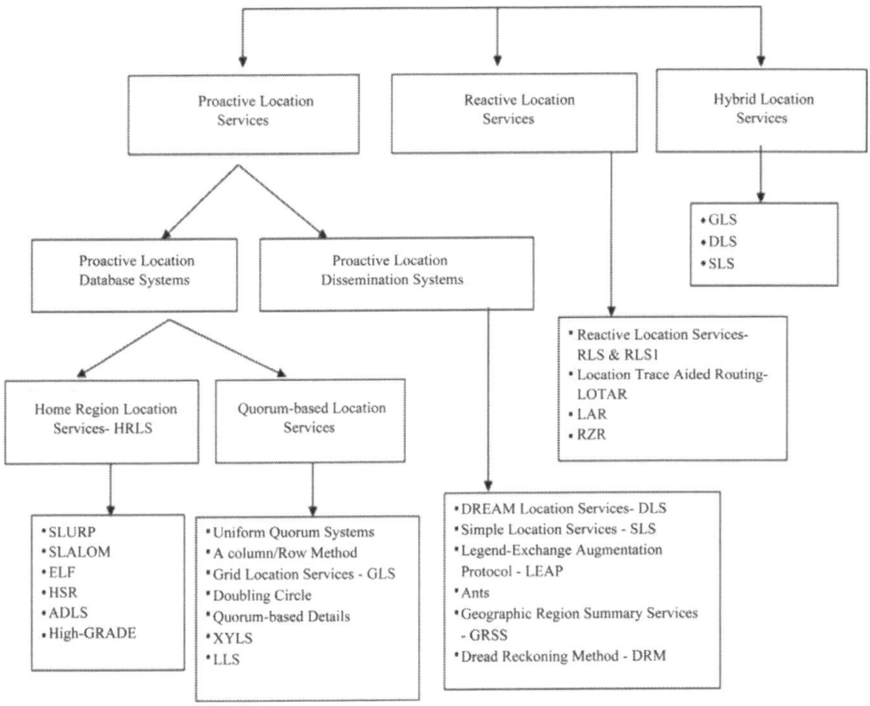

Figure 1. Types of location services in MANET.

4. SIMULATION

For simulation purposes, we have used GloMoSim (Global Mobile Information System Simulator-Zeng et al., [14] 1998). GloMoSim is a discrete event parallel environment for large wireless and wireline communication networks. GloMoSim uses a parallel discrete-event simulation capability provided by PARSEC (PARallel Simulation Environment for Complex systems) (Bagrodia [15], 1998). PARSEC is a C-based discrete-event simulation language developed by the Parallel computing laboratory at UCLA, for sequential and parallel execution of discrete-event simulation models. It can also be used as a parallel programming language. GloMoSim is developed at UCLA (California, USA) and is the second most popular wireless network simulator.

5. PERFORMANCE ANALYSIS OF CBOLS

In this simulation work we have compared the metrics with Grid Location Services (GLS) and Home Region Location Services (HRLS) with our proposed ClusterBased Object Location Services (CBOLS). Our simulation result shows the average location registration cost at 550 nodes at the mobility rate at 10 m/s compared with GLS and HRLS.

The below **Figure 2** depicts that our CBOLS (ClusterBased Object Location Services) shows the minimum registration cost when compared with GLS and HRLS. Even though the GLS and HRLS results are similar, the CBOLS show better result as the cost of a node to register in the network is very low. Each node in the network gets registered with each cluster while the cluster is being formed.

Figure 3 shows the average location update cost of all the nodes in the network. In CBOLS, we see, the location update cost grows much more slowly than GLS and HRLS so we can define CBOLS update cost as O (v log N) vs O (v $\sqrt{N}$). When the number of nodes (N) of the network density (order O) grows, the number of location update cost (v log N) also grows along with the varied network density.

Figure 4 shows that the average location finding cost at each node differs with High Region Location Service (HRLS) which is basically without cluster based network. This is a usually a static network where all the nodes are stable in routing and location information services. Whereas, the GLS and CBOLS illustrate similar results with location finding cost at each node, CBOLS exhibits better result than GLS, in its overall finding cost scale.

The **Figure 5** shows that the average location maintenance cost at each cluster is minimum with CBOLS, compared to GLS. However, GLS and CBOLS show similar results. The location maintenance cost grows as the number of nodes in the network increases. Moreover HRLS cost is very high and performs very poor as node density grows.

The **Figure 6** illustrates the average control overheadcost at each node where CBOLS is stable and increases control overhead while network density grows. But HRLS average overhead cost is showing worst performance. However, it is stable between CBOLS and GLS and the result shows that they are similar as the number of nodes increases. But still CBOLS perform better in comparison with GLS.

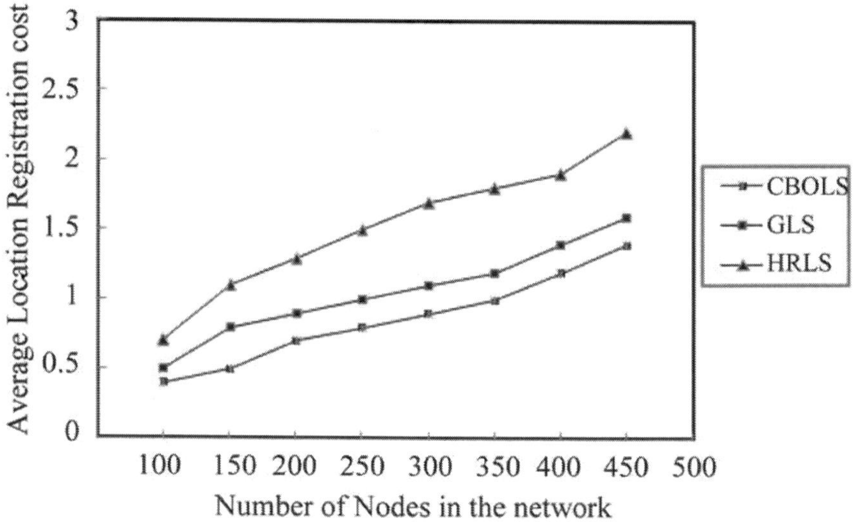

Figure 2. Average location registration cost per node in the network.

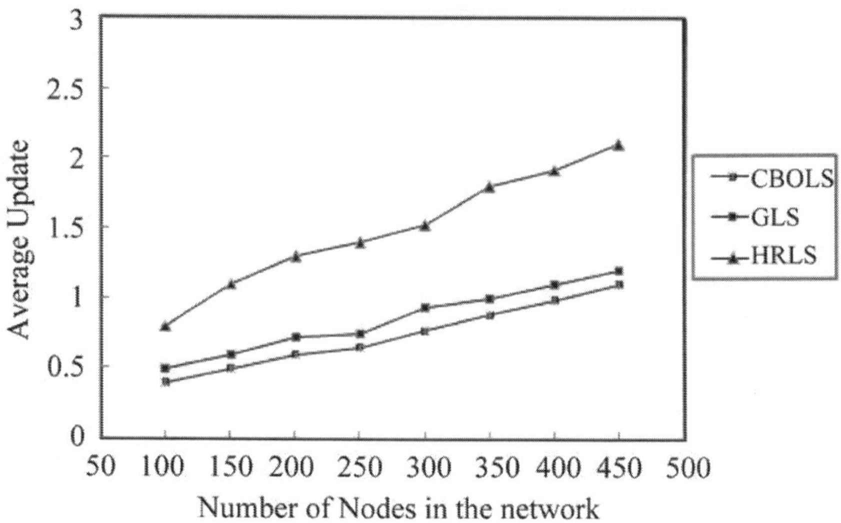

Figure 3. Average location update per each node in the network.

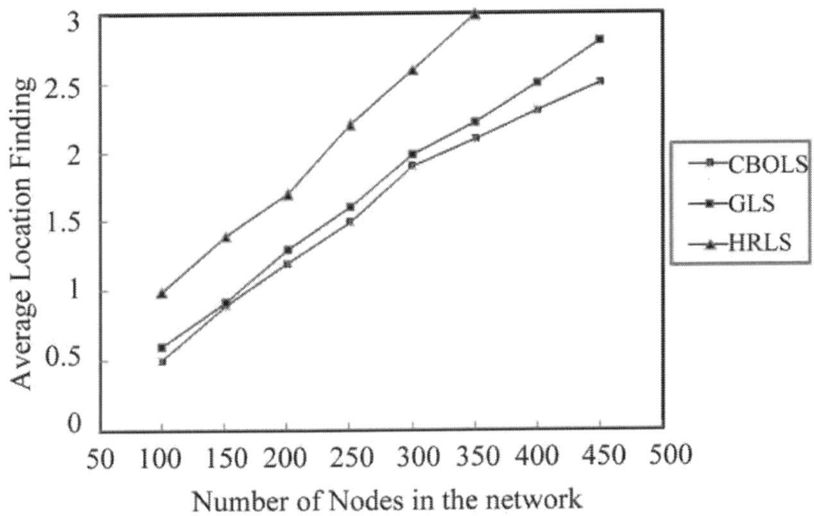

Figure 4. Average location finding cost at the mobility of the node up to 10 m/s (about 22 miles per hour). Each line corresponds to a different movement threshold.

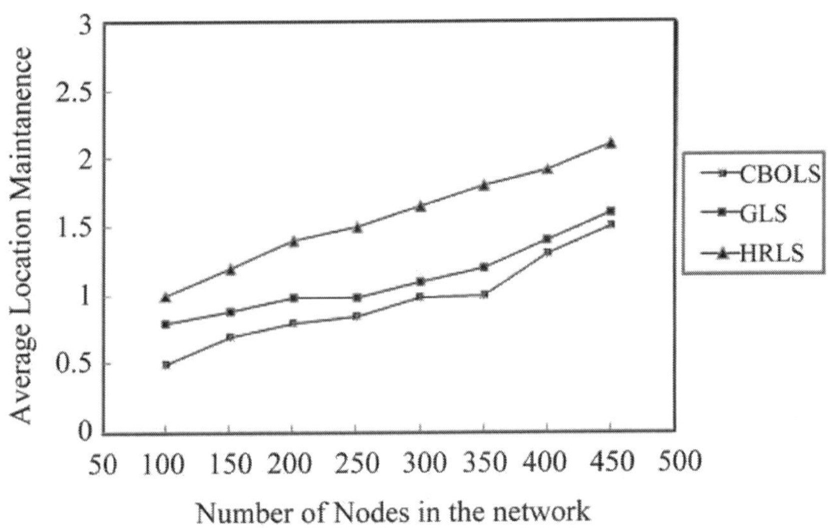

Figure 5. Average location maintenance cost at the mobility speed of 10 m/s.

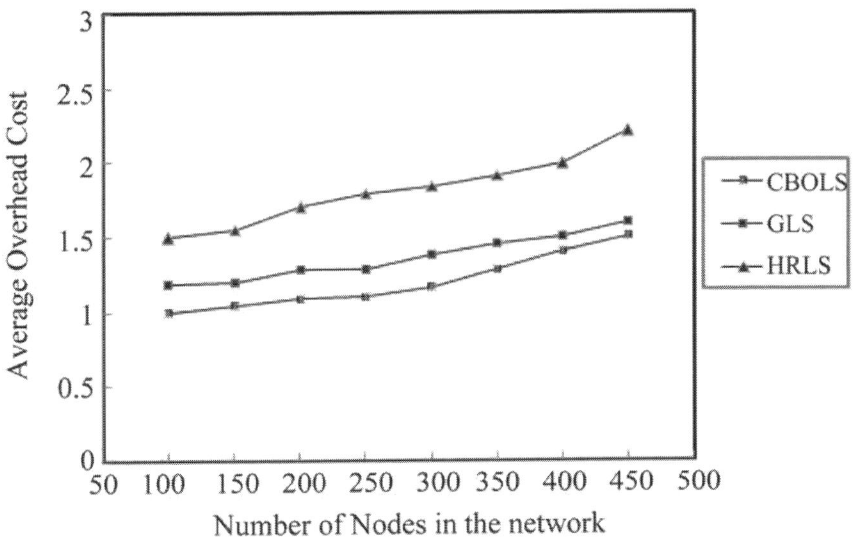

Figure 6. Average overhead cost at 500 nodes in the network.

Figure 7 shows the number of packet transmissions for each location request over the number of location requests answered as speed increases (We include the "hello" packets, to determine the number of packet transmissions). The number of packets transmitted in CBOLS is equivalent to the number of location, location request, and location response packets transmitted. Whereas the number of packets transmitted in GLS and HRLS consists of only the number of location server update packets and location server query packets. However, performance wise the CBOLS is quite constant compared to GLS and HRLS which show poor performance.

Figure 8 illustrates the effect of the node movement speed on the CBOLS location query success rate for 500 nodes. As nodes move faster, the clusters of the node are more likely to be out of date. On the other hand, the nodes also generate updates faster. The effect of the query success rate is relatively insensitive to the node speed. The graph shows CBOLS and GLS have relatively similar results whereas HRLS is very poor in its performance.

Figure 9 plots the average end-to-end delay on a response to a location request versus number of nodes in the network. This figure indicates that the HRLS and GLS have largest percentage of location request delay provided by the requesting nodes. As location request increases, and its control overhead also increased. CBOLS have the lowest percentage right away.

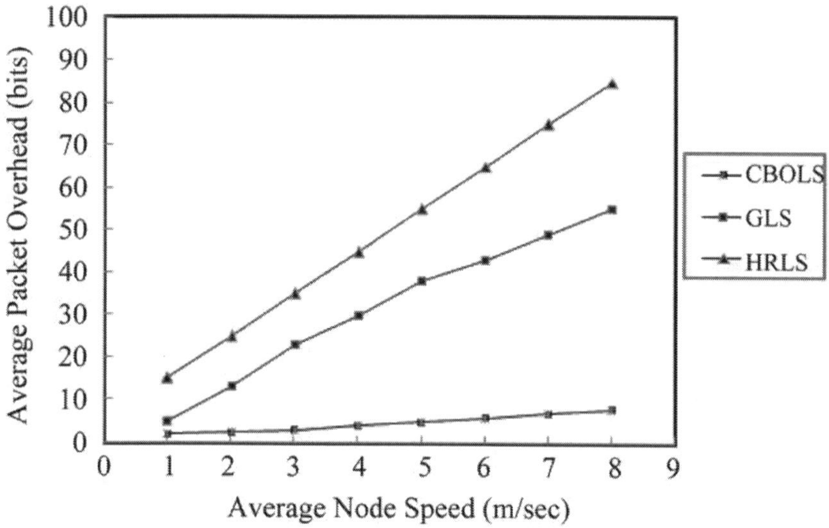

Figure 7. Average packet overhead at average speed of the node (m/sec).

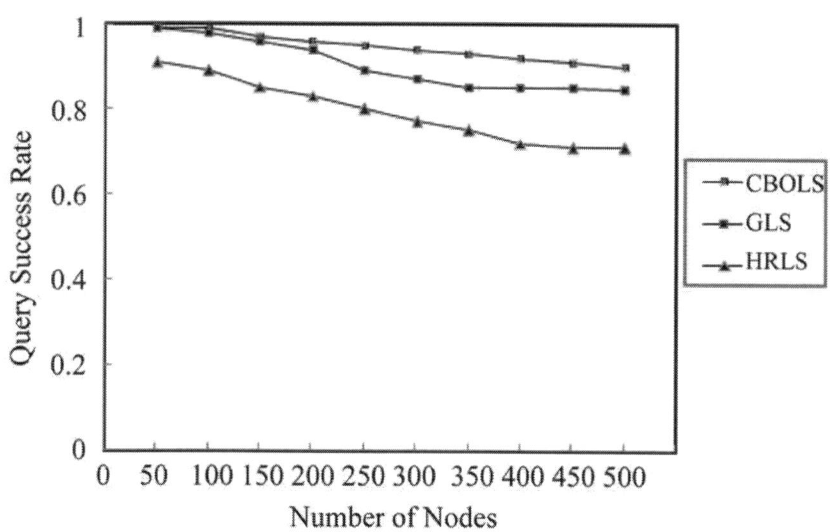

Figure 8. Average query success rate for 500 nodes in the network.

The **Figure 10** shows the average end-to-end delay with regard to the increase in the function of nodes. It depicts that, a slight increase is inevitable as node-count increases in CBOLS and GLS due location updates generated by number of nodes, as it has to traverse a longdistance which will cost the overhead on clusters, whereas HRLS performs poorly.

The **Figure 11** shows that the average end-to-end delay shows slight increase in our scheme with node speed, while the other two schemes are above the normal level. However, GLS is still stable after a certain point, but HRLS shows worst performance.

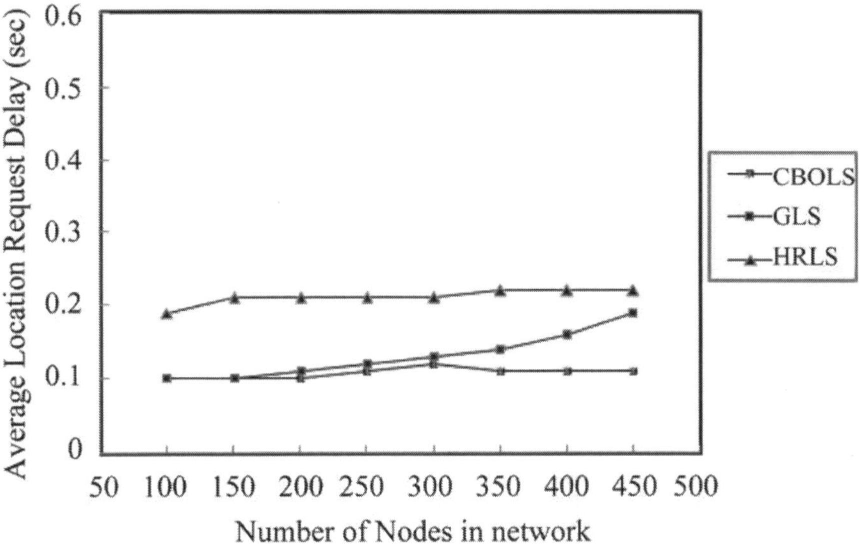

Figure 9. Average location request delay vs number of nodes.

Figure 12 depicts the normalized throughput as a function of increasing the number of nodes at different traffic scenarios. The normalized throughput is defined as the total number of packets actually delivered to their respective destinations divided by the total number of packets generated within the whole network. The throughput in GLS and HRLS scheme is higher than that of CBOLS; the throughputs in both schemes tend to increase as the number of nodes increases.

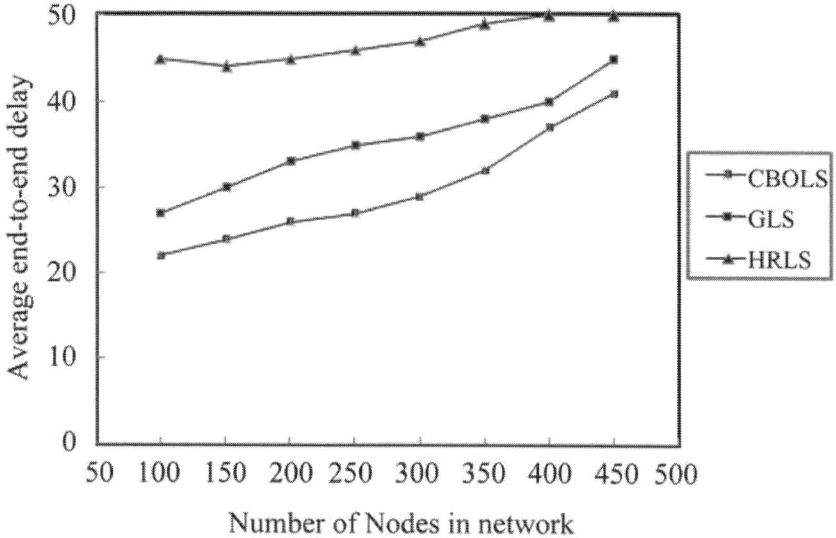

Figure 10. Average end-to-end delay as a function of increasing node-density.

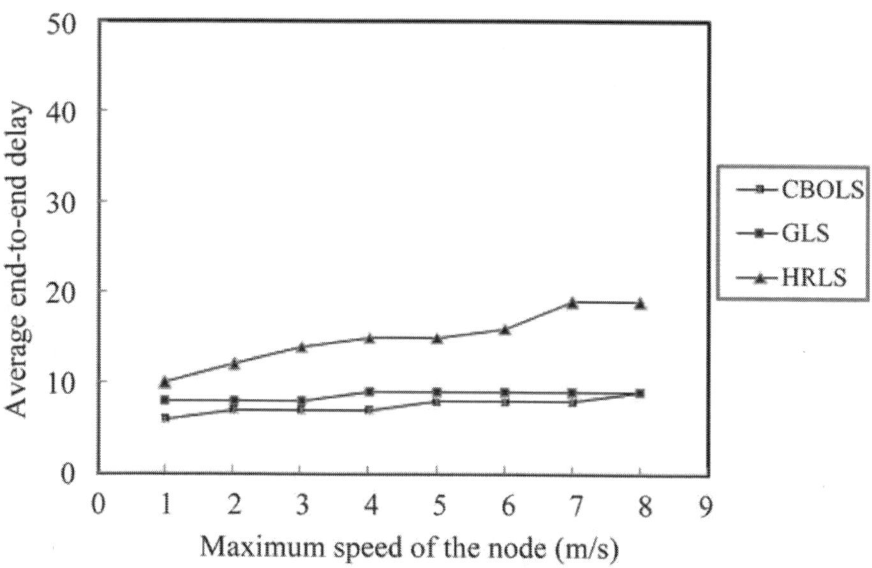

Figure 11. Average end-to-end delay (seconds) as a function of increasing node-speed.

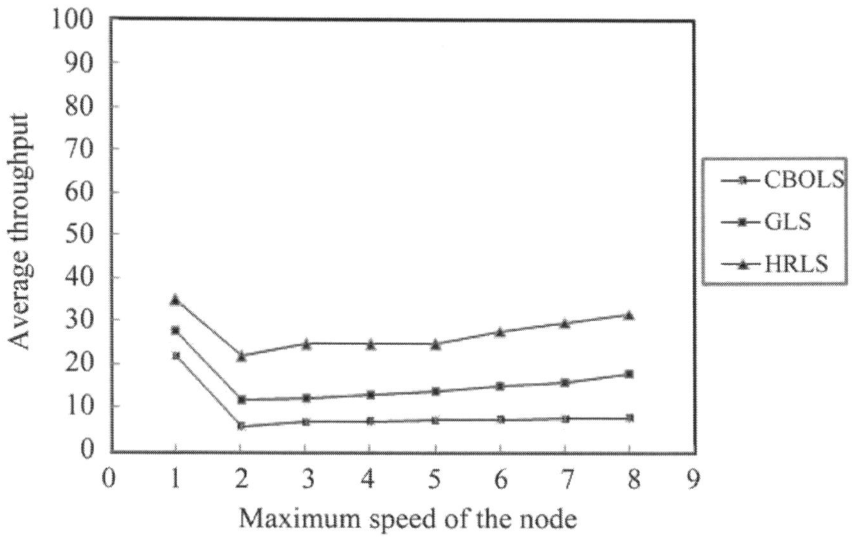

Figure 12. The average throughput vs number of nodes in the network.

Figure 13 shows the average throughput of the network with node speed increasing from 0 to 10 m/s, with pause-time 5 seconds. The throughput performance is impaired by increasing node-speed, but the extent of its effect in our scheme is very low. However, when the node density reaches a certain threshold, the normalized throughput of the network tends to drop gradually because of the IEEE 802.11 wireless channel that has fixed capacity of 2 Mbps, which is saturated due to collisions when the node-density exceeds a threshold.

6. OLC ALGORITHM

1) set Transmission range
2) set all nodes to "initial state"
3) while ClusterHead (CH) is selected do
4) define HelloMsg;
5) broadcast HelloMsg;
6) if (HelloMsg received by initial node = true) do

```
7) Start Timer();
8) call computeWeight();
9) if (initial node weight<=other node) do
10) select as CH;
11) return CH;
12) else do{
13) select as member;
14) return member;
15) else if (a node received HelloMsg by more than two CH)
16) select as Gateway (GW);
17) repeat step 6 - 16;
18) end loop;}
19) int broadcast HelloMsg (){
20) broadcast HelloMsg to all nodes;
21) return HelloMsg;}
22) int calculate Neighborsnode(){
23) Dc = Nodes within transmission range;
24) return Dc;}
25) int compute Mobility(){
26) Mb = Mb = 10log10 (RxTx) new X -> Y/(RxTx) old X->Y;
27) return Mb;}
28) int computeBr(){
29) Bn = Fn/Rn (t);
30) return Bn;}
31) int compute_Weight(){
32) call calculate Neighborsnode();
33) call compute Mobility();
```

34) call computeBr();

35) Wc = (W1 × Dc) + (W2 × Mb) + (W3 × Br) + (W4 × Mr) + (W5 × Ps);

36) return Wc;}

37) Exit Application();

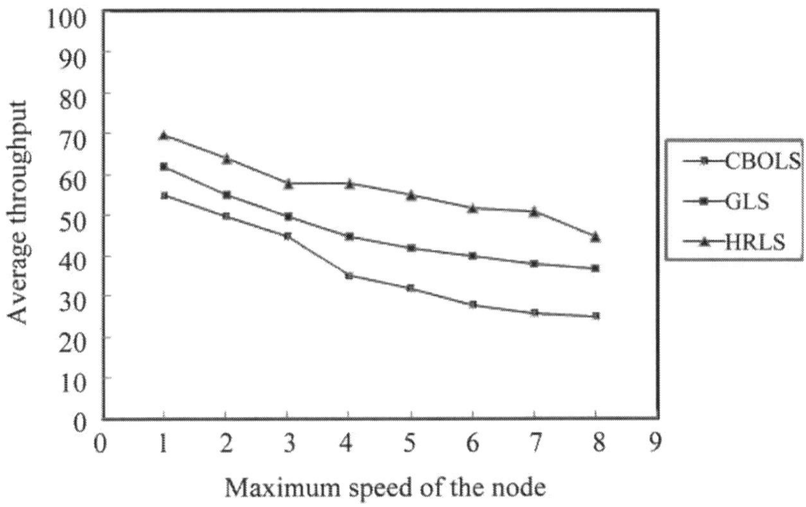

Figure 13. Average throughput as a function of increasing node-speed.

7. PERFORMANCE ANALYSIS OF OLCA

We have used the network region of 2000 × 2000 m^2. Nodes follow Random waypoint mobility model and connections are established between nodes using CBR (Constant Bit Rate) traffic. Nodes pause for a few seconds and then move to a randomly chosen location at a fixed speed of 10 m/s. We consider 50 nodes in the constant area and vary the node density by increasing the number of nodes from 100 to 500.

Figure 14 shows that the network size of 500 nodes with average cluster formation property. Using LowestID, more number of clusters formed, and thus degraded performance of the network. Considering the routing tables in the network, this proves that Lowest-ID has limitations.

As shown in **Figure 15**, at Mobility speed of 10 m/s the total number rate of cluster re-affiliation is slowed down with OLCA and stable in increasing while network density grows, whereas with Lowest-ID the result shows that the number of cluster changes is much higher with network density of 500 nodes. However, at initial and end point the Lowest-ID also shows that the rate of cluster formation is lower and equally similar graph with our OLCA as shown in Figure15.

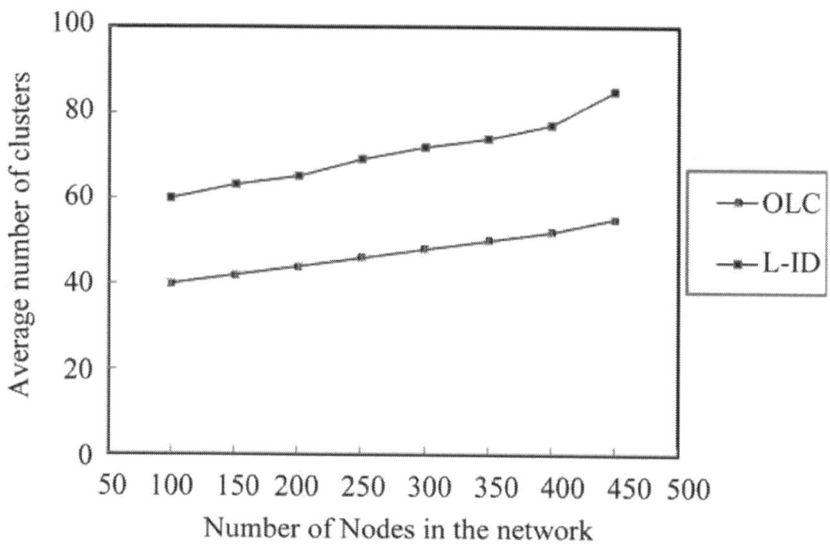

Figure 14. Total number of cluster formation with lowestID and OLCA using the network density of 500 nodes at mobility speed of 10 m/s.

Figure 16 shows the average number of cluster head re-election at Mobility speed of 10 m/s with network density of 500 nodes, this metric result shows our OLCA has tremendous advantage over lowest-ID as it has very less number of cluster head re-elections happening at the mobility rate as defined 10 m/s by us. Our OLCA has been able to make less number of cluster head re-elections and thus the network is stable and robust in terms of cluster heads which can hold their status for a long time causing greater improvement in network throughput.

Figure 17 shows the results of end-to-end throughput of CBR traffics. OLCA gave lower throughput as the node density and mobility increased. Regardless of the number of nodes and speed, OLCA gave consistently better end-to-end throughput in comparison with L-ID.

Figure 18 shows the overhead of packets generated per node during the initial clustering set up phase. In L-ID the overhead is increased with node speed and the number of nodes. On the other hand, the proposed OLCA produced stable and consistent overhead regardless of speed and density of the network. Such result can be obtained, since our algorithm uses neighbor information table to form clusters and eliminates delivery of packets with weight information of nodes that are not within transmission range.

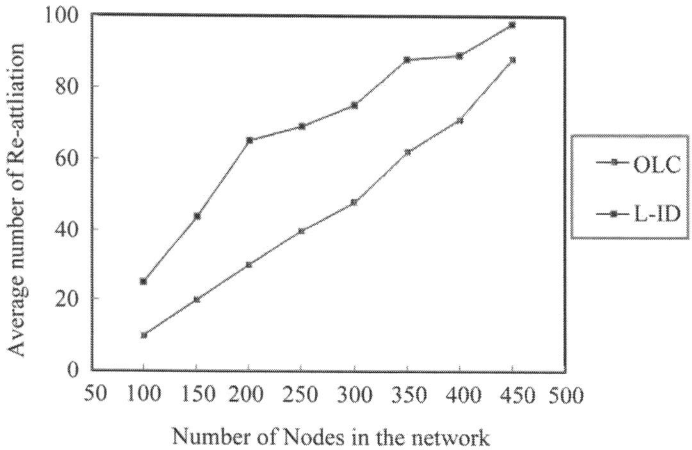

Figure 15. Total number of cluster re-election using network density of 500 nodes at mobility speed of 10 m/s.

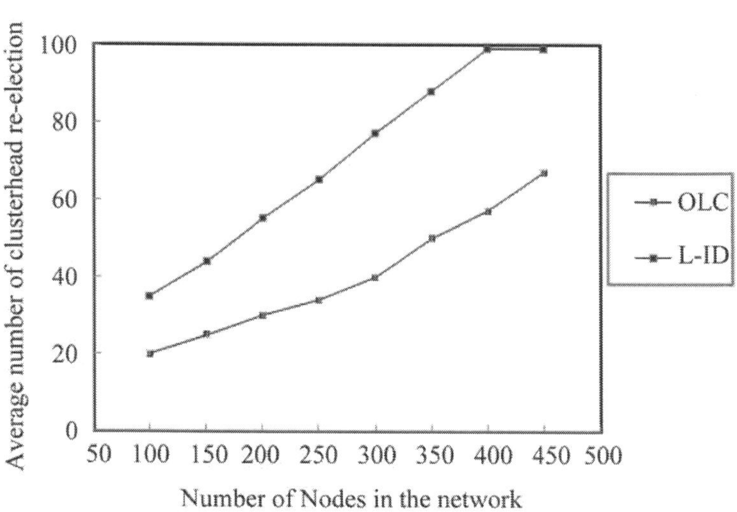

Figure 16. Total number of cluster head re-election using network density of 500 nodes at mobility speed of 10 m/s.

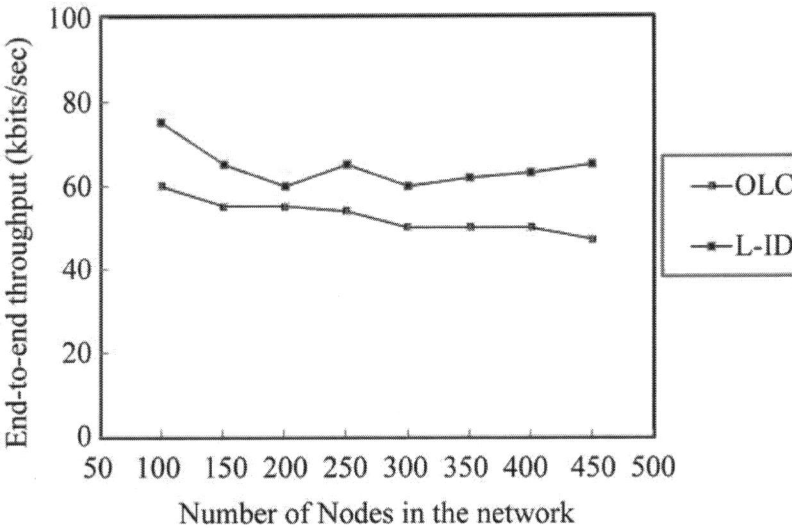

Figure 17. End-to-end throughput in OLCA and L-ID.

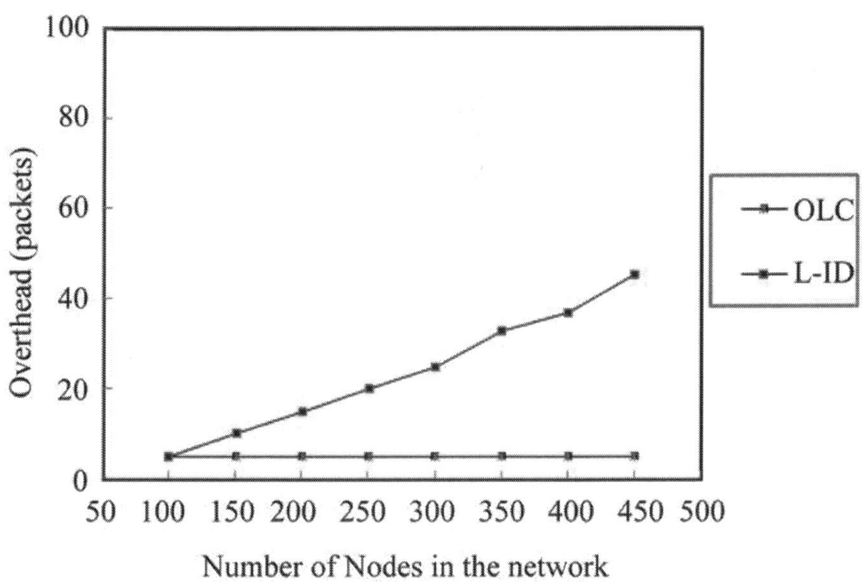

Figure 18. Overhead packets are generated during clustering setup phase.

8. CONCLUSION

The overall performance of the CBOLS is much more effective and efficient for object location services compared with the GLS and HRLS. It is a technology which is cost efficient and time-saving with easy connectivity which can be very useful for the location services. We are also working on possibilities of comparing it with more tools and technologies in order to obtain better results, in order to make it more effectual.

REFERENCES

1. C. K. Toh, "Ad Hoc Mobile Wireless Networks: Protocols & Systems," 2nd Edition, Prentice Hall, Inc., Upper Saddle River, 2002.

2. D. B. Johnson and D. A. Maltz, "Dynamic Source Routing in Ad Hoc Wireless Networks," SpringerLink, 2007, pp. 153-181.

3. C. E. Perkins and E. M. Royer, "Ad-Hoc On-Demand Distance Vector Routing," Workshop on Mobile Computing Systems and Applications, 1999, p. 90.

4. N. Beijar, "Zone Routing Protocol." www.netlab.tkk.fi/ opetus/ s38030/k02/Papers/08-Niclas.pdf

5. Y.-B. Ko and N. H. Vaidya, "Location-Aided Routing (LAR) in Mobile Ad Hoc Networks," Wireless Networks, Vol. 6, No. 4, 2000, pp. 307-321.

6. S. Basagni, I. Chlamtac, V. R. Syrotiuk and B. A. Woodward, "A Distance Routing Effect Algorithm for Mobility," ACM Digital Library, 1998, pp. 76-84.

7. T. Camp, J. Boleng and L. Wilcox, "Location Information Services in Mobile Ad Hoc Networks," Proceedings of the IEEE International Conference on Communications, 2002, pp. 3318-3324.

8. M. Kasemann, H. Fubler, H. Hartenstein and M. Mauve, "A Reactive Location Service for Mobile Ad Hoc Networks," Report, 2002.

9. N. K. Guba and T. Camp, "GLS: A Location Service for an Ad Hoc Network," http://toilers.mines.edu

10. G. Owen and M. Adda, "SOLS: Self Organizing Distributed Location Server for Wireless Ad Hoc Networks," International Journal of Computer Networks & Communications, Vol. 1, No. 1, 2009.

11. Stojmenovic, "Location Updates for Efficient Routing in Ad Hoc Networks," Handbook of Wireless Networks and Mobile Computing, John Wiley & Sons, Inc., New York, 2002.

12. R. Jain, A. Puri and R. Sengupta, "Geographical Routing Using Partial Information for Wireless Ad Hoc Networks," IEEE Personal Communications, February 2001.

13. Garmin, "GPS Beginner's Guide," July 2008.

14. J. Nuevo, "Comprehensible GloMoSim Tutorial," 2004. INRS—Universite du Quebec Nuevo@inrstelecom. Uquebec.ca

15. R. A. Meyer and R. Bagrodia, "PARSEC User Manual for PARSEC," 1999. http://pcl.cs.ucla.edu/

CHAPTER 3

Integration of Body Sensor Networks and Vehicular *Ad-hoc* Networks for Traffic Safety

Angelica Reyes-Muñoz [1,*], Mari Carmen Domingo [2], Marco Antonio López-Trinidad [3] and José Luis Delgado [3]

[1]Computer Architecture Department, UPC BarcelonaTech, Esteve Terradas, Castelldefels 7-08860, Spain

[2]Electrical Engineering Department, UPC BarcelonaTech, Esteve Terradas, Castelldefels 7-08860, Spain

[3]Laboratorio Nacional de Informática Avanzada (LANIA), Monterrey IT Cluster, Technological Research and Innovation Park (PIIT), Km. 10 Autopista al Aeropuerto Internacional Mariano Escobedo, Monterrey-Nuevo León 66629, México

ABSTRACT

The emergence of Body Sensor Networks (BSNs) constitutes a new and fast growing trend for the development of daily routine applications. However, in the case of heterogeneous BSNs integration with Vehicular *ad hoc* Networks (VANETs) a large number of difficulties remain, that must be solved, especially when talking about the detection of human state factors that impair the driving of motor vehicles. The main contributions of this investigation are principally three: (1) an exhaustive review of the current mechanisms to detect four basic physiological behavior states (drowsy, drunk, driving under emotional state disorders and distracted driving) that may cause traffic accidents is presented; (2) A middleware architecture is proposed. This architecture can communicate with the car dashboard, emergency services, vehicles belonging to the VANET and road or street facilities. This architecture seeks on the one hand to improve the car driving experience of the driver and on the other hand to extend security mechanisms for the surrounding individuals; and (3) as a proof of concept, an Android real-time attention low level detection application that runs in a next-generation smartphone is developed. The application features mechanisms that allow one to measure the degree of attention of a driver on the base of her/his EEG signals, establish wireless communication links via various standard wireless means, GPRS, Bluetooth and WiFi and issue alarms of critical low driver attention levels.

KEYWORDS

body sensor network; vehicular *ad hoc* networks; driver behavior

1. INTRODUCTION

The behavior of the driver is essential for traffic safety. Fatigue, alcohol, on-road distractions and emotional state disorders deteriorate the driver's performance, his/her assessment capability and may lead to loss of vehicular control and traffic accidents. Drowsiness is a significant contributing factor in traffic crashes. The American Automobile Association (AAA) estimates that 21% of deadly traffic accidents and 13% of crashes requiring hospitalization of car drivers or passengers are due to drowsy driving [1].

Drunk driving increases the likelihood of a road traffic crash and that death or serious injury will result [2]. Statistics show that in most high-income countries the proportion of fatally-injured drivers with excess alcohol is about 20%. In addition, in low-income countries drivers had consumed alcohol in 33% to 69% of crashes in which drivers were fatally injured and in 8% to 29% of crashes in which drivers were not fatally injured [3].

Distractions can also lead to impaired driving. The National Highway Traffic Safety Administration (NHTSA) estimates that 10% of the fatalities in 2014 were caused by a driver's distraction and 3179 people died as a result in the United States [4].

The emotions of drivers (stress, frustration, *etc.*) may also endanger traffic safety. The inability to manage emotions has been identified as one of the major causes of accidents [5].

A Body Sensor Network is formed by multiple sensors placed at the human body to monitor the vital signs of a person [6]. The physiological states of the person are being sensed, sampled and processed by specific implant and body surface sensors. On the other hand, Vehicular *ad hoc* Networks (VANETs) [7] are mobile *ad-hoc* networks that enable the communication among nearby vehicles, and between vehicles and roadside equipment. In this work, an integrated BSN-VANET architecture is introduced. The proposed architecture focuses on how to avoid traffic accidents caused by an inadequate behavior of the driver.

This paper identifies how BSNs are useful to detect four basic behavior states (drowsy, drunk, driving under emotional state disorders and distracted driving) that may cause traffic accidents. If the driver's state impairs driving, notification messages will be sent to the VANET to alert other vehicles and/or the emergency services. In addition, experiments in real driving conditions have been carried out to validate our proposal.

The structure of the paper is as follows: Section 2 discusses the state of art. Section 3 introduces our scenario. Section 4explains in depth each one of the components of the proposed architecture. In Section 5, the monitoring station architecture is described. Section 6 compares the proposed architecture. Section 7 shows our experiments in a real life scenario. Section 8discusses the performance of the proposed architecture. Finally, the main research challenges to be addressed and conclusions are summarized in Section 9 and Section 10, respectively.

2. STATE OF THE ART

Until now there is no agreement on how to measure and classify emotions. Some studies have been made such as a research area called Driving Psychology which is a behavioral engineering tool that operates in three separate but interacting behavioral areas: affective, cognitive, and sensorimotor [8].

We argue in this paper that some traffic accidents can be avoided thanks to a proper integration of BSNs and VANETs. The BSNs help us to detect if the emotional state of the driver could produce driving impairment. Our research focuses on four behaviour states that cause serious driving impairments:

drowsy driver, drunk driver, driver with emotional disorders and distracted driver.

2.1. Drowsy Driving Detection

The typical visual clues when a person feels drowsy are frequent yawning, frequent eye-blinking, pupil movement (gaze), head movement and facial expression. Several systems have been developed for the detection of drowsiness driving using physiological parameters such as eye movement measures (electrooculogram, EOG), heart activity (electrocardiogram, ECG), skin electrical potential (electromyogram, EMG) and brain activity (electroencephalogram, EEG). In [9], a real-time wireless EEG-based computer interface system for drowsiness detection is proposed. It consists of a wireless physiological signal-acquisition module, which collects EEG signals with an electrode, amplifies, filters, pre-processes and sends them to the embedded signal-processing module using wireless communication. The signal-processing module detects real-time drowsiness. The wireless physiological signal-acquisition module can be embedded into a headband as a wearable device being part of the BSN. A warning tone is triggered to warn the driver when a drowsy state occurs. In [10], a driver fatigue recognition model based on the dynamic Bayesian network is proposed. Multiple features (contextual such as sleeping quality or work environment, contact physiological such as ECG or EEG and contactless physiological such as eye movements) were used; it is shown that the EEG and ECG signals contribute significantly to fatigue detection. The first-order Hidden Markov Model (HMM) has been employed to compute the dynamics of a Bayesian network. Simulation-based experiments were performed to validate the proposed model. In [11], a driver fatigue and drowsiness monitoring system based on an ECG sensor attached to the steering wheel is proposed. The heart rate variability of the ECG signals measured from the driver palms is analyzed; it enables the non-intrusive detection of drowsiness and fatigue condition in the driver. In [12], eyelid parameters are extracted from the EOG data collected in a simulated driving experiment; Support Vector Machine (SVM) is the technique used to detect successfully the drowsiness of the drivers. In [13], a non-invasive driver assistance system is introduced. It is able to detect ECG/EEG signals through cloth or hair without direct skin-contact. Eye blinking can also be detected at a distance of 10 cm. The experiments carried out using a driving simulator show that the blinking duration as well as the heart rate variability (HRV) are useful physiological measures to distinguish between alertness and drowsiness. In [14] authors propose a system that indicates the driver's fatigue level using electrocardiography, heart rate variability, blood pressure and photoplethymosgraphy signals collected from an indoor driving simulation.

If their fuzzy Bayesian network probabilities are between the values of 0.30 and 0.54, this means that the subject is fully awake, if the probability interval increases to 0.60 the driver is starting to get drowsy and between 0.60 and 0.75 it is considered that the driver is in the partial-sleep condition. In [15], the authors state that the reliability and accuracy of driver drowsiness detection by using physiological signals is very high compared to other methods such as vehicle-based measures and behavioral measures.

There are some techniques that measure physical changes during fatigue such as computer vision. A digital camera is used in [16] to compute the driver's eye state and eye blinking frequency, head movement and sagging body posture. In [17], a driver monitoring and event detection system based on 3D information from a range camera is presented. A Kinect sensor integrated in a commercial vehicle allows head pose estimation, which enables the detection of driver's drowsiness or inattention.

2.2. Drunk Driving Detection

Alcohol affects eye-to-hand reaction times and the brain control of eye movements is also highly vulnerable to alcohol. Blood alcohol concentrations (0.03% to 0.05%) interfere with voluntary eye movements and impair the eye's ability to rapidly track a moving target.

Blood alcohol concentration can be measured using interstitial fluid alcohol level sensors belonging to a BSN. The authors in [18] have developed an armband hosting an interstitial fluid based alcohol sensor that enables real-time collection of blood-alcohol level. The sensor responds to a drinking event and the data is highly correlated with the blood alcohol concentration. The data is made available to an attached mote which processes it, stores it locally, and transmits it to a remote server via a mobile phone. In [19] the authors propose to sense the level of driver's alcohol using the PAS 32U alcohol sensor. If the sensor detects 10% of alcohol in the breath of the driver, then the speed of the vehicle is cut down to 80 km/h automatically. Between 20% and 30% of alcohol content the speed of the vehicle is maintained at 60 km/h. When an alcohol content of more than 30% is detected, a caution message is displayed on the LCD screen. If the driver ignores the message and does not stop the vehicle in the stipulated time, the system stops the vehicle automatically and sends an SMS alert to law and enforcement authority with the GPS location. In [20], the authors define a sensing phase to get information about alcohol levels in the driver's blood, the direction of driver's eyes, *etc.* The reasoning phase is responsible for extracting the situation of the driver and calculating corrective actions for other vehicles on the road. Finally the application phase disseminates warning messages for other vehicles on the road and warns the driver to prevent the occurrence of accidents.

In [21] the system authenticates the driver by combining the function of alcohol detection and a face identification system based on image recognition. It offers to eradicate the fraudulent conduct of drunk driver and driver changing. A sensor reads the alcohol concentration of the air around the driver and determines whether it is less than the original standard. If it is higher, the ignition circuit of the engine is cut off by the On Board Unit (OBU) to hinder driving. It will only be possible to start the car if the alcohol concentration is reduced.

In [22] the authors propose a seat incorporating a sensor that can be retrofitted into an automobile seat for detection of impairment of a driver who has consumed alcohol. Body-trunk plethysmogram and respiration are detected from the back of the driver using the body sensor. The extracted signal was defined as a pulse wave that allows a quick detection of alcohol-impaired driving. In [23] alcohol content in the driver's body is detected by means of an infrared breath analyser placed in the steering wheel. The alcohol level of the driver is continuously monitored and calibrated on a scale. When it exceeds a particular limit the fuel supply is cut-off.

In [24] there is an overview that focuses on in-vehicle capability to detect impairment before a vehicle can be operated. They mention a biometric fingerprint device capable of detecting alcohol levels (this device is placed on the steering wheel to detect alcohol through the pores of the skin); alcohol sniffers to measure the driver's' breath (placed on the driver's seat, behind the driver's shoulder); transdermal sensors that measure blood alcohol concentration based on how much alcohol is present in perspiration (this device is worn around the ankle).

2.3. Detection for Driving under Emotional State Disorders

Emotions are mental and physiological states associated with a wide variety of feelings, thoughts, and behaviors. Emotional state disorders impair driving. Some works have evaluated with BSNs the emotional state of the drivers in simulated environments. In [25], a methodology and a wearable system for the evaluation of the emotional states of car-racing drivers in simulated racing conditions have been introduced. The emotional states high or low stress, euphoria and disappointment have been determined by classifying features extracted from the facial electromyogram (EMG), electrocardiogram (ECG), respiration, and electrodermal activity (EDA) sensors. Support vector machines (SVMs) and Adaptive Neuro-Fuzzy Inference System (ANFIS) have been used for the classification of the emotions with overall classification rates of 79.3% and 76.7%, respectively. In [26], a real time, wearable system for remote monitoring of the affective condition of car racing drivers has been presented. The emotional classes identified are high stress, low stress, dysphoria and euphoria. It has been validated with 10 subjects in simulated racing conditions with a high classification. In [27], the impact of drivers' emotions on driving performance has been investigated with fifteen participants in two driving simulation experiments. The results indicate the driver's task performance varies according to different emotional states. In [28], the electroencephalogram (EEG) signals have been analyzed in a car simulation environment with and without billboards. It has been observed that the registration of billboards generates a specific brain signal; consequently, the blinking rate and the driver's stress level are increased. In [29], the authors evaluate the driver's stress level analysing the autonomic nervous system changes using sensors to measure heart rate variability, respiration activity and electrodermal response along with mechanical information such as that coming from steering wheel angle corrections, velocity changes and time responses. Fifteen subjects have performed a driving simulation experiment consisting of a first session keeping a constant speed in a motorway and two additional sessions in the same environment with incremental stress load. In [30], the authors propose a monitoring system that alerts people before they become sick and prevents them from having motion sickness symptoms while driving a car. The authors use EEG features that have been extracted online from five motion sickness-related brain areas. A virtual reality-based dynamic driving simulator has been constructed to perform experiments. The results show that motion sickness has been successfully detected in more than 80% of the subjects. The experiments of [25,26,27,28,29,30] have been taken in simulated conditions. However, emotions do not always correlate with specific driving events [25] and subjects experience different emotions to driving events on simulation environments from those in real conditions.

Other empirical studies have also analyzed with BSNs the driver's emotions in a real life scenario. In [31], the authors show that driver's physiological signals were measured with acceptable quality of analysis without interrupting driving. Authors defined two categories of stresses using nonintrusive sensors (electrocardiogram, photoplethysmogram, galvanic skin response and respiration) on the steering wheel, driver's seat, and seat belt. In [32], physiological sensing has been applied to determine the driver's stress level during real-world driving tasks. ECG, EMG, EDA and respiration have been recorded during a set route, which included periods of rest, highway and city driving. A driver questionnaire and a score derived from observable events and actions coded from a videotape taken during the drives have been used to assess the stress levels. The results show that three stress levels (low, medium, and high) could be recognized with an overall accuracy of 97.4% using 5 min intervals of data and that heart rate and skin conductivity metrics provide the highest overall correlations with continuous driver stress levels. The authors in [33] describe how to use combinational fusion to select features and fuse physiological sensor data to accurately detect stress level during driving. They use the data acquired by Healey and Picard's experiments [31] for feature extraction. In [34], a real-time methodology for the assessment of drivers' stress has been introduced. The detection has been based on physiological signals (ECG, EDA and respiration) as well as driving history extracted using GPS and the vehicle's CAN-bus data. This information has been incorporated in a Bayesian network (BN) to estimate the stress probability. Stress events can be detected through monitoring of the driver's physiological reactions to driving events; the results in real driving conditions show an accuracy in stress event detection of 82%. In [35], the driver's affective state has also been monitored using physiological signals (EDA and photoplethysmography (PPG)) during on-road driving experiments. Neural networks have been used to predict the driver's stress levels with an average precision of 89.93%. In [36], the driver's frustration in a real world scenario has been inferred by a BN given the driving environment (e.g., traffic density or road obstructions), speech recognition errors during the interaction with an Automatic Speech Recognition (ASR) system to retrieve and play music, EDA, face expressions and pedal actuation. The system shows a true positive rate in frustration detection of 80% and a false positive rate of 9%. In [37], the authors present a methodology for stress detection in realistic driving conditions. Their signal acquisition process considers an ECG sensor which is placed on the subject's chest, electrodermal activity sensors are attached on the subject's middle, index fingers on the right hand, and a respiration sensor is placed around the subject‘s thorax. The most significant indicators have been selected and a dataset has been collected during real-world driving. Experiments have been carried out in a simulated environment to study how the estimated changes of driver's state affect driving performance. In [38] heart rate, respiration rate and hand pressure is used to measure stress. Authors analyze the loss of peripheral vision and explain that the car could compensate for this by auto-adjusting the field of view of headlights; also authors propose to change the color of the dashboard based on physiological changes (green and red colours could indicate a more relaxed or stressed driver, respectively).

2.4. Distracted Driving Detection

A distraction is anything that diverts the driver's attention from the primary task of navigating the vehicle and responding to critical events. In [39] motion sensors are used to detect distractions. The abnormal movements of the head or leg are an indication of driver distractions (such as an abrupt brake or a sharp turn), which can be detected using accelerometers and gyroscopes. The current vehicle signals vehicle speed, brake, acceleration and steering angle are extracted from the Controller Area Network (CAN) bus and are combined with motion sensor data to identify the distractions. This way, a high accuracy of distraction detection of over 90% is achieved. In [40], a driver distraction monitoring system based on dual compass motion sensing is proposed; it is able to recognize driver's head pose by removing the vehicle motion component, which also affects head pose recognition. The driver's distraction index was computed and compared to a threshold to warn the driver if necessary. In [41], a non-intrusive distracted driving warning system based on motion capture technology is introduced. It is composed of: (i) the Microsoft Kinect motion sensing hardware for tracking head and skeletal movements and (ii) a custom software application for identifying four distractions and outputting audio alerts. Four different distractions can be detected: (a) reaching for a moving object; (b) talking on a cell phone; (c) personal hygiene; and (d) looking at an external object. The system is able to successfully identify these distractions in a driving simulator with accuracy of (a) 100%; (b) 33%; (c) 50%; and (d) 66%. Drivers are alerted of their distractions with audio signals.

In [42], the distraction level of a driver performing secondary tasks (talking in the phone or to a passenger, operating a navigation system or changing radio stations) is analyzed. The driver's distractions are detected in real-world scenarios by the CAN bus, a frontal camera facing the driver and a microphone. The CAN bus provides relevant car data such as brake value, acceleration, vehicle speed, steering wheel angle, brakes and gas pedal pressures. A video camera captures the facial expressions and head orientation of the driver and a microphone array provides audio. Another camera is placed facing the road. Separate binary classifiers are trained to recognize whether the driver is performing some secondary tasks, achieving an average accuracy of 77.2%. A joint multi-class classifier is trained and achieves an accuracy of 40.8%. Afterwards, a regression model to predict the level of distraction of the driver is built; it highly correlates with the perceived driver distraction scores from subjective evaluations. In [43], regression models were used to predict the perceived distraction level of the drivers. The independent variables are features extracted from the CAN-bus signal, a microphone array and two video cameras facing the road and the driver. Four different distraction modes were identified using the proposed system. In [44], algorithms and experimental results to detect distraction by using in-vehicle signals are introduced. The variance of steering angle and average steering speed were selected as most distinguishing signals between normal and distracted driving. Two kinds of machine learning schemes (unsupervised learning and supervised learning together) are used to classify normal and distracted driving features in real driving situations.

In [45], a distributed camera framework for continuously monitoring the driver's head dynamics is proposed. The system has been evaluated during on-road driving with spatial head turns. The results show that the proposed system was reliable over 90% of the time in comparison with the single-perspective approach (reliability less than 72% of the time). In [46], a distributed camera framework for head movement analysis is introduced. Two approaches for facial feature tracking to compute the head pose and different configurations of multi-camera systems have been analyzed. The head movement could be tracked by the best system over 96% of the time. Evaluations were performed in real-world scenarios to capture spatially large head turns (away from the driving direction) during different maneuvers (e.g., merge and lane change) on urban streets and freeways. The system in [47] requires monocular video for real-time driver head pose estimation, since head pose indicates the current focus of attention of the driver. New algorithms for automotive head pose estimation and tracking have been introduced. A new detection method based on video camera is proposed in [48]. The new algorithm includes driver's face location based on gray variance, and segmentation of separate areas of facial organs using the projection curve pole position. It is able to distinguish between distraction and fatigue states according to the driver's head rotation angle. The results show a good average real-time performance (32 ms) and a high accuracy rate.

In [49] texting during driving is detected with the aid of smartphones. Motion sensors integrated in the smartphone are able to detect who the driver is (sitting on the front seat and right side of the car) recognizing micro-movements. A naïve Bayesian classifier has been chosen; it achieves an accuracy of 87.18% and a precision of 96.67%.

The online monitoring system in [50] detects early driver distractions using brain activity measured by EEG signals. The proposed method predicts the start and end of a distraction period. 24 subjects were asked to drive from an initial position to a destination using a city map in a simulated driving environment. The experimental results showed that the algorithm is able to predict the start and end of distraction periods with relatively high accuracy (81% and 70%, respectively). In [51], the driver's EEG signal is analyzed to detect cognitive distractions. A new EEG analysis method based on Singular Value Decomposition (SVD) is introduced. The proposed method has been analyzed in a highway-driving simulated environment with a high accurate detection of the driver's cognitive state.

Table 1 summarizes the various different body sensors used to detect drowsy driving, drunk driving, driving under emotional state disorders and distracted driving.

Table 1. Sensors to detect four behavior states that cause driving impairments.

State	Sensor	Data Rate	Bandwidth
Drowsy driver	ECG	288 Kbps	100–1000 Hz
	EEG	43.2 Kbps	0–150 Hz
	EOG	1.2 Kbps	0.05–35 Hz
	EMG	320 Kbps	0–10,000 Hz
Drunk driver	Interstitial fluid	–	–
	Plethysmogram	2400 bps	0.5–4 Hz
	Respiration	800 bps	0.1–10 Hz
Driver with emotional disorders	Respiration	800 bps	0.1–10 Hz
	EDA	1.2 Kbps	0–35 Hz
	Glucose	1600 bps	0–50 Hz
	Facial EMG	320 Kbps	0–10,000 Hz
	ECG	288 Kbps	100–1000 Hz
Distracted driver	EEG	43.2 Kbps	0–150 Hz
	EOG	1.2 Kbps	0.05–35 Hz
	Accelerometers, gyroscopes	35 Kbps	0–500 Hz

3. PROPOSED SCENARIO

We propose a scenario (see Figure 1) where the behavior of the driver is monitored to avoid traffic accidents. Vital signs (body temperature, heart rate, blood pressure, respiratory rate, *etc.*) of the driver are measured and sent to a gateway located on the body surface, which forwards this data to the monitoring station. The monitoring station is a wireless device such as cell phone, tablet PC, smartphone, *etc.*, which is able to connect to the vehicle's OBU. The OBU is a network device that communicates with other vehicles (VANET) and with fixed infrastructure.

In this scenario, the vital signs sent by the BSN are analyzed in the monitoring station to determine the driver's state. Four common causes of traffic accidents due to an irresponsible behavior of the driver have been selected: drowsy, drunk, driving under emotional state disorders, and distracted driving. Since these ways of driving constitute a danger to road users, the surrounding vehicles and pedestrians should be advised for safety reasons.

Figure 1. Proposed scenario.

If the behavior of the driver is inadequate, notification messages are sent from the monitoring station to the vehicle's OBU, which forwards them to the VANET and/or the Road Side Units (RSUs). Our architecture contemplates that the notification messages in the VANET use the current VANET protocols. Notification messages between the OBU and the emergency services or the RSUs use the available communications platforms such as 4G, WiMAX, *etc.* Pedestrians should also be warned through these notification messages, which are forwarded to their own monitoring stations (e.g., smart phones) using Vehicle to Pedestrian (V2P) or Infrastructure to Pedestrian (I2P) communications. Next, we introduce the proposed system architecture.

4. MODULAR INTEGRATION OF BSN AND VANET

The proposed integrated BSN and VANET architecture is shown in Figure 2. It consists of: (1) the BSN; (2) the monitoring station; (3) the vehicle's OBU and (4) the emergency services. Next, we describe its components and functionalities in detail.

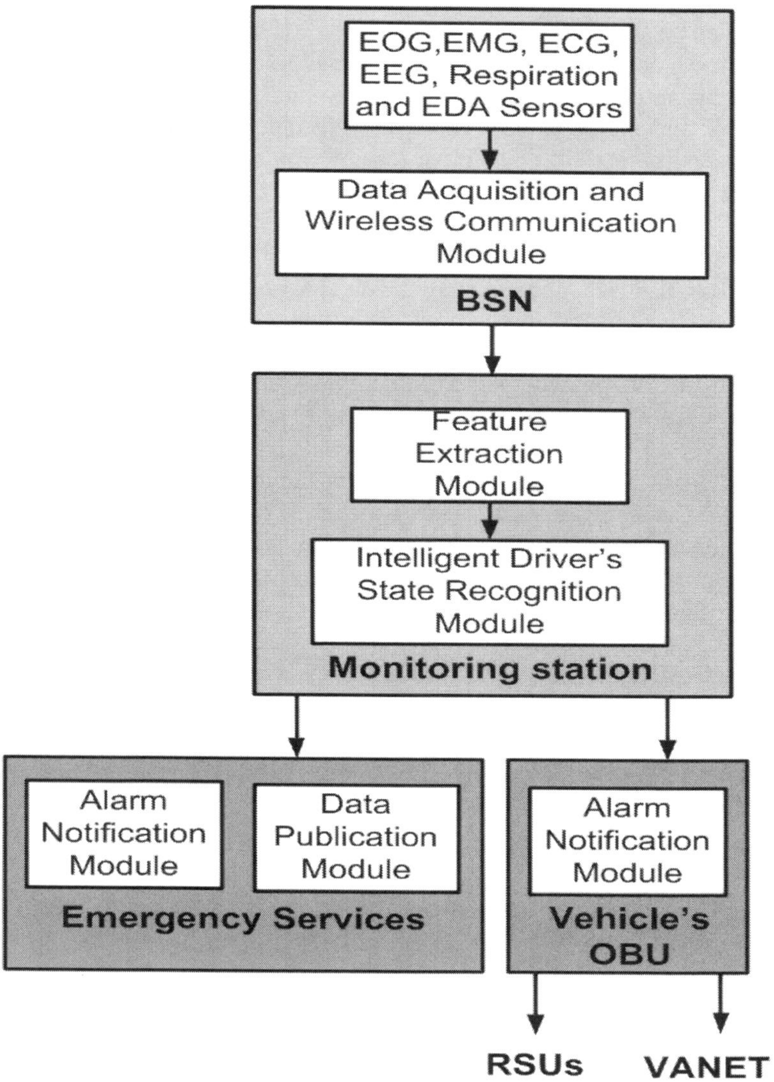

Figure 2. Integrated BSN and VANET architecture.

4.1. Body Sensor Network

The following sensors have been used to monitor the driver state at a specific moment: electrocardiogram (ECG), electroencephalogram (EEG), electrooculogram (EOG), facial electromyogram (EMG), interstitial fluid, plethysmogram, respiration, electrodermal activity (EDA), glucose and motion sensors (accelerometers and gyroscopes).

ECG is a graphic record of the heart's electrical activity. The ECG sensors are located on the thorax of the driver. The EEG sensor of the head measures the electrical activity within the brain. The EOG is the resulting signal when the resting potential of the retina is measured. It records eye movements. The EOG sensors are placed around the eye. The EMG sensor measures the muscle activity or the frequency of tension of a certain muscle. A balaclava contains the EMG sensors.

The interstitial fluid based alcohol sensor enables real-time collection of blood-alcohol level. Interstitial fluid is harvested via micro pores and assayed in real time for blood alcohol content. An arm band hosts this sensor.The plethysmogram shows fluctuations in pulse or heartbeat frequency to judge whether a subject has been drinking alcohol. The plethysmogram is detected from the back of the driver.

Respiration is an indicator of how deep and fast a person is breathing. Respiration sensors are located on the thorax of the driver. EDA refers to the skin conductance activity. The EDA sensor could be placed inside a driver's glove or on the neck. The glucose sensor placed under the skin measures the amount of glucose circulating in the blood.

An accelerometer is used to recognize and monitor body posture. A gyroscope is used for measuring or maintaining orientation, based on the principle of conservation of angular momentum. Gyroscopes together with accelerometers monitor the physical movements. Motion sensors can be placed on the leg and the head.

The acquired data is transmitted via a wireless communication module. Ultra-wideband or IEEE 802.15.6 [52] is used for wireless transmission between the sensors and the gateway. Bluetooth or ZigBee can be used to forward the physiological data from the gateway to the monitoring station [53]. Different MAC protocols have also been developed for the communication in wireless body sensor networks [54,55] and cognitive radio wireless body sensor networks [56].

4.2. Monitoring Station

The acquired data from the BSN is processed in the monitoring station because the BSN gateway is restricted by its low capabilities and limited battery capacity. The monitoring station is the core component of the system. It is divided into two major modules, namely: the feature extraction module and the intelligent driver's state recognition module. The first module extracts features from the selected bio signals. These features are used by the intelligent driver's state recognition module to determine if the driver has one of the four predefined subject's states (drowsy, drunk, emotional state disorder or distracted driver). The state is being monitored during the driving task. More details about monitoring station components are explained in Section 5.

4.3. Vehicle's OBU

The OBU has an alarm notification module. If impaired driving is detected due to an inadequate behavior of the driver, then alarm notification messages are sent from the monitoring station towards the OBU, which forwards them to the VANET and/or the RSUs.

4.4. Emergency Services

We distinguish between the alarm notification and the data publication modules. The emergency services can also be notified of an inadequate driver's state if it is required to assist the driver. The collected information of body sensors is also sent from the monitoring station to the emergency services for police control and/or medical reasons. OpenXDF has been selected as an open XML-based standard for the digital storage and exchange of time-series physiological signals and metadata between the monitoring station and the vital sign monitoring server of the emergency services. The resulting XML documents are sent to this server to be published and accessed by authorized users. Next, we describe the components of the monitoring station architecture.

5. MONITORING STATION COMPONENTS

The monitoring station architecture is shown in Figure 3. The architecture consists of connectivity and an abstraction layer. The connectivity layer has an interface for the BSN, another for the emergency services and one last for the OBU. In the abstraction layer, body sensor data should be processed, formatted and sent to the emergency services in case of impaired driving due to the driver's state.

The registration, authentication and authorization module controls the security and privacy between the monitoring station and the OBU and between the monitoring station and the emergency services. Afterwards, subscription authorization policies are defined for the monitoring station interaction with the OBU and between the monitoring station and the emergency services.

We incorporate policy rules to prioritize information previously defined and stored in the policies repository. These rules are related to the appropriate laws of the driver's country (e.g., the legal blood alcohol concentration limit for driving) and the steps to take in case of impaired driving due to an inadequate behavior of the driver (see Section 5.1). Also, there is a driver's context aware information module in charge of feeding the policy repository with personal information such as: age, driving experience, *etc*. The purpose of all these rules is to help in the decision that determines if a person has a specific state that produces driving impairment.

The acquired data from the BSN is processed in the monitoring station where data aggregation and consistency checking techniques are applied. Afterwards, this data is stored in the information repository. Next, it is analyzed by the policy decision points. The information repository provides information to the policy decision module using OpenXDF.

The policy decision points are the architecture elements where all decisions are taken according to the established policies from the policy repository and the body sensor data which is stored in the information repository. The decision points select the adequate policy that should be applied in the enforcement points. The information repository uses OpenXDF for the digital storage and exchange of time-series physiological signals and metadata.

The enforcement points are involved in the execution of the policies. This module receives the action that should be applied in the OBU, as well as the transmission of notification messages to the OBU and to the emergency services. It should also send the sensor data to the vital sign monitoring server of the emergency services, which will be published based on the publication policies defined at the monitoring station.

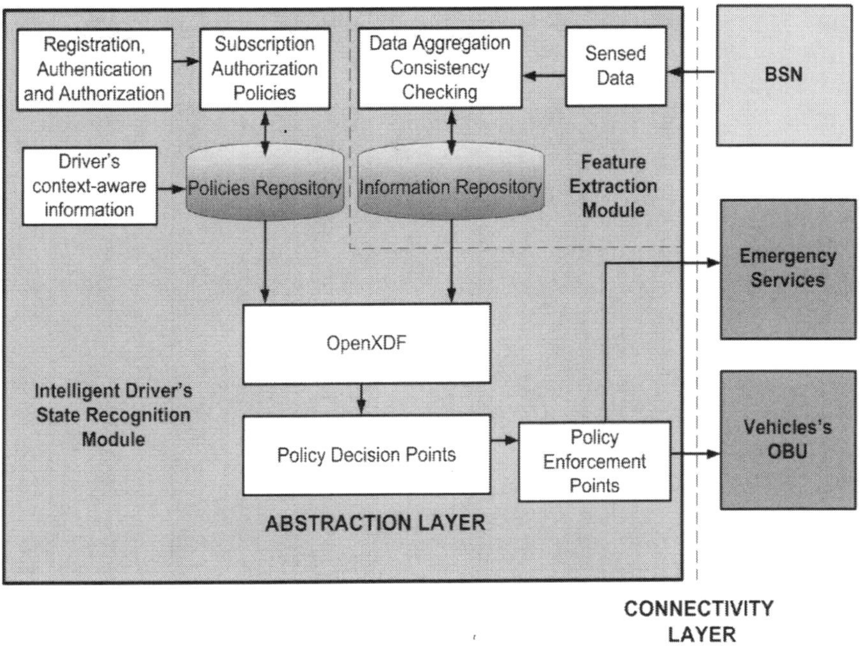

Figure 3. Monitoring Station Architecture.

5.1. Enforcement Points According to the Driver's State

Once our architecture has detected impaired driving, we propose to have a variety of enforcement points and also linkages between multiple emergency services, for example having accessible the Driver's context-aware information (seeFigure 3) such as: driver identity confirmed through data and digital photo, contact information, conviction history, license status, medical problems, age, driving experience, *etc.* In [57] there is a proposal that law enforcement agencies may use the driver history to identify violators who have been encountered driving under impaired conditions.

Roadside information would be also useful as context-aware data, for example: traffic density and weather conditions (this process shall manage data directly from collection equipment located at the roadside.). Figure 4 summarises the enforcement points in a general way for the four behavior states.

Next subsections detail the enforcement points when a detection alert (for drowsy driving, drunk driving, driving under emotional state disorders and distracted driving) is sent to the OBU.

5.1.1. Enforcement Points for Drowsy Driving

The statistics from Section 1 demonstrate that drowsiness is a significant contributing factor in traffic accidents. Therefore, the driver should be notified when a drowsy state occurs so that he/she stops. Experts recommend drowsy drivers [58] to either pull over for a twenty-minute nap or let someone alert drive instead. It has been demonstrated that a short nap has the greatest effect on the driver's performance and the effects last for several hours [59].

In addition, a drowsy detection alert is sent from the OBU to warn the other drivers (VANET) and pedestrians. This way, they could increase the security distance with respect to this vehicle and react more quickly in case of accident danger.

It is necessary to identify safe places for a nap [60]. For this purpose, Global Positioning System (GPS) applications for VANETs can be used [61]; they provide enhanced route guidance and navigation. Once the drowsy driver's state is detected, the OBU enforces the GPS to locate the next road exit or service station. Information concerning hotels and accommodations could also be offered. The emergency lights are automatically switched on by the OBU.

In addition, the driver's alert can be kept in his/her way towards the next service/road exit using specific alert strategies: opening the window, turning on the air conditioning, or playing loud music. These strategies are only emergency transient measures that give the driver some time to pull off the road [62]; however, its effectiveness to improve alertness when sleepy has not been demonstrated [58].

In case the driver refuses to stop, a notification message is automatically sent towards police cars using the VANET and/or towards the nearest police station. In the meantime, the fuel is cut off to prevent him/her from driving. If the driver decides to start again the vehicle and the BSN detects he/she is still drowsy, a notification message is sent to the OBU, which prevents driving by immobilizing the vehicle's motor.

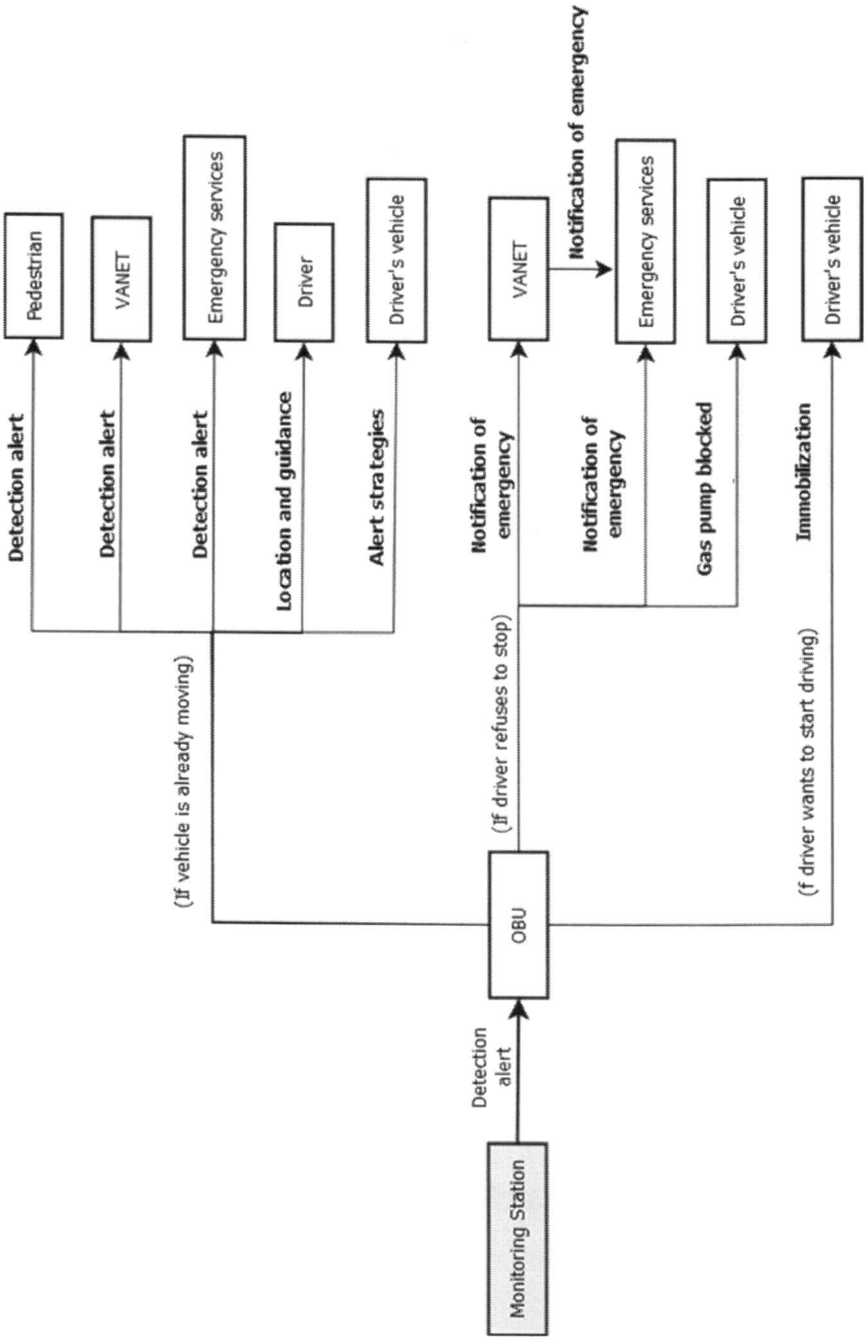

Figure 4. Enforcement points.

5.1.2. Enforcement Points for Drunk Driving

The statistics from Section 1 demonstrate that alcohol is a significant contributing factor in traffic accidents. Some factors that affect the absorption of alcohol include: person's weight, age, individual biomedical/chemical make-up, rate of metabolism and food in the body. This information is managed by the driver's context aware information module (seeFigure 3).

If a driver wants to start driving, but the BSN detects a higher alcohol concentration than the allowed concentration by law (in each country is different) then the vehicle will not start. The ignition will be locked out for some period of time. This method can ensure that the driver is sober prior to operating a motor vehicle [63]. Authors in [64] said that alcohol interlocks are associated with reductions in drunk driving by an average of 64%. In [65] showed that alcohol interlocks reduced the risk of committing an alcohol traffic violation within the first year by 65% while the device was installed.

Date, time, driver's data and his/her ethanol concentration are sent to the emergency services. After some period of time the vital signs of the driver are sensed again. If the vehicle is already moving and the BSN detects an alcohol concentration that impairs driving, then the OBU of the vehicle should notify the driver about his or her own alcohol concentration and the GPS indicates the place to immediately stop. If the driver does not obey, the 3G system notifies the police indicating the GPS position of the vehicle. In the meantime, visual and auditory annoying warnings are signaled to the driver [66]. Another measure is to cut off the fuel [23] (the vehicle slows down, it does not stop abruptly) to prevent him/her from driving. Also, the OBU will send an alert message to the other vehicles in their geographical range using the VANET to increase the security distance from the drunk driver. This way, the rest of drivers have more time to react in case of a dangerous situation. Alert messages will be sent to pedestrians as well.

5.1.3. Enforcement Points for Emotional State Disorders

The affective state recognition of drivers is essential for traffic safety. Driving under unacceptable levels of accumulated stress deteriorates vehicle control. During driving, drivers are affected by [67] events (sequential maneuvers such as stopping for the light, putting on the brakes, *etc.*) and sudden incidents like unanticipated pedestrian crossing, abrupt lane change by another vehicle, *etc.* Some stressors for urban bus drivers [68] include increased road traffic, violent passengers, and increasingly tight running schedules from commercial pressure.

The statistics from Section 1 demonstrate that emotional state disorders are a significant contributing factor in traffic accidents. For this reason it is required to monitor the driver's affective state continuously, detecting on-road stress-trends and cumulatively accounting for increasing stress level [69]. Therefore, if the driver wants to start driving but the BSN detects impairment due to an emotional disorder, some countermeasures are taken to reduce anger and stress [70]: asking questions to the driver, offering breathing exercises, playing music, *etc.* Other strategies that can help the driver to better manage his/her stress are lowering the volume of music or listening to a more relaxing audio, temperature adaptation, corrective headlight [38] (see Section 2.3), reflective dashboard (see Section 2.3), *etc.* If the driver is still emotionally impaired, the vehicle will not start. If the vehicle is already moving and the BSN detects an abnormal emotional behavior, then the GPS system of the vehicle indicates the closest possible place to stop.

If the driver does not obey, the 3G system will notify it to the emergency services indicating the GPS position of the vehicle. Also, the OBU will send an alert message to the other vehicles in their geographical range using the VANET to help them to decide how to be as far away as possible of the indicated vehicle. This way, the rest of drivers have more time to react in case of a dangerous situation. Alert messages will be sent to pedestrians as well.

5.1.4. Enforcement Points for Distracted Driving

The causes of distraction can be broadly classified into visual, cognitive, biomechanical and auditory [71]. On the other hand, researchers have found out that the distraction 'latency' lasts an average of 27 s [72], which means that, even after drivers put down the phone or stop fiddling with the navigation system, drivers aren't fully engaged with the driving task. The statistics from Section 1 demonstrate that distractions are a significant contributing factor in traffic accidents. Teen drivers were distracted almost a quarter of the time they were behind the wheel [73]. 7% of the identified distractions were related to electronic devices such as texting, e-mails, and downloading music [73]. Other distractions included adjusting controls, eating or drinking, personal hygiene, reading, turning around, reaching for an object, and communicating with someone outside the vehicle. Using a cellphone while driving can also pose serious risks for traffic safety [74]. Therefore, the driver should be notified when he/she is distracted. If the glance-monitoring system detects that the driver is not looking ahead in some risky situations (e.g., when the radar detects a potential crash), the driver will receive a voice warning [75].

Other enforcement points include the use of GPS to locate and advertise the next road exit and voice alert suggestions of rest areas that offer services such as Internet access, which could encourage drivers to defer engagement in secondary tasks until they arrive at the rest area [75].

After three times advertising without any change of the behavior of the driver, he/she should be forced to abandon the road and take a break of a minimal time period. In case the driver refuses to stop, a notification message via the VANET will be automatically sent towards police cars and/or towards the nearest police station. In the meantime, the fuel will be cut off to prevent him/her from driving. In addition, once driver distractions are detected by the BSN, the system should notify it to the other drivers using the VANET. This way, the other drivers are warned and can slow down their vehicles or change lane to maintain a proper safety distance to prevent a possible accident.

6. ARCHITECTURE COMPARISON

In Table 2, the main components of the proposed architecture are listed and then as a sort of comparison, the literature projects characteristics are crossed against our project listed features.

The BSN column refers to the body sensor signals collected and processed to infer the driver's emotional or intoxication states. It must be noted that not in all the cases refer to body signals, some projects realise indirect measurements of the driver performance via external instrumentation, for instance the car facilities such as: steering speed, car velocity, braking behavior, *etc.*, or video cameras that allow determine the driver postures.

The Monitoring state column refers to the driver emotional or intoxication state measurements such as: distraction drowsiness, drunkenness, *etc.* It should be noted that because in some projects the car driver state inference is realised on the base of external instrumentation the column holds those variables, for instance, the car kinematics such as the steering speed, velocity speed, braking performance, acceleration, or via the use of cameras installed inside the car cockpit driver that allow determine the driver postures, *etc.*

Table 2. Comparison of platform features offered by the current literature developments.

Platform	BSN	Behavior State	Monitoring Station	OBU	Emergency Services	Communication Interface	VANET
[9]	EEG	Drowsiness	No	No	No	Bluetooth	No
[10]	ECG,EEG	Fatigue	No	No	No	No	No
[11]	ECG	Fatigue, Drowsiness	No	No	No	No	No
[12]	EOG	Drowsiness	No	No	No	No	No
[13]	ECG,EEG	Alertness, Drowsiness	No	No	No	No	No
[14]	ECG, heart rate variability, blood pressure, photoplethysmosgram	Drowsiness	No	No	No	No	No
[15]	ECG,EMG,EOG, EEG	Drowsiness	No	No	No	No	No
[16]	Camera	Fatigue	No	No	No	No	No
[17]	Kinect System	Drowsiness	No	No	No	No	No
[18]	Interstitial fluid	Drunkness	Yes	No	Yes	TDMA 2.4Ghz. RF radio, Bluetooth	No
[19]	Fuel cells, breath analyser	Drunkness	No	No	Yes	No	No
[21]	Infrared breath analyser, camera	Drunkness	No	Yes	Yes	No	No
[22]	Back-pack sensor, body-trunk plethymogram and respiration	Drunkness	No	No	No	No	No

The Monitoring station column indicates whether there is a project element where the sensor signals are collected, processed and analysed in-situ by the prototype or the data analysis is left for posterior study in a laboratory, for instance.

The OBU column considers whether the project features mechanisms that enable to issue alarms to the VANET, or the authorities and emergency services of potential accidents in course.

The Emergency services column shows whether the platform implements any kind software that enables the interaction with the car facilities (worn, radio, interior lights, engine, *etc.*); in order to make the driver reacts; the VANET, or the pedestrians to prevent potential fatal accidents in course.

The Communication interfaces column considers whether the project incorporates software interfaces and the technologies employed; Bluetooth, Wi-Fi, ZigBee, GPRS or others; to enable communication with the car, external networks, facilities or pedestrians.

The VANET column shows whether the project considers shaping the cars and road or street facilities network up. As it can be observed from Table 2, it is still hard to find projects that merge a global interaction among different sort of networks such as: BSN, VANET, GPRS and the Internet.

7. EXPERIMENTATION

At present, the implementation of the proposed architecture considers the interactions of only one BSN sensor node, the monitoring station, and an Internet server that enable communication links with other networks, for instance the emergency services and the road or street facilities. On the one hand, the sensor node collects data signals and periodically transmits the data to the station. The station is a communication gateway that receives the sensor data, processes it and on the base of the car driver attention critical level issues alarms to the server. On the other hand, the server broadcasts the alarms to the VANET, and pedestrians located nearby the position of the warning station. It follows in the next sections more detailed explanations of the architecture implementations, experimental tests and results.

7.1. Monitoring Station Implementation

We have developed an Android real-time attention low level detection application that runs in a next-generation smartphone. The application features mechanisms that allow: to measure the degree of attention of a driver on the base of her/his EEG signals, establish wireless communication links via various standard wireless means, GPRS, Bluetooth and WiFi, and issue alarms of critical low driver attention levels.

In the driving process, the EEG device periodically gathers raw readings of the driver brain waves and sends the readings via a Bluetooth wireless link to the Android application. Once the smartphone has received the EEG data, it processes the data to extract meaningful features; these features then serve as input models that analyse the driver attention levels, then an alert system is triggered if the results indicate that the driver attention is low.

The application works on the base of the attention values that are ranged within a scale of 0 to 100 units. Alarms are issued by the application whether within an adaptable time window, the driver attention value gets critically low levels for determined time durations. Currently, the application performs evaluations over three attention level intervals, (i) values within 40–100 units indicate the driver is fully focused; (ii) values within 20–40 units mean low attention, and iii) critical low attention levels for values less than 10 units.

A client-server communication scheme is used to receive the alarms issued by the monitor and to broadcast message to the VANET, the road or street facilities, and pedestrians. Two sort of alarms are triggered by the application, warning messages and emergency messages. Warning messages are issued when the driver attention levels are within the 20–40 units. Emergency messages are transmitted when the driver attention levels are under the 10 units.

Whilst warning messages are addressed to the vehicles and pedestrians that are nearby the driver vehicle low levels of attention. Emergency messages are broadcasted to the emergency services, the nearest vehicles (those within a 1 km distance) and pedestrians. Eventually, it is considered to make actions over the vehicle controls such as slowing the car velocity, increasing the car radio volume, switching on the turn and stop lamps, and switch the engine off, for instance. InFigure 5 is shown a snapshot of the data collection interface of the developed Android application.

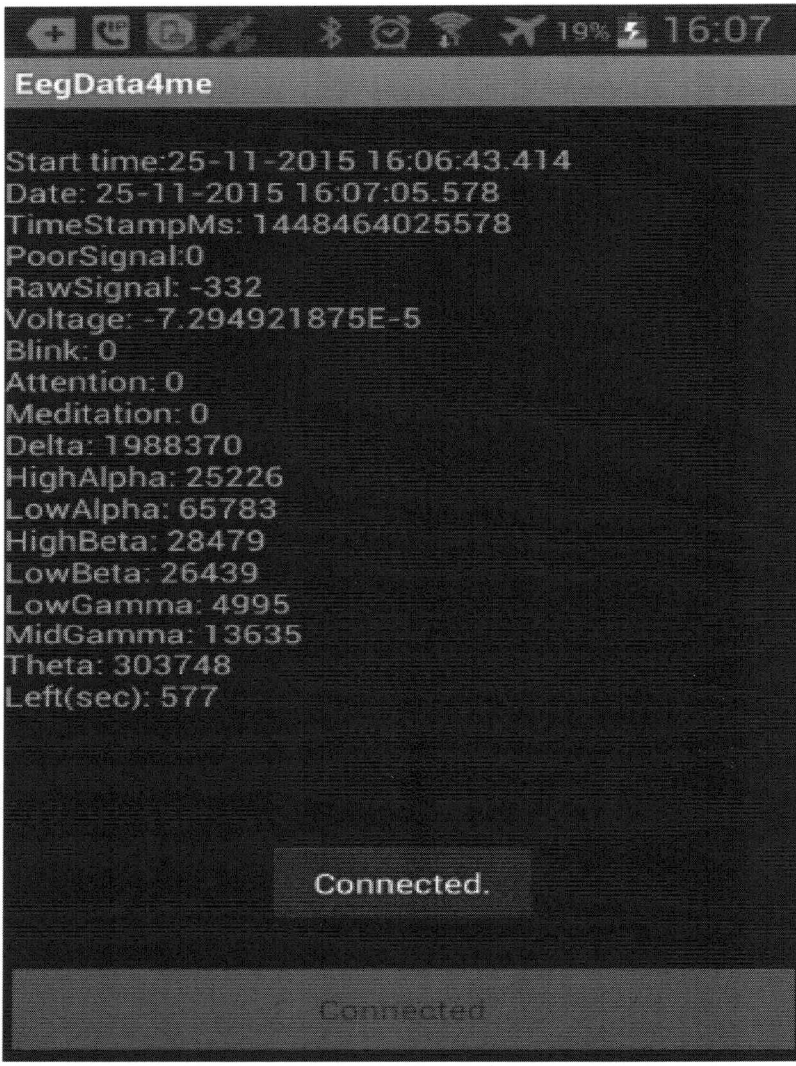

Figure 5. Android application to collect the EEG data.

7.2. Instrumentation Device

In the experimentation process, the Neurosky Mindwave mobile, that is an unobtrusive low-cost (€136) sensor device for EEG data acquisition is employed, see Figure 6. The device consists of a headband with three sensors, the reference and ground electrodes that are clipped onto the earlobe, whilst the EEG recorder electrode is positioned on the forehead.

The sensors require no gel or saline for recording, and no expertise is required for set up. The sensor provides raw EEG signal, alpha, beta, gamma delta and theta, the EEG power spectrum, and the measurements for 'attention', 'meditation' and 'eye blink'. Neurosky employs Bluetooth wireless communication which features: a RF data rate of 250 Kbits/s, 10 m RF range and UART baud rate of 57,600 Baud. Attention, meditation, and blink measurements are computed by Neurosky proprietary algorithms with a calculation rate of 1 Hz, and the measurement values range within the scale of 0 to 100 units.

Figure 6. Participant with the EEG acquisition device.

7.3. Participants

A total of three healthy women drivers aged between 35 and 50 years old with more than 15 years of experience driving participated in the test. The participants, *P1*, *P2*, and *P3*, were asked to get a full night of sleep time in the lead up to their study appointments. Participants were also requested to avoid drinking alcohol at least 24 h before their test, and abstain from caffeine on the day before of the study. Informed consent was obtained from all participants.

7.4. Procedure

The experiment was developed within three consecutive days starting at 9:30 a.m. Each participant drove during 10 min in her own vehicle. All participants followed the same route from the BarcelonaTech parking to the Port Ginesta of Castelldefels, Spain. See Figure 7. The speed limit that applies to the road-related area was 40 Km/h and the traffic density was very low.

Figure 7. Route of the experiment.

7.5. Dataset

Ten minutes of attention and meditation signals at a sampling rate of 512 samples per second were registered. In Figure 8, two minute readings of the signals of the three car drivers *P1*, *P2* and *P3*, are shown.

In the left column the attention signals are graphed and in the right column the readings of the meditation signals are plotted. In the ordinate, the magnitude of the signals, attention and meditation, are displayed and in the abscissa the sample numbers are shown. In the case of the attention signals, it can be observed that the readings of the *P1* individual are distributed along a value range of 0–60 units, the *P2* readings fall within the range of 0–80 units and the *P3* reading values are allocated within the range of 0–100 units. In the case of meditation values, *P1* presents readings are distributed along 0–90 units, *P2* readings fall within the range of 0–80 units, and *P3* has readings falling within the range of 0–80 units.

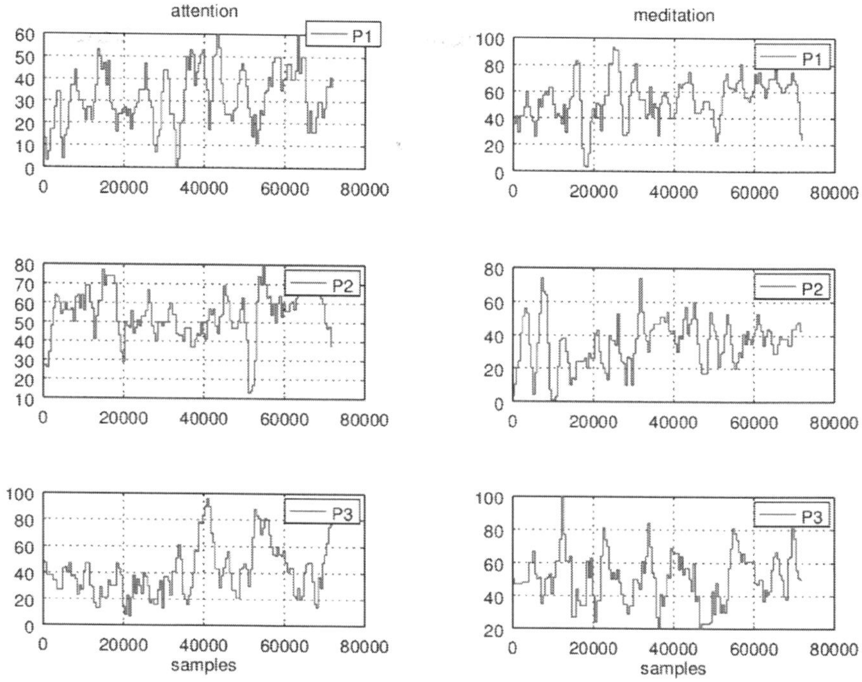

Figure 8. Attention and meditation readings of three individuals, *P1*, *P2*, and *P3* car drivers.

From Figure 8, it must be observed that the values apparently do not follow a distinguishable pattern. This is due to the large changes in the signal magnitude and frequency, so the values do not present a predictable behavior and in this manner it is not possible to determine the drivers' state conditions. Therefore a number of signal processing tasks should be performed before the application can make any decision.

Signal Processing

Signal average. The values of the readings, attention and meditation, are passed through a point to point averaging module. This procedure has the purpose of cutting high frequency changes out from the signals. This process implies the implementation of low pass filters, more precisely adaptive low pass filters. The outcome is a signal which presents less abrupt changes in the signal amplitude. The average output is passed to the signal variance module, see Figure 9.

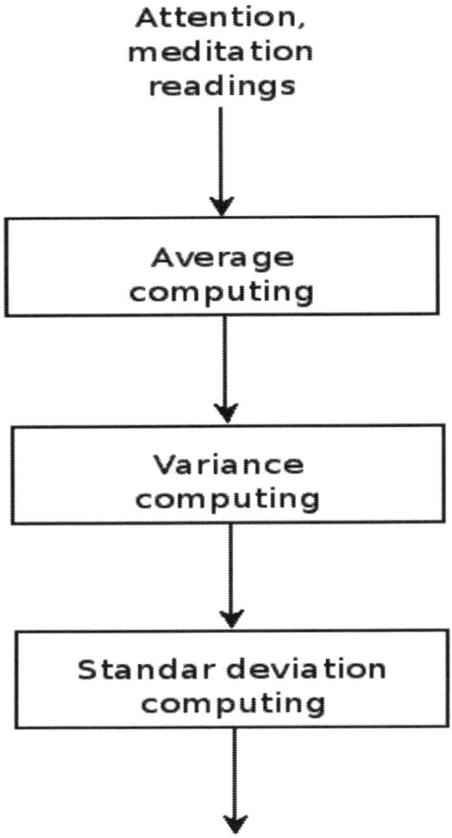

Figure 9. Application signal processing module, adaptive low pass filter, variance and standard deviation computations.

Signal variance. In the same manner, a software module computes a point to point variance. The purpose of this step leads to enhance the differences between the sensor signal and the average data. In this manner, the variance amplifies little changes in the differences whilst large difference values are kept almost without change. The variance output is passed to the standard deviation module, see Figure 9.

Signal standard deviation. In this step a software module calculates a point to point standard deviation. The purpose of this operation is to provide a measurement of the data dispersion.

Figure 9 shows the calculation sequence followed by the application signal processing layer that operates over the signals, attention and meditation of each one of the individuals *P1*, *P2* and *P3*.

The attention and meditation signals, and the average and standard deviation computations for the *P1*, *P2*, and *P3*individuals are plotted in Figure 10. In the ordinate, the magnitude of the signals, attention, meditation, average, and standard deviation, are displayed and the abscissa shows the sample numbers. It should be noticed that the average, and standard deviation adaptive algorithms take around 1536 samples (three seconds) to settle down to the actual signal average and standard deviation values. In both cases, it is observed that the average estimations give a more stable reference with respect the changes observed in the amplitude and frequency of the input signal, attention and meditation readings. In the same manner, the standard deviation of the signals peacefully follows the average computation changes.

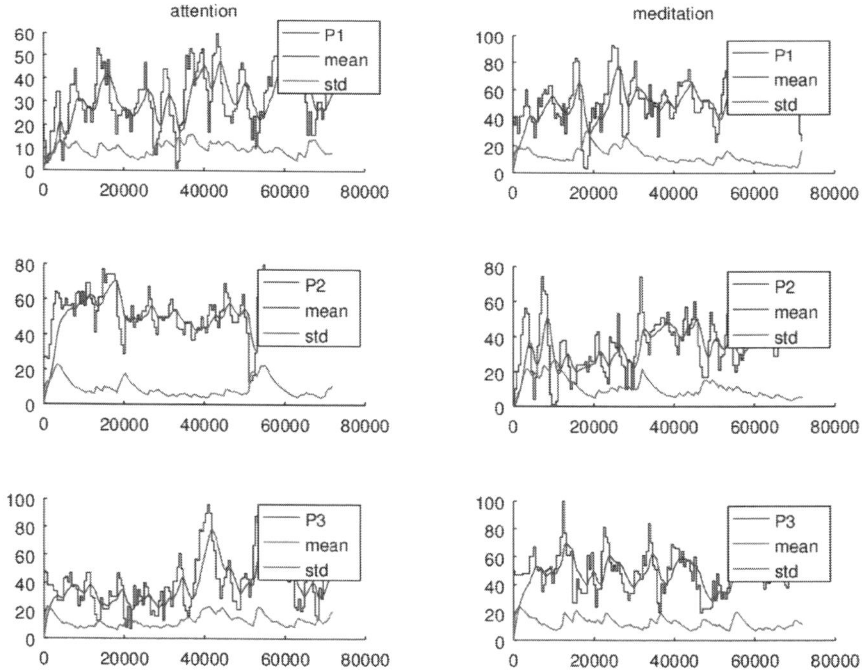

Figure 10. Statistic, average and standard deviation, computations of the attention and meditation signals of the individuals *P1*, *P2*, and *P3*.

Additionally, in both cases it is observed that within some intervals the standard deviation preserves a uniform distance with respect the average values. For instance, it is noticed that individual *P2* can focus (average and standard deviation differences larger than 40 units) for longer time periods (samples 1536 to 50,000) than *P1* and *P3*. Also, it can be observed that in the smallest attention levels the distance between the average and the standard deviation becomes quite closer. On the other hand, the graphs show that *P1* and *P3* are able to keep calm for longer periods of time compared with respect to*P2*, although *P3* presents the lower focusing levels.

Interestingly, running a comparison between the attention and meditation values it is noticed that having high levels of attention does not necessarily imply having higher levels of meditation or peacefulness. In fact, being more focused can be a cause of high stress levels, as it can be seen for individual *P2* whose attention average and standard deviation difference values are the highest, while the meditation average and standard deviation difference values are lower with respect to the individuals *P1* and *P3*, see Figure 10.

7.6. Low Level Attention Driving State Detection

In this manner the distance between average and standard deviation values can be employed to have in a way a measurement of the attention level. Furthermore, the observed distance can be combined with other measurements: such as the data collection timestamps, the car speed, orientation, steering speed, *etc.* that can be a measurement of the driver performance.

In the particular case of the developed application two variables are under consideration to detect a possible impaired driving performance: (1) the difference between the attention average and standard deviation values and (2) the elapsed time the driver performs with low attention average and standard deviation values. In this manner, alarms are issued given the condition, large time periods with low attention differences. To do this, on the one hand, the attention difference measurements are grouped within three ranges: (I) the values that fall between 10 and 20 units are considered low; (II) the difference values that are within the 20 and 60 units mean elevated cognitive load and (III) the difference values below 10 units are interpreted as lowered levels. On the other hand, assuming the maximum driving velocity of 40 km/h, approximately the time required to advance a distance of 10 m is close to one second.

8. PERFORMANCE OF THE ARCHITECTURE

The performance of the integrated architecture is evaluated in terms of alarm triggering, the BSN bandwidth estimation and the Monitoring Station bandwidth estimation.

8.1. Alarm Triggering

The architecture has been tested with the EEG signals of the *P1* driver under two car driving cases: in phase 1 the drivers are asked to just guide the car without any secondary task and in phase 2 the drivers are asked to drive while performing secondary tasks. In both field studies, participants drove while EEG data were recorded.

For phase 2, in addition to the primary driving task, participants had to complete two secondary cognitive demand tasks that increase the workload. Within the first three minutes, the drivers, via the hands-free set, must pick up and answer a phone call that lasts one minute. Then a rest period of 2 min is introduced. The second procedure consists of presenting a digit span test, it means, an auditory presentation of the single digits 0–9, one at a time in a randomly ordered sequence. As each new item was presented, participants were required to say out loud the digit two items back in the current sequence. This secondary task requires auditory perception and cognitive processing involving working memory [76]. The test considers a set of 30 number series of three digits, between each series there is a pause period of two seconds. Finally, the rest of the time the driver is left guiding with no load until she/he arrives the destiny.

In Figure 11, row one, the *P1* EEG signals are plotted for the conditions of phases 1 and 2. In row two, the statistical EEG values (average and standard deviation) and the difference between the average and the standard deviation are graphed. In row three the alarms triggered by the triggering module are shown. The triggering limit is set to a difference value of 10 units. In both cases, phases 1 and 2, within the first 47 s the triggering module issues several alarms. It is because this is the time required by the adaptive average and standard deviation algorithms to adjust their computations to a settled estimation value, therefore these alarms are discarded from the test results. In case of phase 1, after the settling time period has elapsed, as expected there are no alarms triggered along all the resting time of the test. In case of phase 2, within the time period of the phone call, there are no alarms issued. Then, two alarm sets are triggered along the rest of the test time period. The first alarms are centered around the 100,000th sample (6.53 min) and around the 230,000th sample (15.033 min). The alarm at minute 6.53 corresponds to the digit span test and the alarm in the 13.033 min is out of the car guiding period, therefore this may be discarded.

It must be observed that the triggering module sensibility is controlled by the triggering limit. In fact, if the triggering limit is raised the number of triggers is increased. For instance, in Figure 12, the triggers obtained for the setting of the triggering limit to a value of 15 units are shown in row 3. In the case of phase 1, the triggering module issues alarms within the 100,000th to 150,000th samples interval. These triggers are false positives because the expected result is no alarms under the condition of no cognitive load. In the case of phase 2, there are six points where alarms are triggered, the first set is issued between the 13,000th and 15,000th sample period (50 s to 60 s). The second group is centred at the 100,000th sample (6.53 min). The third group lays around the 150,000th sample (minute 15.033) that is out of the test time period, and the other alarm groups are also outside the test time period, therefore as previously has been mentioned these alarms may be discarded.

In Figure 13, row 3, the issued alarms for a triggering limit of 20 units are plotted. In both cases, phase 1 and phase 2, the number of triggers has been incremented, appearing alarms in the places where the difference between the average and standard deviation are less than 20 units. In this case, the alarms appearing in the phase one can all be considered as false positives. In the phase 2, it is expected the triggers appear in the places where the phone call answering and the digit span test take place.

From the previous discussion it can be seen that a tuning process should be run in order to find out the triggering limit that best points the critical degree out of the driver attention.

8.2. BSN Bandwidth Estimation

The BSN is made up of one single hop transmission star topology network, with at most seven sensor slaves, and one master played by the monitoring station. It is assumed a 2.4 GHz radio transmission link with data rates within the range of 1 Mbit/s to 3 Mbit/s, such as the featured by the Bluetooth low energy or Zigbee IEEE 802.15.4 RF radio transceivers. It should be observed that with the use of the Bluetooth technology there is no possibility of data packet collisions. In fact, sensors data requests are synchronised by the master in a round-robin fashion. Differently, Zigbee would manage a larger number of slaves rather requiring the implementation of a contention access media protocol.

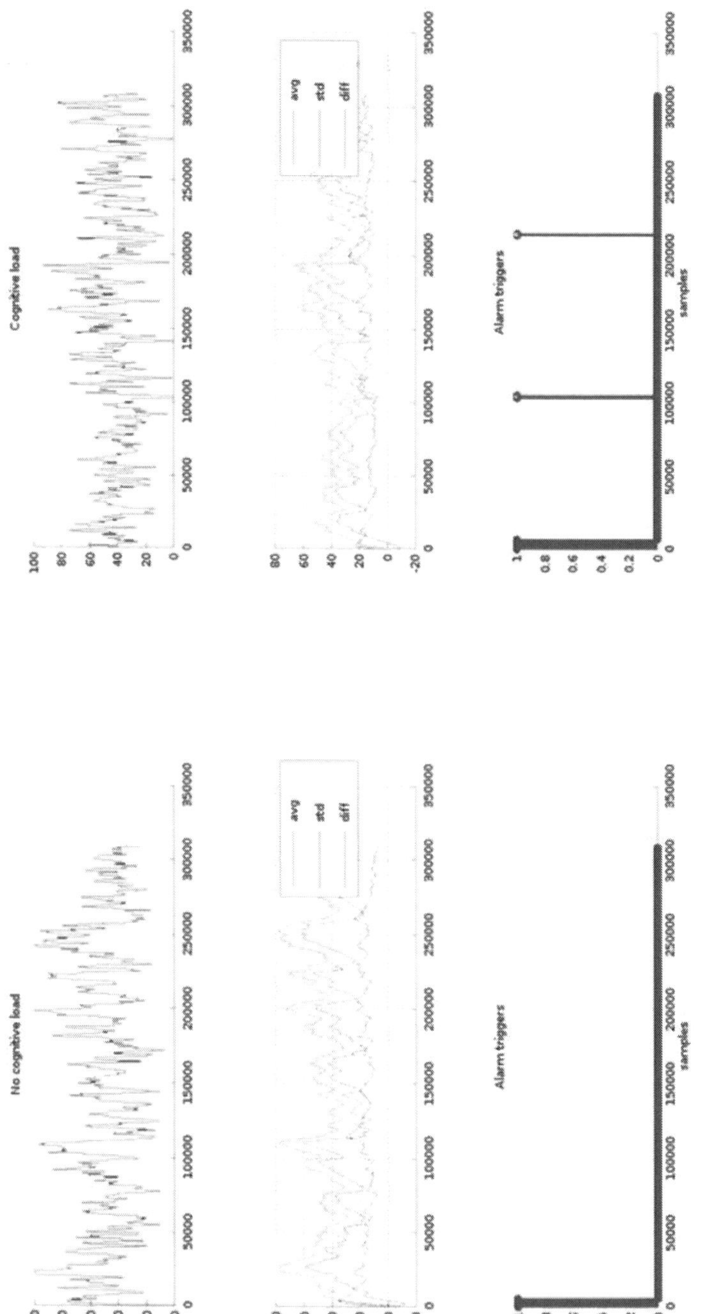

Figure 11. Row 1, *P1* EEG signals for the no cognitive load and cognitive load. Row 2, average, standard deviation and difference of the EEG signal values. Row 3 alarm triggers for difference values of less than 10 units.

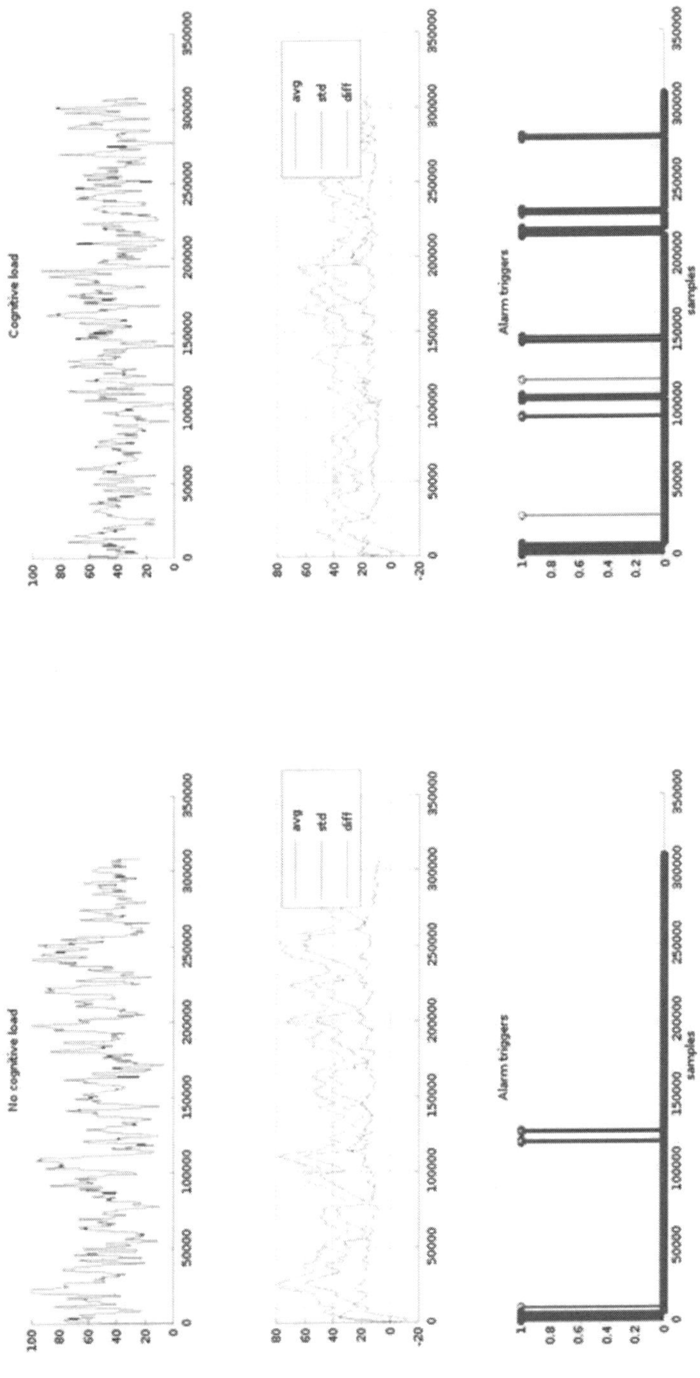

Figure 12. Row 1, *P1* EEG signals for the no cognitive load and cognitive load. Row 2, average, standard deviation and difference of the EEG signal values. Row 3, alarm triggers for difference values less than 15 units.

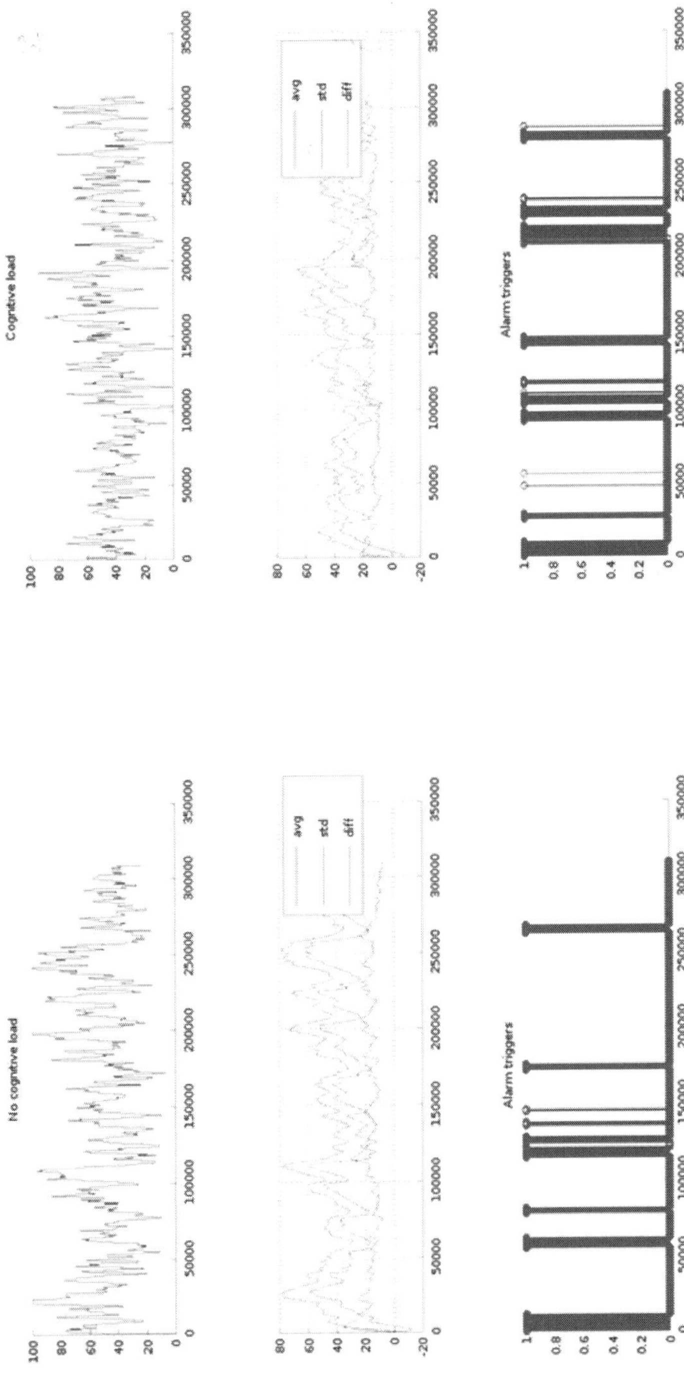

Figure 13. Row 1, *P1* EEG signals for the no cognitive load and cognitive load. Row 2, average, standard deviation and difference of the EEG signal values. Row 3, alarm triggers for difference values less than 20 units.

The prototype architecture considers the monitoring of two physiology EEG signals: drowsy and attention. The EEG sensor requires one second to compute one drowsy and one attention level estimations, then the sensor transmits within the Bluetooth wireless channel a data packet. The data packet structure of the EEG sensor consists of three sections: (i) a 3 bytes header; (ii) a 0–169 bytes payload and (iii) a 1 byte checksum. In the worst of the cases the data payload length of the EEG Bluetooth packet is 173 bytes. Each EEG data inserted in the packet payload is identified by a code number, a data type, and the sensor reading value. The code number is one byte and labels the physiology state, blink or attention, the data type is one byte and shows the variable length, and the value field that is the sensor reading value, generally a two bytes integer value. In our case the data packet payload starts with the blink code, the data type, and the two bytes of the sensor value. Secondly, the attention code, the data type and the two bytes integer sensor value. In this manner, the total data payload packet is eight bytes, two bytes for the command codes, two bytes for the value types, and four bytes for the two state values. The data transmissions among the slaves and the monitoring station are limited to the the RF data rate that is 32 Kbytes per second. Therefore, assuming a full packet payload, the time required to transmit an EEG data packet of payload length is 3.27 ms.

From the discussion in Section 2.4, the respiration monitoring can serve to detect drunkenness and emotional disorders, therefore the design of the prototype considers respiration sensors. The sensor data rate is 800 bps (100 Bps) and the frequency to estimate one state value is around the 0.1–10 Hz (10 s–100 ms). Then, assuming a Bluetooth transmission link, a data packet of length 173, the time required to transmit one sensor data at the maximum frequency, 100 ms, is 103.27 ms.

8.3. Monitoring Station Bandwidth Estimation

After receiving the sensor signals, EEG and respiration. Separately, the monitoring station computes the impaired driver degree for each signal. Whether is found in any or both signals critical levels alarms are triggered via an event based detection algorithm. In this case events are abnormalities in the course that potentially would become an incident. In principle, events rarely happen therefore the most of the time the wireless channel links between the monitoring station, the services server, GPRS or WiFi, and the VANET, WiFi, are available.

9. RESEARCH CHALLENGES

Next, the challenges concerning the integration of BSNs and VANETs are introduced. Information security and privacy preservation are essential challenges. It must be strictly guaranteed that sensitive and private driver-related data is only accessed by authorized users. For this reason, ordinary notification messages should warn about an improper driver's state but not specify the state or incorporate related body sensor data. In addition, the emergency services should also be notified if driver's assistance is required and body sensor data should be forwarded. It is essential to ensure the secure delivery of patient-related data, since the inability to securely store and transfer authentic data can prevent the driver from being treated effectively.

However, the integration of a high-level security mechanism in low-power and resource-constrained body sensors increases the computational, communication and management costs [77]. Therefore, simple and effective biometrics-based methods that use the intrinsic human body characteristics for user authentication and secure key cipher transmission should be designed to protect the privacy of drivers. Data should be protected against modifications of malicious vehicles [78] (such as replay attack) and against node failures.

Furthermore, ensuring comfort during driving while preserving security is essential. Safety belts are sometimes considered uncomfortable, since they restrict movement but they prevent deaths in many traffic accidents. The same would apply to BSNs. In addition, as technology evolves, a limited number of highly sensitive, miniaturized sensors will be worn more comfortably and will continuously measure the vital signs and brain activity without disrupting the driver.

Another key challenge is the provision of Quality of Service (QoS) in this architecture. In BSNs loss-sensitive and delay-sensitive applications require efficient error detection strategies to guarantee a high level of QoS. The Bit Error Rate (BER) can be reduced applying error correction and interference-avoidance methods at the MAC and physical layers. End-to-end delay and jitter are important parameters to ensure a fast delivery of high-priority traffic. The link quality conditions are dramatically affected by the spatial and temporal variability of the vehicular channel. If safety-related notification messages are delayed, lost or corrupted, the reliability of the network would be seriously damaged and in a worst case scenario the non-detection of a traffic driving impairment could be fatal. It is required to develop adaptive QoS routing schemes that can quickly redirect traffic when the established routes are no longer available. Important QoS metrics such as the packet delivery ratio and connection duration require in-depth research and improvement.

Furthermore, position-based information dissemination should be accurate and reliable. Since the BSN-VANET integration is strongly dependent on the geographic location of the vehicle that sends notification messages, positional information is crucial. Wrong position information due to malfunction or intentionally falsified by attackers degrades the performance of the system and should be quickly detected and corrected.

The accuracy of the impaired driving detection systems is also challenging. Detecting emotional state disorders is especially difficult, since there is no agreement on how emotions can be measured and classified.

The impact of false positives in real life scenarios should also be analysed. In this sense, body sensor networks technologies have been incrementally improved and tuned to the point where claims of near-perfect accuracy are not unheard of, despite relatively high recording noise levels and high complexity of the collected signals [79]. So there is an increasing need to compare and evaluate the performance of different behavior state detection methods using BSNs. In future work, we will explore the relationship between classification accuracy and driver performance that we think may reveal interesting correlations.

Some legal and ethical issues arise from the BSN-VANET integration. Regulations about the use of BSNs while driving should be defined. Its use could be mandatory for every driver or just restricted to the control of drivers with prior driving while impaired convictions. In this last case, BSNs could be effectively used to prevent accidents, since statistics demonstrate that drivers with a blood alcohol concentration of 0.08% or higher involved in fatal crashes were four times more likely to have a prior driving while impaired conviction than were drivers with no alcohol (8% and 2%, respectively) [80]. The use of BSNs by drivers is also a controversial issue from a social and ethical viewpoint. Many people could be concerned about illicit access or accidental revelation of personal information through the VANET to others, since this occurrence may be undesirable from the driver's perspective and could violate civil liberties. Since inappropriate use of the drivers' states could lead to discrimination, the proper degree of protection of these data is essential. Therefore, a regulation that determines the ownership of the data and its legal liabilities should be explicitly defined.

Energy efficiency in BSNs is a challenging issue as well. The battery capacity is limited by the dimension of the nodes. Using human energy harvesting as secondary energy source to supplement batteries sounds promising but arises different challenges such as the amount and availability of the collected energy [81]. In addition, it is possible to improve the energy efficiency and robustness to link failures of BSNs by exploiting the benefits of Random Linear Network Coding (RLNC)-based cooperation and Compressed Sensing (CS)-based signal processing algorithms [82]. RLNC is based on the transmission of linear combinations over a block of original data packets, created by multiplying each packet with a random coefficient drawn by a finite Galois field. RLNC techniques can also be applied to provide reliability. In [83], the authors propose a cloud-assisted MAC protocol that guarantees the delivery of all data packets to the destination by enabling the coordination among the relays of a relay sensor network, that is, a network that enables the transmission of information between a BSN and the medical data center.

10. CONCLUSIONS

If we focus on the driver behaviours, traffic accidents are likely to happen when drivers make a mistake or manifest improper driving behaviors while they misjudge the risks of driving environments. Such driving behaviours are mainly caused by four factors: drunk driving, drowsy driving, distracted driving and drivers with emotional states disorders.

In this paper an architecture for the integration of BSNs and VANETs to detect driving impairments has been introduced. Its main components and relevant driver's states have been described. Thanks to this integration it is possible to monitor the driver's state and take the necessary actions to avoid accidents.

In our BSN-VANET integration proposal four behavior states have been addressed: drowsy, drunk, emotional state disorders and distracted while driving. Future work will detect other human states via the BSN such as abrupt health problems (e.g., heart attack) that produce driving impairment.

ACKNOWLEDGMENTS

This work was supported by the Spanish Ministry of Education and Science under the projects TRA2013-45119-R and TEC2013-47960-C4-1-P. Jose Luis Delgado is partially supported by the National Science and Technology Council (CONACyT) of Mexico with a scholarship that allowed him staying in the spring season, at the Computer Architecture Department in the UPC.

CONFLICTS OF INTEREST

The authors declare no conflict of interest.

REFERENCES

1. Tefft, B.C.; AAA Foundation for Traffic Safety. Prevalence of Motor Vehicle Crashes Involving Drowsy Drivers. Available online: https://www.aaafoundation.org/sites/default/files/AAAFoundation-DrowsyDriving-Nov2014.pdf(accessed on 13 January 2016).

2. World Health Organization. Global Status Report on Road Safety. Available online: http://www.who.int/violence_injury_prevention/road_safety_status/2015/GSRRS2015_Summary_EN_final2.pdf?ua=1 (accessed on 13 January 2016).

3. World Health Organization. Report on Road Traffic Injury Prevention. Available online: http://apps.who.int/iris/bitstream/10665/ 42871/1/9241562609.pdf (accessed on 13 January 2016).

4. National Highway Traffic Safety Administration. National Center for Statistics and Analysis; Crash Data Key Findings (Traffic Safety Facts Crash Stats. Report No. DOT HS 812219); National Highway Traffic Safety Administration: Washington, DC, USA, 2014.

5. James, L.; Nahl, D. Road Rage and Aggressive Driving: Steering Clear of Highway Warfare; Prometheus Books: Amherst, NY, USA, 2000.

6. Omeni, O.; Wong, A.; Burdett, A.J.; Toumazou, C. Energy Efficient Medium Access Protocol for Wireless Medical Body Area Sensor Networks. IEEE Trans. Biomed. Circuits Syst. 2008, 2, 251–259.

7. Hartenstein, H.; Laberteaux, K.P. A Tutorial Survey on Vehicular Ad Hoc networks. IEEE Commun. Mag. 2008, 46, 164–171.

8. James, L. Traffic Psychology Research at the University of Hawaii. Available online: http://www.soc.hawaii.edu/leonj/leonj/leonpsy/traffic/tpintro.html (accessed on 13 January 2016).

9. Lin, C.-T.; Chang, C.-J.; Lin, B.-S.; Hung, S.-H.; Chao, C.-F.; Wang, I.-J. A Real-Time Wireless Brain—Computer Interface System for Drowsiness Detection. IEEE Trans. Biomed. Circuits Syst. 2010, 4, 214–222.

10. Yang, G.; Lin, Y.; Bhattacharya, P. A Driver Fatigue Recognition Model based on Information Fusion and Dynamic Bayesian Network. Inf. Sci. 2010, 10, 1942–1954.

11. Jung, S.-J.; Shin, H.-S.; Chung, W.-Y. Driver Fatigue and Drowsiness Monitoring System with Embedded Electrocardiogram Sensor on Steering Wheel. IET Intell. Transp. Syst. 2014, 8, 43–50.

12. Hu, S.; Zheng, G. Driver Drowsiness Detection with Eyelid related Parameters by Support Vector Machine. Expert Syst. Appl. 2009, 36, 7651–7658.

13. Sun, Y.; Yu, X.B. An Innovative Nonintrusive Driver Assistance System for Vital Signal Monitoring. IEEE J. Biomed. Health Inform. 2014, 6, 1932–1939.

14. Lee, B.-G.; Chung, W.-Y. A Smartphone-based Driver Safety Monitoring System using Data Fusion. Sensors 2012, 12, 17536–17552.

15. Sahayadhas, A.; Sundaraj, K.; Murugappan, M. Detecting Driver Drowsiness Based on Sensors: A Review. Sensors2012, 12, 16937–16953.

16. Flores, M.J.; Armingol, J.M.; Escalera, A. Driver Drowsiness Warning System Using Visual Information for both Diurnal and Nocturnal Illumination Conditions. EURASIP J. Adv. Signal Process. 2010, 2010, 1–20.

17. Gustavo, A.; Pelaez, C.; Garcia, F.; de la Escalera, A.; Armingol, J.M. Driver Monitoring Based on Low-Cost 3-D Sensors. IEEE Trans. Intell. Transp. Syst. 2014, 15, 1855–1860.

18. Ertin, E.; Kumar, S.; al'Absi, M.; Kedia, S.; Scott, M.; Venugopal, M.; Ward, K.; Feuvrel, K.; Ghosh, A.; Guha, S.; et al. AutoSense: A Wireless Sensor System to Quantify Personal Exposures to Psychosocial Stress and Alcohol in Natural Environment. ISES 2009, 15, 1–9.

19. Geeta, B.; Marur, D. Smart Drunken Driver Detection and Speed Monitoring System for Vehicles. Int. J. Adv. Technol. Eng. Sci. 2015, 3, 67–73.

20. Al-Sultan, S.; Al-Bayatti, A.; Zedan, H. Context-aware Driver Behaviour Detection System in Intelligent Transportation systems. IEEE Trans. Veh. Technol. 2013, 62, 4264–4275.

21. Wu, Y.-C.; Xia, Y.-Q.; Xie, P.; Ji, X.-W. The Design of an Automotive Anti-Drunk Driving System to Guarantee the Uniqueness of Driver. Int. Conf. Inform. Eng. Comput. Sci. 2009, 62, 1–4.

22. Murata, K.; Fujita, E.; Kojima, S.; Maeda, S.; Ogura, Y.; Kamei, T.; Tsuji, T.; Kaneko, S.; Yoshizumi, M.; Suzuki, N. Noninvasive Biological Sensor System for Detection of Drunk Driving. IEEE Trans. Inform. Technol. Biomed. 2011, 15, 19–25.

23. Ramanath, S.; Sudharsan, A. Drunken Driving and Rash Driving Prevention System. In Proceedings of the International Conference on Mechanical and Electrical Technology (ICMET), Singapore, 10–12 September 2010; pp. 599–603.

24. American Beverage Institute. Alcohol Detection Technologies: Present and Future. Available online: http://interlockfacts.com/pdfs/ 090724_ ABI_AlcoholDetectionTech_PresentandFuture.pdf (accessed on 13 January 2016).

25. Katsis, C.D.; Katertsidis, N.; Ganiatsas, G.; Fotiadis, D.I. Toward Emotion Recognition in Car-Racing Drivers: A Biosignal Processing Approach. IEEE Trans. Syst. Man Cybern. A Syst. Hum. 2008, 38, 502–512.

26. Katsis, C.D.; Goletsis, Y.; Rigas, G.; Fotiadis, D.I. A Wearable System for the Affective Monitoring of Car Racing Drivers during Simulated Conditions. Transp. Res. C Emerg. Technol. 2011, 19, 541–551.

27. Cai, H.; Lin, Y. Modelling of Operators' Emotion and Task Performance in a Virtual Driving Environment. Int. J. Hum. Comput. Stud. 2011, 9, 571–587.

28. Haak, P.V.D.; Lon, R.V.; Meer, J.V.D.; Rothkrantz, L. Stress Assessment of Car-Drivers using EEG-analysis. In Proceedings of the International Conference on Computer Systems and Technologies (CompSysTech), Sofia, Bulgaria, 17–18 June 2010; pp. 473–477.

29. Lanatà, A.; Valenza, G.; Greco, A.; Gentili, C.; Bartolozzi, R.; Bucchi, F.; Frendo, F.; Scilingo, E.P. How the Autonomic Nervous System and Driving Style Change With Incremental Stressing Conditions During Simulated Driving. IEEE Trans. Intell. Transp. Syst. 2015, 16, 1505–1517.

30. Lin, C.; Tsai, S.; Ko, L. EEG-based Learning System for Online Motion Sickness Level Estimation in a Dynamic Vehicle Environment. IEEE Trans. Neural Netw. Learn. Syst. 2013, 24, 1689–1700. [PubMed]

31. Baek, H.J.; Lee, H.B.; Kim, J.S.; Choi, J.M.; Kim, K.K.; Park, K.S. Nonintrusive Biological Signal Monitoring in a Car to Evaluate a Driver's Stress and Health State. Telemed. e-Health 2009, 15, 182–189.

32. Healey, J.; Picard, R. Detecting Stress During Real-World Driving Tasks Using Physiological Sensors. IEEE Trans. Intell. Transp. Syst. 2005, 6, 156–166.

33. Deng, Y.; Wu, Z.; Chu, C.; Zhang, Q.; Hsu, F. Sensor Feature Selection and Combination for Stress Identification Using Combinatorial Fusion. Int. J. Adv. Robot. Syst. 2013, 10, 1–10.

34. Rigas, G.; Goletsis, Y.; Fotiadis, D.I. Real-Time Driver's Stress Event Detection. IEEE Trans. Intell. Transp. Syst. 2012,13, 221–234.

35. Singh, R.R.; Conjeti, S.; Banerjee, R. A Comparative Evaluation of Neural Network Classifiers for Stress Level Analysis of Automotive Drivers using Physiological Signals. Biomed. Signal Process. Control 2013, 8, 740–754.

36. Malta, L.; Miyajima, C.; Kitaoka, N.; Takeda, K. Analysis of Real-World Driver's Frustration. IEEE Trans. Intell. Transp. Syst. 2011, 12, 109–118.

37. Rigas, G.; Goletis, Y.; Bougia, P.; Fotiadis, D. Towards Driver's State Recognition on Real Driving Conditions. Int. J. Veh. Technol. 2011, 2011, 1–14.

38. Hernandez, J.; McDuff, D.; Benavides, X.; Amores, J.; Maes, P.; Picard, R. AutoEmotive: Bringing Empathy to the Driving Experience to Manage Stress. In Proceedings of the Designing Interactive Systems (DIS Companion), Vancouver, BC, Canada, 21–25 June 2014; pp. 53–56.

39. Sathyanarayana, A.; Nageswaren, S.; Ghasemzadeh, H.; Jafari, R.; Hansen, J.H.L. Body Sensor Networks for Driver Distraction Identification. In Proceedings of the IEEE International Conference on Vehicular Electronics and Safety (ICVES), Columbus, OH, USA, 22–24 September 2008; pp. 120–125.

40. Chou, W.-Y.; Yang, C.-H.; Tasi, H.-C.; Lin, Y.-C.; Chuang, C.-F.; Chen, K.-H. Driver Distraction Recognition Based on Dual Compass Motion Sensoring. In Proceedings of the IEEE 17th International Conference on Intelligent Transportation Systems (ITSC), Qingdao, China, 8–11 October 2014; pp. 1375–1380.

41. Gallahan, S.L.; Golzar, G.F.; Jain, A.P.; Samay, A.E.; Trerotola, T.J.; Weisskopf, J.G.; Lau, N. Detecting and Mitigating Driver Distraction with Motion Capture Technology: Distracted Driving Warning System. In Proceedings of the IEEE Systems and Information Engineering Design Symposium (SIEDS), Charlottesville, VA, USA, 26–26 April 2013; pp. 76–81.

42. Li, N.; Jain, J.J.; Busso, C. Modeling of Driver Behavior in Real World Scenarios using Multiple Noninvasive Sensors.IEEE Trans. Multimed. 2013, 15, 1213–1225.

43. Li, N.; Busso, C. Predicting Perceived Visual and Cognitive Distractions of Drivers with Multimodal Features. IEEE Trans. Intell. Transp. Syst. 2015, 16, 51–65.

44. Im, S.; Lee, C.; Yang, S.; Kim, J.; You, B. Driver Distraction Detection by In-vehicle Signal Processing. In Proceedings of the IEEE Symposium on Computational Intelligence in Vehicles and Transportation Systems (CIVTS), Orlando, FL, USA, 9–12 December 2014; pp. 64–68.

45. Martin, S.; Tawari, A.; Trivedi, M.M. Monitoring Head Dynamics for Driver Assistance Systems: A Multi-Perspective Approach. In Proceedings of the IEEE International Conference on Intelligent Transportation Systems (ITSC), The Hague, The Netherlands, 6–9 October 2013; pp. 2286–2291.

46. Tawari, A.; Martin, S.; Trivedi, M.M. Continuous Head Movement Estimator for Driver Assistance: Issues, Algorithms, and On-Road Evaluations. IEEE Trans. Intell. Transp. Syst. 2014, 15, 818–830.

47. Murphy-Chutorian, E.; Trivedi, M.M. Head Pose Estimation and Augmented Reality Tracking: An Integrated System and Evaluation for Monitoring Driver Awareness. IEEE Trans. Intell. Transp. Syst. 2010, 11, 300–311.

48. Jiang, Y.; Wu, Y.; Xu, H. A Surveillance Method for Driver's Fatigue and Distraction Based on Machine Vision. In Proceedings of the International Conference on Transportation, Mechanical, and Electrical Engineering (TMEE), Changchun, China, 16–18 December 2011; pp. 727–730.

49. Bo, C.; Jian, X.; Li, X.-Y.; Mao, X.; Wang, Y.; Li, F. You're Driving and Texting: Detecting Drivers Using Personal Smart Phones by Leveraging Inertial Sensors. In Proceedings of the 19th Annual International Conference On Mobile Computing & Networking

(MobiCom), Miami, FL, USA, 30 September–4 October 2013; pp. 199–202.

50. Wang, S.; Zhang, Y.; Wu, C.; Darvas, F.; Chaovalitwongse, W.A. Online Prediction of Driver Distraction Based on Brain Activity Patterns. IEEE Trans. Intell. Transp. Syst. 2015, 16, 136–150.

51. Almahasneh, H.S.; Kamel, N.; Malik, A.S.; Wlater, N.; Chooi, W.T. EEG based Driver Cognitive Distraction Assessment. In Proceedings of the 5th International Conference on Intelligent and Advanced Systems (ICIAS), Kuala Lumpur, Malaysia, 3–5 June 2014; pp. 1–4.

52. IEEE Standards Association. 802.15.6–2012—IEEE Standard for Local and Metropolitan Area Networks—Part 15.6: Wireless Body Area Networks; LAN/MAN Standards Committee of the IEEE Computer Society: Piscataway, NJ, USA, 2012.

53. Kartsakli, E.; Lalos, A.S.; Antonopoulos, A.; Tennina, S.; Renzo, M.D.; Alonso, L.; Verikoukis, C. A Survey on M2M Systems for mHealth: A Wireless Communications Perspective. Sensors 2014, 14, 18009–18052.

54. Shu, M.; Yuan, D.; Zhang, C.; Wang, Y.; Chen, C. A MAC Protocol for Medical Monitoring Applications of Wireless Body Area Networks. Sensors 2015, 15, 12906–12931.

55. Li, C.; Yuan, X.; Yang, L.; Song, Y. A Hybrid Lifetime Extended Directional Approach for WBANs. Sensors 2015, 15, 28005–28030.

56. Bhandari, S.; Moh, S. A Survey of MAC Protocols for Cognitive Radio Body Area Networks. Sensors 2015, 15, 9189–9209.

57. Traffic Injury Research Foundation. Effective Strategies to Reduce Drunk Driving. Working Group on DMI Systems Improvements. Available online: http://tirf.ca/publications/PDF_publications/ 2011_DWI_WG_Full_Report_11.pdf(accessed on 13 January 2016).

58. Department of Transportation (US), National Highway Traffic Safety Administration (NHTSA). Drowsy Driving and Automobile Crashes. Report and Recommendations. Available online: https://www.nhlbi.nih.gov/files/docs/resources/sleep/drsy_drv.pdf (accessed on 13 January 2016).

59. Dinges, D. An Overview of Sleepiness and Accidents. J. Sleep Res. 1995, 4, 4–14.

60. AAA Foundation for Traffic Safety. How to Avoid Drowsy Driving. 2013. Available online: http://exchange.aaa.com/wp.content/ uploads/

2012/10/AAA-FTS-Drowsy-Driving-Brochure.pdf (accessed on 13 January 2016).

61. Domingo, M.C.; Reyes, A. A Clean Slate Architecture Design for VANETs. Wirel. Pers. Commun. 2012, 67, 315–333.
62. Rail Safety and Standards Board Limited (RSSB). Driving for Work: Managing Fatigue Risks. A Guide for Road Vehicle Drivers. Available online: http://www.rssb.co.uk/Library/improving-industry-performance/2013- guide-t997-driving-for-work-a5.pdf (accessed on 13 January 2016).
63. McCartt, A.T.; Geary, L.L.; Berning, A. Observational Study of the Extent of Driving While Suspended for Alcohol Impaired Driving. Inj. Prev. 2003, 9, 133–137.
64. Willis, C.; Lybrand, S.; Bellamy, N. Alcohol Ignition Interlock Programmes for Reducing Drink Driving Recidivism.Cochrane Database Syst. Rev. 2004, 18.
65. Beck, K.H.; Rauch, W.J.; Baker, E.A.; Williams, A.F. Effects of Ignition Interlock License Restrictions on Drivers with Multiple Alcohol Offenses: A Randomized Trial in Maryland. Am. J. Public Health 1999, 89, 1696–1700.
66. Stan, O.; Miclea, L. Road Traffic Safety Solution. In Proceedings of the IEEE International Conference on Automation, Quality and Testing, Robotics, Cluj-Napoca, Romania, 22–24 May 2014; pp. 1–5.
67. James, L.; Nahl, D. Chapter 3 in Driving lessons: Exploring Systems that Make Traffic Safer. In Dealing with Stress and Pressure in the Vehicle. Taxonomy of Driving Behavior: Affective, Cognitive, Sensorimotor; Rothe, J.P., Ed.; University of Alberta Press: Edmonton, AB, Canada, 2003; pp. 21–50.
68. Tse, J.L.M.; Flin, R.; Mearns, K. Bus Driver Well-Being Review: 50 Years of Research. Transp. Res. F 2006, 9, 89–114.
69. Singh, R.R.; Conjeti, S.; Banerjee, R. Assessment of Driver Stress from Physiological Signals Collected under Real-Time Semi-Urban Driving Scenarios. Int. J. Comput. Intell. Syst. 2014, 7, 740–754.
70. Swan, M. Connected Car: Quantified Self becomes Quantified Car. J. Sens. Actuator Netw. 2015, 4, 2–29.
71. Sathyaranayana, A.; Angkititrakul, P.; Hansen, J.H.L. Detecting and Classifying Driver Distraction. In Proceedings of the Biennial on SP for

In-Vehicle and Mobile Systems, Istanbul, Turkey, 17–19 June 2007; pp. 214–220.

72. AAA Foundation for Traffic Safety. Measuring Cognitive Distraction in the Automobile III: A Comparison of Ten 2015 In-Vehicle Information Systems. Available online: https://www.aaafoundation.org/sites/ default/ files/strayerIII_FINALREPORT.pdf (accessed on 13 January 2016).

73. AAA Foundation for Traffic Safety. Distracted Driving Among Newly Licensed Teen Drivers. Available online: https://www.aaafoundation.org/sites/default/files/research_reports/DistractedDrivingAmongNewlyLicensedTeenDrivers.pdf(accessed on 13 January 2016).

74. Strayer, D.L.; Drews, F.A.; Crouch, D.J. A Comparison of the Cell Phone Driver and the Drunk Driver. Hum. Factors2006, 48, 381–391.

75. Department of Transportation (US), National Highway Traffic Safety Administration (NHTSA). Driver Distraction: A Review of the Current State-of-Knowledge. Available online: http://www.nhtsa.gov/ DOT/ NHTSA/NRD/Multimedia/PDFs/Crash%20Avoidance/2008/810787.pdf (accessed on 13 January 2016).

76. Reimer, B.; Mehler, B.; Wang, Y.; Coughlin, J.F. A Field Study on the Impact of Variations in Short-Term Memory Demands on Drivers' Visual Attention and Driving Performance Across Three Age Groups. Hum. Factors 2012, 54, 454–468.

77. Saleem, S.; Ullah, S.; Kyung, S.K. Towards Security Issues and Solutions in Wireless Body Area Networks. In Proceedings of the 6th International Conference on Networked Computing (INC), Gyeongju, Korea, 11–13 May 2010; pp. 1–4.

78. Isaac, J.T.; Zeadally, S.; Camara, J.S. Security Attacks and Solutions for Vehicular Ad Hoc Networks. IET Commun.2010, 4, 894–903.

79. Wilson, G.F.; Russell, C.A.; Monnin, J.W.; Estepp, J.R.; Christensen, J.C. How does day to day variability in psychophysiological data affect classifier accuracy? Proc. Hum. Factors Ergon. Soc. Annu. Meet. 2010, 54, 264–268.

80. Department of Transportation (US), National Highway Traffic Safety Administration (NHTSA). Traffic Safety Facts 2010: Alcohol-Impaired Driving. Available online: http://www-nrd.nhtsa.dot.gov/ Pubs/ 811606.PDF (accessed on 13 January 2016).

81. Ibarra, E.; Antonopoulos, A.; Kartsakli, E.; Rodrigues, J.J.P.C.; Verikoukis, C. QoS-Aware Energy Management in Body Sensor Nodes

Powered by Human Energy Harvesting. IEEE Sens. J. 2016, 16, 542–549.

82. Lalos, A.S.; Antonopoulos, A.; Kartsakli, E.; di Renzo, M.; Tennina, S.; Alonso, L.; Verikoukis, C. RLNC-Aided Cooperative Compressed Sensing for Energy Efficient Vital Signal Telemonitoring. IEEE Trans. Wirel. Commun. 2015,14, 3685–3699.

83. Kartsakli, E.; Antonopoulos, A.; Alonso, L.; Verikoukis, C. A Cloud-Assisted Random Linear Network Coding Medium Access Control Protocol for Healthcare Applications. Sensors 2014, 14, 4806–4830.

CHAPTER 4

A Dynamic Reputation Management System for Mobile *Ad Hoc* Networks

Eric Chiejina *, Hannan Xiao and Bruce Christianson

School of Computer Science, University of Hertfordshire, College Lane, Hatfield, Hertfordshire AL10 9AB, UK

ABSTRACT

Nodes in mobile *ad hoc* networks (MANETs) are mandated to utilize their limited energy resources in forwarding routing control and data packets for other nodes. Since a MANET lacks a centralized administration and control, a node may decide to act selfishly, either by refusing to respond to route requests from other nodes or deceitfully by responding to some route requests, but dropping the corresponding data packets that are presented for forwarding. A significant increase in the presence of these misbehaving nodes in a MANET can subsequently degrade network performance. In this paper, we propose a dynamic reputation management system for detecting and isolating misbehaving nodes in MANETs. Our model employs a novel direct monitoring technique to evaluate the reputation of a node in the network, which ensures that nodes that expend their energy in transmitting data and routing control packets for others are allowed to carry out their network activities while the misbehaving nodes are detected and isolated from the network. Simulation results show that our model is effective at curbing and mitigating the effects of misbehaving nodes in the network.

KEYWORDS

selfish nodes; deceitful nodes; direct monitoring; total reputation; reputation management; MANETs

1. INTRODUCTION

Mobile *ad hoc* networks (MANETs) are vital to the advancement of wireless networks. MANETs are characteristically composed of equal nodes that communicate over wireless links without any backbone. Some applications, such as strategic military communication, rescue missions in times of natural disasters and sensor networks, are just a few possible uses of MANETs [1]. The emergence of the MANET technology advocates self-organized wireless interconnection of communication devices that would either extend or operate in concert with the wired networking infrastructure or, possibly, advance to autonomous networks. In either case, the propagation of MANET-based applications depends on a multitude of factors [2].

MANETs generally inherit the conventional problems of wireless and mobile communications. These include issues related to bandwidth optimization, power control and transmission quality enhancement [1,3]. In addition, the multi-hop nature and absence of fixed infrastructure generate new problems, such as configuration advertising, discovery, maintenance, as well as *ad hoc* addressing and self-routing. MANET topology is highly dynamic and random. Furthermore, the distribution of nodes and their ability to self-organize play an important role. Aside from their dynamic topology, due to their wireless transmission, MANETs are affected more by higher loss rates, higher delays and jitter than fixed networks. In addition, nodes in MANETs rely on batteries or other exhaustible power supplies for their energy. The most critical aspect of a MANET is that physical security is limited due to wireless transmission [1–5].

Security in MANETs mainly involves confidentiality and integrity of information, as well as legitimate use and availability of service [6]. Due to some characteristic features, MANETs are vulnerable to various security threats, such as eavesdropping, denial of service attacks (DoS), grey-hole attacks, black-hole attacks, *etc.* [4]. In a grey-hole attack [7,8], the malicious node behaves correctly by sending valid route replies to nodes that initiate route requests. If the malicious node is chosen as the nearest node to the required destination, it periodically drops the data packet to launch a DoS [8–10] attack. In the case of a black hole attack [11], the malicious node waits for neighbouring nodes to send route request messages. It replies to the request by providing a route to the destination over itself. It assigns a high sequence number in the reply message, which enables it to be seen as the best route to the required destination. By taking over all of the route, the malicious node discards all of the packets passing through it, by launching a DoS attack [9,11].

The existence of well-known intrusion prevention mechanisms, such as cryptography or authentication, can reduce threats against MANETs, such as malicious data modification, which aims to reduce data integrity and confidentiality [12]. However, they cannot defend against malicious internal nodes that disrupt the routing of data. Furthermore, conventional cryptography and authentication mechanisms cannot effectively address the above-mentioned threats that arise due to the inherent broadcast wireless medium and decentralized architecture of MANETs.

In general, the absence of a central authorization facility in an open and distributed communication environment is a major challenge, especially due to the need for cooperative network operation. Particularly in MANETs, any node may compromise the routing protocol functionality through a disruption of the route discovery process [2]. In order to ensure the availability of data in a MANET, all nodes in a MANET must act as routers for forwarding data packets from the source to the desired destinations [5]. It is therefore important for all nodes in a MANET to collaborate for the effective and efficient operations of the network.

However, due to the limited network resources and energy-constrained nature of nodes, it is expected that some nodes will exhibit uncooperative behaviours. These behaviours may adversely affect the overall network performance and put a further strain on the limited energy of the cooperative nodes. Specialised protocols have been employed in the network layer of nodes in MANETs to ensure collaboration among nodes. It is usually expected that these nodes will carry out their operations in compliance with the protocol specifications. However, these expectations are not always met.

Nodes sometimes make local decisions on whether to follow the network's basic operations or not. These nodes may decide to act selfishly by not participating in route discovery processes or deceitfully by responding to some route requests, but ensuring that the corresponding data packets are dropped. These misbehaving nodes specialise in conserving their limited energy resources, while the good nodes consume their own energy to ensure that the network is operational. An increase in the number of nodes exhibiting these types of behaviours may result in reduced network efficiency.

Countermeasures for node misbehaviour and selfishness are mandatory requirements in MANETs. Selfishness that causes a lack of node activity cannot be solved using classical security means that aim at verifying the correctness and integrity of an operation. It is therefore essential to employ a management system that will ensure an effective and reliable collaboration of all nodes in a MANET. An effective reputation management system would ensure that a node attains a certain reputation level before it can effectively operate in a network. This would ensure a gradual reduction or elimination of misbehaving nodes trying to disrupt the operations of the network [13].

In this paper, we propose a novel approach in monitoring the packet transmission activities of mobile nodes. The reputation of nodes is evaluated using a data-driven weighted average approach, which is based on the number of successfully transmitted data and control packets that a node carries out for other nodes as against its own transmitted packets. The distinctive direct monitoring approach employed in the proposed dynamic reputation management system is effective at detecting and mitigating various misbehaviours exhibited by nodes in a MANET. The use of directly obtained information to evaluate the reputation of nodes ensures that nodes do not rely on second-hand information before evaluating the reputation of its neighbours. This eliminates the possibility of obtaining false second-hand information, which can be used to carry out attacks, such as bad-mouthing and ballot-stuffing, as described in [14–17]. Furthermore, the reliance on directly obtained information will help in reducing routing overhead and in decreasing additional energy requirements.

The rest of the paper is organised as follows: Section 2 contains related works on trust and reputation management systems in MANETs. Section 3 discusses issues concerning misbehaving nodes in MANETs. Section 4 presents the proposed dynamic reputation management system. Section 5 presents details of the implementation work. Section 6 presents the simulation results and analysis. Section 7 concludes by setting out the benefits of the proposed system and outlines future research works.

2. RELATED WORK

Cooperation enforcement in MANETs using the concept of reputation management systems has received considerable attention by researchers in the *ad hoc* network community. Over the past decade, a lot of research works have been proposed and carried out on trust and reputation management (TRM) systems in MANETs, which employed price-based and reputation-based schemes to enforce cooperation among nodes in the network. The price-based schemes [18–23] treat packet forwarding as a service that can be paid for and, thus, introduce a form of virtual currency to regulate packet-forwarding collaboration among nodes. Most of the price-based schemes require tamperproof hardware [18,19] or virtual banks that all of the nodes in the network can trust [20,21]. These price-based schemes use the virtual currency as a form of reward to nodes that participate in packet forwarding activities. In cases where a trust authority or virtual bank is required, it requires assistance from a fixed communication infrastructure to implement the reward schemes, which is not applicable for a pure*ad hoc* network [24].

On the other hand, reputation-based schemes [7,25–37] employ different monitoring techniques in gathering data, which are used in computing the reputation and trust of nodes in the networks [24]. A significant number of publications have proposed various reputation management-based techniques in which nodes in a MANET monitor the packet forwarding activities of their neighbours. If a node contributes in forwarding packets, the reputation of the node is increased. On the other hand, there is a decrease in the reputation of a node if it discards packets by dropping it. Subsequently, if a node's reputation drops below a certain threshold, the node is either punished or isolated from the network [3]. Several proposed TRM systems rely on first-hand and second-hand reputation information before computing the aggregated reputation of a node in their network. The second-hand reputation is obtained from their neighbouring nodes, while the data used in computing the first-hand reputation of nodes are derived using the watchdog mechanisms, as seen in several research works that are presented below.

Marti *et al.* [7] proposed a reputation-based technique that employs a watchdog and path rater. Each node in their model employs the watchdog to overhear packet transmission and checks if the next-hop node forwards the packet or not. The watchdog mechanism is based on promiscuously listening to packet transmission emanating from the neighbouring node. A monitoring node maintains a buffer of recently sent packets and compares each overheard packet with the packet in the buffer to determine whether there is a match. If a match exists, the packet is removed from the buffer, and the node is determined to be a normal node. However, if a packet stays in the buffer for longer than the expected period and no transmission is overheard, a failure count is incremented. If the count exceeds a certain threshold value, it determines that the node is misbehaving, and the source node is notified.

Buchegger and Boudec [31] modelled reputation system for MANETs using a protocol known as CONFIDANT (cooperation of nodes: fairness in dynamic *ad hoc* networks). The protocol specialises in the detection and isolation of nodes exhibiting anomalies in the network. The CONFIDANT protocol employs a monitoring system for observations. This includes a reputation system that specialises in knowledge creation based on first-hand and second-hand observations, a trust manager that manages incoming and outgoing second-hand reports from neighbouring nodes and a path manager that implements routing decisions through the elimination of paths containing misbehaving nodes and re-ranking of the other path based on the reputation of the nodes on the paths. Furthermore, CONFIDANT also utilises a passive acknowledgement scheme. This scheme confirms when the next-hop node in a routing path has forwarded a data packet. Although CONFIDANT ensures that low ranking nodes are denied data forwarding services, the monitoring scheme employed in the protocol will not be able to detect selfish nodes that do not participate in route discovery processes, because these nodes will never be presented packets for forwarding.

He *et al.* [29] proposed a secure and objective reputation-based incentive scheme for MANETs. The reputation of nodes in their proposed model is quantified by objective measures, and the propagation of reputation is efficiently secured by a one-way hash chain-based authentication scheme, which is computationally efficient and eliminates the need for a public key infrastructure (PKI) or other forms of authentication infrastructures. Their model uses punishment as a way of encouraging packet forwarding and disciplines selfish nodes by probabilistically dropping packets that originate from those nodes.

In [38], the authors proposed a trust management system (TMS), which includes a reputation system and a watchdog. Watchdogs normally monitor the events of data forwarding and count the arrival of the acknowledgement packets (ACKs) with respect to the forwarded data. The watchdog in their model employs a positive feedback message (PFM) as the evidence of the forwarding behaviour of a node. The trust evaluation in their model is a combination of both direct and indirect observation of nodes activities. Their model aimed at detecting malicious nodes' attempts to degrade the network performance through dropping or arbitrarily forwarding data.

Banerjee *et al.* [8] proposed a reputation-based trust management system for detecting and preventing vulnerabilities in MANETs. In their model, the node evaluates and exchanges the reputation values with its one-hop neighbours in the form of trust vectors. Trust vectors in their system signify the outcomes of previous transactions, and it is preserved for each neighbour that it had transactions with in the past. Every time a node intends to forward a packet, it checks the trust rating of the nodes connected downstream from its routing table. If the node is trusted, the packet is then forwarded. On the other hand, if the node is not trusted, a different downstream node is chosen randomly among the trusted nodes. Their proposed scheme works in a purely distributed manner, whereby attacks are detected by collaborative monitoring and information exchange among the nodes. The monitoring scheme employed in their model requires a node to monitor its upstream node, and trust computation is based on the received acknowledgement from the node.

Gupta and Kumar [39] proposed a novel routing strategy that deals with nodes that, due to loss of power, become selfish after previously being classified as trustworthy. Their strategy assumes that the selfish nodes are not malicious in nature, thus ensuring that they are mandated to provide accurate information about their current energy level. The information containing the status of a node's energy level is exchanged through periodic updates with its neighbours. The knowledge about the power status of the neighbours helps a node to avoid those nodes with very low power. This is based on the assumption that a node with low energy level may drop the packets presented to it for forwarding in a selfish manner in order to save energy.

Gong *et al.* [40,41] emphasized the importance of identifying selfish and malicious nodes to enable proper functioning of a MANET. They carried out critical reviews of some existing secure routing techniques and proposed an approach that incorporates a trust vector model within existing routing protocols. In their proposed model, each node monitors the traffic of its neighbours and evaluates its local trust vector about its neighbours. The nodes in their model monitor the packet forwarding activities using promiscuous listening of traffic. When a node overhears its immediate neighbour node forwarding a packet, it first checks the integrity of the packet in order to ensure that the packet had not been modified. If the neighbour being monitored passes the integrity test and the packet is forwarded, its trust vector is computed. Performance evaluation of their system shows that their mechanism successfully detected malicious nodes and avoided them in the routing path.

Bakar and Irvine [42] proposed a new mechanism to detect selfish nodes, which specializes in dropping control packets to avoid them being asked to forward data packets. Each node in their model operates in promiscuous mode to monitor both data and control packets that are transmitted within its receiving range. The monitoring node stores successfully observed transactions carried out by its neighbouring nodes. Nodes in their proposed model are expected to contribute to the network within a time frame. Those that fail to contribute to the network activities will undergo a test for their suspicious behaviours. Performance evaluation shows that their scheme was able to detect selfish nodes in a network.

In [43], the authors proposed a 2ACK scheme, which focuses on detecting misbehaving links instead of misbehaving nodes to avoid several issues, such as ambiguous collisions, receiver collisions and limited transmission power, which affect the general watchdog detection mechanism. The 2ACK scheme detects misbehaviour through the use of a new type of acknowledgement packet, termed 2ACK. A 2ACK packet is assigned a fixed route of two hops (three nodes) in the opposite direction of the data traffic route. When a node wishes to communicate with another node, a methodology is performed by the sending and receiving nodes, which ensures authentication and integrity. Security in their model is achieved through the use of cryptographic algorithms.

Ayday and Fekri [17] proposed a belief propagation-based trust and reputation management for P2P networks, which can also be utilized by social and mesh networks. In their proposed algorithm, the reputation and trustworthiness of a network node is computed by the Belief Propagation-based distributed message passing algorithm between peers (network nodes), which is presented on a chosen factor graph. The reputation of peers is based on the quality of service a node receives, and trustworthiness is based on the ratings that each node provides after successful transactions. Performance evaluation of their proposed model shows that it iteratively decreases the error in the reputation values of peers due to the malicious ratings with a high probability.

Further works were carried out by Ayday and Fekri [16] in which they proposed a trust management and adversary detection scheme for delay-tolerant networks (DTNs). Their proposed scheme was further extended in [15], which comprises a comparison of their proposed model with some well-known and commonly-used reputation management techniques (e.g., EigenTrust and Bayesian framework). The evaluation in their work shows the preeminence of their proposed scheme in terms of robustness against malicious behaviour. The performance evaluation described in [15,16] shows that their proposed model provided high data availability and packet-delivery ratio with low latency in DTNs under various adversary attacks. These attacks attempted to both undermine the trust and detection scheme and the packet delivery protocol employed in their proposed model. In particular, their proposed model was very effective and efficient at curbing Byzantine attacks in which one or more genuine nodes have been compromised. Despite relying on second-hand reputations from other nodes, their proposed model was able to mitigate the effects of bad mouthing and ballot stuffing attacks. However, one form of attack that may go undetected when employing this scheme is the selective existence attack carried out by totally selfish nodes. The nature of these nodes means that they will not participate in route discovery processes for other nodes. Thus, these nodes will never be presented data packets for forwarding. This type of node can never act as a service provider in a MANET, making it difficult for existing watchdog mechanisms that rely on feedback to compute the direct reputation of nodes.

When we compared some of the above-mentioned related works to our proposed model, one significant difference is in the monitoring technique that we employ in detecting misbehaving nodes. For instance, the watchdog monitoring techniques employed in [7,8,29,31,38–42,44] have the ability to detect when a node forwards a packet by listening to the traffic of the forwarding node. When it overhears the packet being forwarded, it uses the information to compute the corresponding reputation or trust values. Although, the watchdog mechanism is effective at detecting successful packet dropping and forwarding activities of nodes in MANETs, the watchdog mechanism has its own limitations. The watchdog mechanism is prone to ambiguous collisions, receiver collisions and limited transmission power, which may lead to false detection. More significantly, the watchdog monitoring technique will not be able to monitor and detect the network activities of selfish nodes that do not participate in the route discovery processes for other nodes. Nodes exhibiting this type of selfish behaviour will not be presented packets to forward for other nodes, which ensures that they will not act as service providers for other nodes in the network. However, the limitation of the watchdog mechanism in reference to monitoring the network activities of nodes exhibiting totally selfish behaviours is addressed by the monitoring scheme employed in this work. In our proposed work, a node relies only on first-hand information in computing the reputation of its neighbours. It captures packets through promiscuous listening of transmissions carried out by all of its neighbours and on packets it received from the target nodes that are being monitored. It employs a novel technique to analyse and filter each received and captured packet to identify if the node being monitored is the originator or just a forwarder. A full description of the monitoring technique is described in Section 4.1.

3. THREAT MODEL

MANETs generally suffer from several vulnerabilities, which are exploited by misbehaving nodes in the networks. Some of these exploitations occur at the routing layer, and the resulting attacks are mostly carried out by these misbehaving nodes operating inside the network. Some of these attacks are explained below.

3.1. Selective Existence (Totally Selfish Behaviour)

A misbehaving node is said to exhibit a totally selfish behaviour if it does not participate in network operations, but uses the network for its advantage to enhance its performance and save its own resources, such as energy. This selfish node only makes its presence known to other nodes in the network whenever it wants to send its own packets. These selfish behaviours are known as selective existence attacks [3]. When a selfish node wants to send its own packet to another node, it performs a route discovery and then sends the required packets. When the node no longer needs to use the network, it returns to the silent mode. It ensures that all control packets that are presented during route discovery requests by other nodes are dropped. After a given period, its neighbouring nodes update their various route entries and delete their entries with routes with the destination to this node; this makes the node invisible to the network. Employing the passive acknowledgement mechanism used by some of the existing TRM systems mentioned in Section 2 will not be able to detect these totally selfish behaviours.

For instance, Figure 1 shows a MANET with nine nodes consisting of various paths from a source to a destination. If Node 1 wants to send a packet to Node 9, there are several possible paths to the destination assuming that all of the nodes are cooperative. If Node 4 and Node 6 were non-cooperative nodes exhibiting totally selfish behaviours, this means that all data from Node 1 must go through Node 3 (1-3-5-8-9) or through Node 5 (1-5-8-9), as seen in Figure 2.

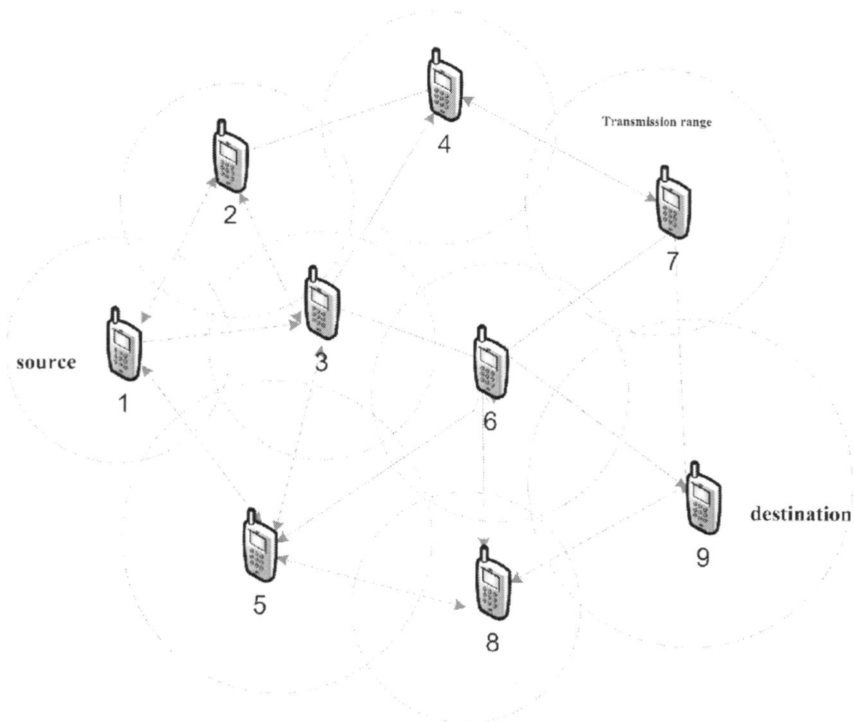

Figure 1. A MANET with nine cooperative nodes.

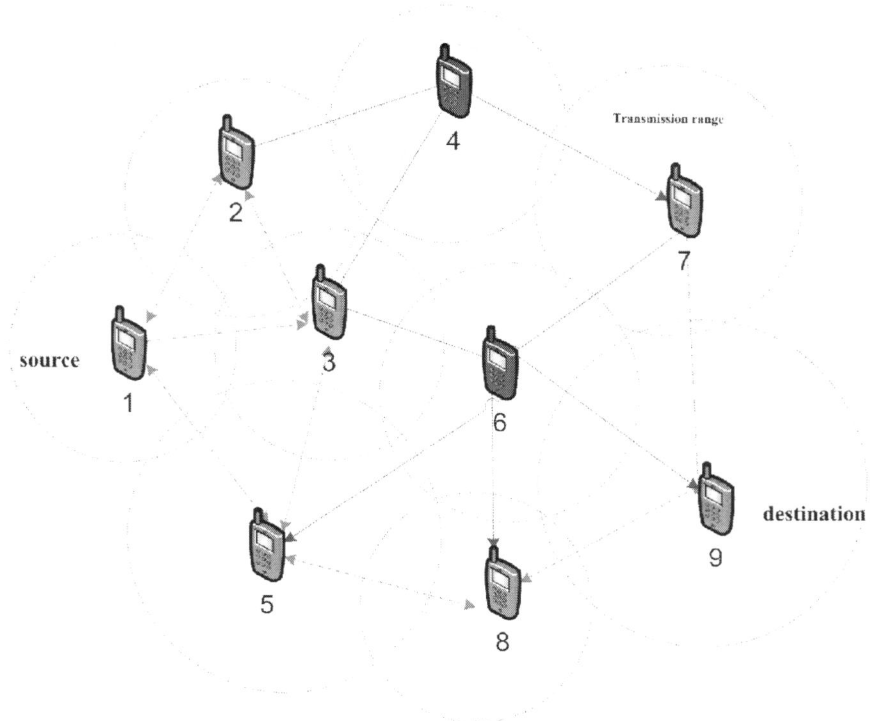

Figure 2. A MANET with two uncooperative nodes.

Consequently, if Node 2 or Node 3 wants to send a packet to Node 7, Node 8 or Node 9, it must go through Node 5. As a result of the totally selfish behaviours exhibited by Node 4 and Node 6, Node 5 is at a high risk of exhausting its limited energy resources due to the energy-constrained nature of nodes in MANETs. This type of behaviour creates an unfair environment if left unchecked. If Node 4 and Node 6 were cooperative, this will lessen the burden on Node 5, due to the fact that the amount of energy consumed during packet forwarding will be shared amongst the three nodes (with the assumption that the costs of the links of the three paths are almost the same). This will, in turn, elongate the life-time of the overall network.

3.2. Selective Dropping (Deceitful Behaviour)

A misbehaving node can act deceitfully in order to conserve its energy. It periodically participates in route discovery processes by forwarding control packets for other nodes. This is because control packets are smaller in size than data packets and consume a low amount of energy during transmission. Whenever a data packet is presented to this node for onward transmission, the data packet is dropped. Nodes that forward data packets to this node perceive the link as broken when they do not receive acknowledgements for the first set of data sent. The connection to this node is then deleted from their route entries, but after a given period, the connection is later re-added when the deceitful node participates in the route discovery process again.

4. THE PROPOSED REPUTATION MANAGEMENT SYSTEM

The proposed reputation model consists of a monitor, a reputation manager, a punishment scheme and a path administrator. The following assumptions are employed in our reputation management system.

- Nodes in our network do not maliciously modify packets before forwarding.
- Every node operates in a promiscuous mode, such that each node listens to every packet transmitted by its neighbours, even if the packet is not intended for the node.
- A node may be selfish in terms of conservation of power and computing resources, but not malicious, which means that it will not try something that could directly target another node.

These assumptions are very important for the proposed model, because we are more focused on detecting nodes that exhibit totally selfish and deceitful behaviours in the network. A depiction of the various core components of the proposed model is given in Figure 3. These core components make up the modules of the reputation management system.

4.1. Monitoring Module (Monitor)

The monitor is an important part of the proposed model. It promiscuously listens to traffic and captures packets transmitted by a node. The monitor registers and records the number of packets being transmitted by a target node.

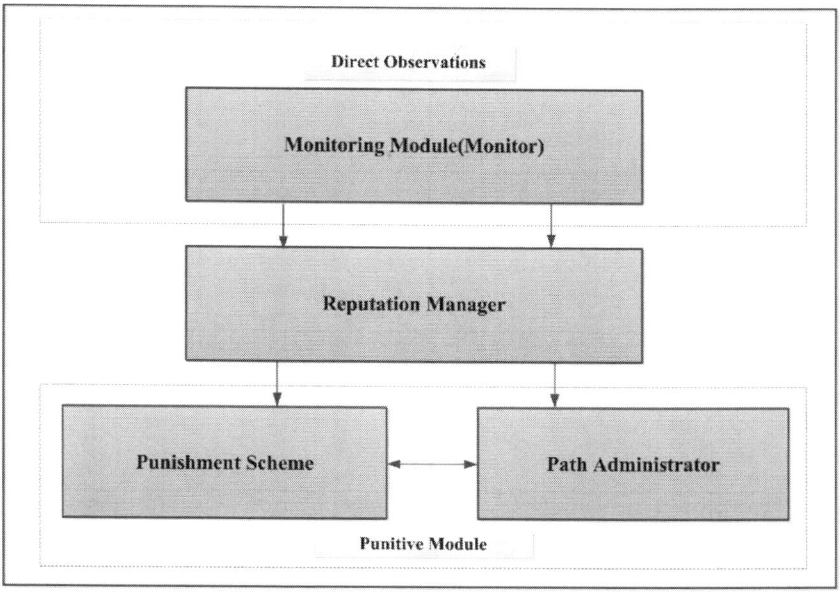

Figure 3. The schematic diagram of the reputation management system.

The monitor carries out a basic analysis for every captured packet to determine the type of packet being transmitted. It also checks if the node being observed (target node) is the originator of the packet or just a forwarder by comparing the source IP address of the packet against the IP address of the node being monitored. It has an inbuilt counter that increments and registers these data that are then stored in a node table.

Figure 4 gives insight into how the monitor captures and filters various packets using promiscuous listening. In order to cater to situations where a node has not had enough time to promiscuously listen to the traffic of its neighbours, the monitor relies on the packets that a node receives from its neighbours. Figure 5 shows how the received packets from the monitored node are filtered.

For every packet it receives, the node analyses the packet to check if the sender is the originator or just a forwarder. Table 1 shows a brief summary of the information that could be derived from monitoring nodes' activities. The stored data are passed on to the reputation manager for onward computation.

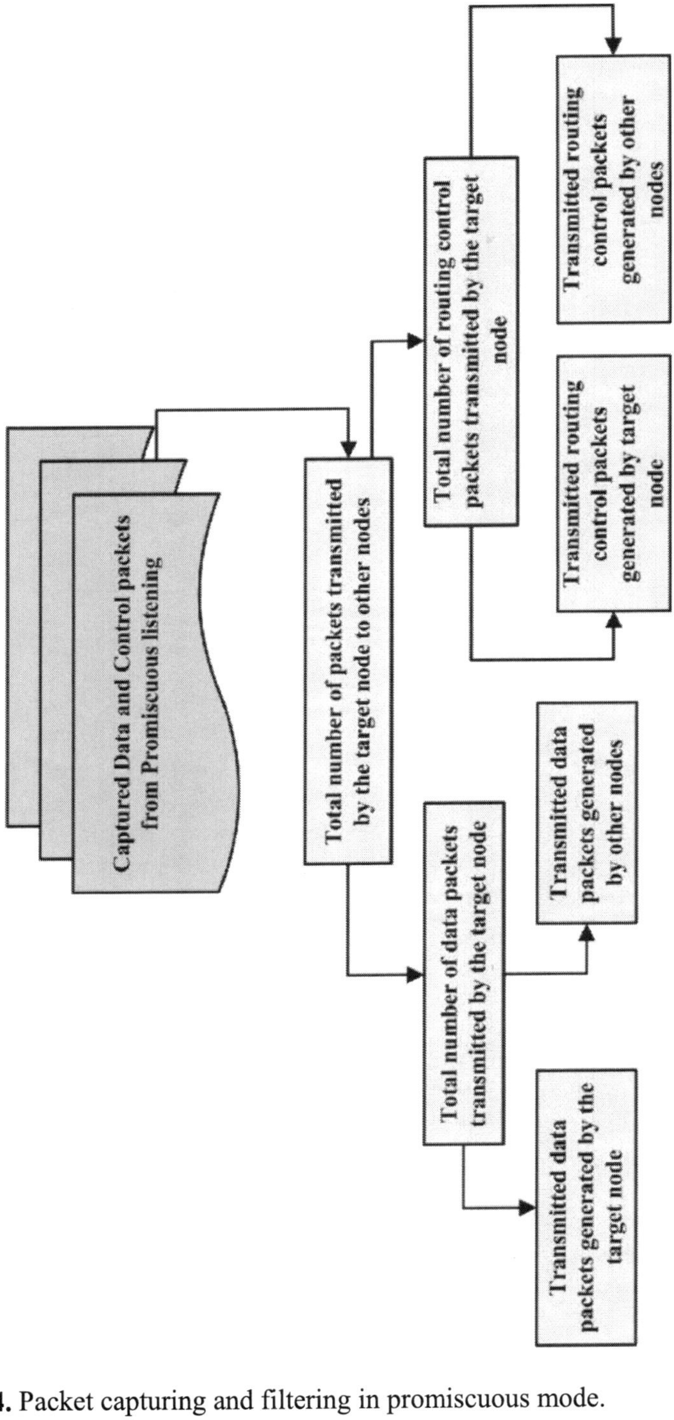

Figure 4. Packet capturing and filtering in promiscuous mode.

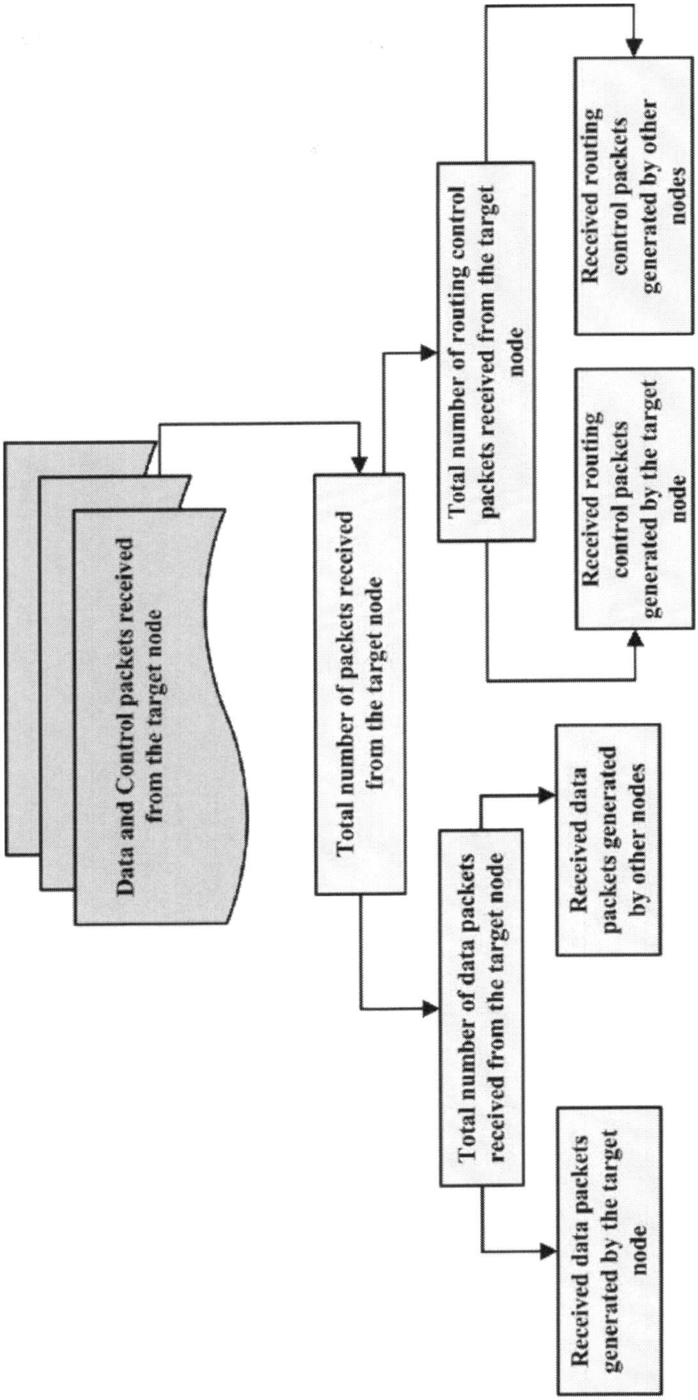

Figure 5. Filtering of received packets.

Table 1. Summary of monitoring details stored in the node table.

Packet Variable	Packet Count Details
P_T	Packets transmitted by the target node.
P_{Tdata}	Data packets transmitted by the target node.
$P_{Tdata-self}$	Transmitted data packets generated by the target node.
$P_{Tdata-others}$	Transmitted data packets generated by other nodes.
$P_{Tcontrol}$	Routing control packets transmitted by the target node.
$P_{Tctrl-self}$	Transmitted routing control packets generated by the target node.
$P_{Tctrl-others}$	Transmitted routing control packets generated by other nodes.
P_{Rdata}	Data packets received from the target node.
$P_{Rdata-self}$	Data packets received from the target node generated by itself.
$P_{Rdata-others}$	Data packets received from the target node generated by other nodes.
$P_{Rcontrol}$	Control packets received from the target node.
$P_{Rctrl-self}$	Received routing control packets generated by the target node.
$P_{Rctrl-others}$	Received routing control packets from the target node generated by other nodes.

4.2. Reputation Manager

The reputation manager computes the reputation values of a node from the information it obtains from the monitor. Nodes generally consume more energy when they transmit data packets than routing control packets. The proposed reputation model focuses more on the number of data packets a node transmits for other nodes than the number of routing control packets it transmits. To compute the reputation of a node, we evaluate the information derived from the monitor in two phases.

Let $\hbar_1$ represent the reputation of the node based on the data packets it transmits for others, and let ψ_1 represent the reputation of the node based on the routing control packets it transmits for other nodes. We computed $\hbar_1$ as shown inEquation (1):

$$\hbar_1 = P_{Tdata-others} / (P_{Tdata-self} + P_{Tdata-others}) \tag{1}$$

Similarly, ψ_1 is given as:

$$\psi_1 = P_{Tctrl-others} / (P_{Tctrl-self} + P_{Tctrl-others}) \tag{2}$$

To compute the reputation of a node based on the number of data and routing control packets it receives from the target node, which was generated by other nodes, let $\hbar_2$ represent the reputation value based on received data packets generated by other nodes and let ψ_2 represent the reputation value based on received routing control packets generated by other nodes. We compute $\hbar_2$ and ψ_2 as follows:

$$\hbar_2 = \quad P_{Rdata-others} / (P_{Rdata-self} + P_{Rdata-others}) \tag{3}$$

$$\psi_2 = \quad P_{Rctrl-others} / (P_{Rctrl-others} + P_{Rctrl-self}) \tag{4}$$

The variables employed in computing the reputations $\hbar_1$, ψ_1, $\hbar_2$ and ψ_2 in Equations (1)–(4) are presented in Table 2.

To compute the final reputation of a node in terms of data packets it has transmitted for other nodes, we combine $\hbar_1$ and$\hbar_2$. Thus, the final reputation of a monitored node in terms of data packets it has transmitted for other nodes is given as:

$$\hbar_{\mathbf{data}} = \quad \hbar_1 + \quad \hbar_2 \tag{5}$$

Table 2. Terminology used in our proposed model.

Notation	Definitions
$\hbar_1, \hbar_2$	Reputations in terms of data packets transmitted.
ψ_1, ψ_2	Reputations in terms of routing control packets transmitted.
$\hbar_{data}$	Final reputations in terms of data packets transmitted.
$\psi_{control}$	Final reputations in terms of routing control packets transmitted.
$\mathfrak{H}_T$	Evaluated total reputation.
$\mathfrak{H}_0$	Initial total reputation.
λ	Weight assigned to final reputations in terms of data packets transmitted.
ρ	Weight assigned to final reputations in terms of control packets transmitted.
ω	Decay factor for computed reputation value.

Similarly, the final reputation of the nodes based on the number of routing control packets it has transmitted for other nodes is given by:

$$\psi_{\mathbf{control}} = \psi_{\mathbf{1}} + \psi_{\mathbf{2}} \tag{6}$$

4.2.1. Total Reputation Value of Nodes

The total reputation of a node in the proposed model denoted by $\mathfrak{H}_T$ is the combination of the individual final reputation values of a node in terms of the data packets transmitted, $\hbar_{data}$, and the routing control packets transmitted, $\psi_{control}$. Mathematically, R_T is given by the equation below:

$$\mathfrak{H}_{\mathbf{T}} = \lambda \hbar_{\mathbf{data}} + \rho \psi_{\mathbf{control}} \tag{7}$$

where λ and ρ are given as 0.8 and 0.2, respectively. The values of λ and ρ are based on the relative importance placed on the final reputation value of a node in regards to the type of packets it transmits continuously for other nodes.

4.2.2. Initial Reputation of Nodes in the Networks

At the onset of network operations, nodes in the network will not have interacted or have had the opportunity to monitor their neighbouring nodes for long enough time before computing their respective reputation values. In order to cater to this kind of situation, a default reputation value is introduced for all of the nodes in the network. This value is also assigned to a node that newly joins the network. From Subsection 4.2.1, we estimated that the total reputation of a node ɧ_T will always be between [0, 2]. Considering this range of values, the default reputation value for all nodes in the network is defined as ɧ_0. This means that every node in the network is assigned a default reputation value, which is also their total reputation value at time t equal to zero. Mathematically, the total direct reputation of a node when they newly join the network or at the onset of network activities is given as:

$$\text{ɧ}_T = \text{ɧ}_0 \tag{8}$$

After monitoring the various activities of nodes for a given period of time, a node would have gathered enough evidence to compute the individual reputation of its neighbouring nodes. The total reputation in this case is a combination of the initial default reputation value and the currently measured reputation value. Let us denote the new total reputation $\text{ɧ}_T = \text{ɧ}_1$. We can evaluate the new total reputation ɧ_1 as:

$$\text{ɧ}_1 = \omega \text{ɧ}_0 + (1-\omega)\text{ɧ}_{M1} \tag{9}$$

where ω is a small value between [0, 1] and R_{M1} is the currently measured reputation value of a node based on new evidence collected from monitoring activities. As more evidence becomes available, the direct reputation of the nodes will be regularly updated at a specific time interval. For instance, we evaluated the direct reputation of node at a given period of time t as ɧ_1. We can therefore say that after a time interval of (t + 1), ɧ_2 will be given as:

$$\text{ɧ}_2 = \omega \text{ɧ}_1 + (1-\omega)\text{ɧ}_{M2} \tag{10}$$

We can conclude that the direct total reputation of a node in our model can be evaluated using the equation below:

$$\text{ɧ}_n = \omega^n \text{ɧ}_0 + \omega^{n-1}(1-\omega)\text{ɧ}_{M1} + \omega^{n-2}(1-\omega)\text{ɧ}_{M2} + \omega^{n-i}(1-\omega)\text{ɧ}_{Mi} \tag{11}$$

where ɧ_1, ɧ_{M2} and ɧ_{Mi} are the newly-measured direct reputation values at regular intervals. Equation (11) can be further simplified as:

$$\text{ɧ}_n = \omega^n \text{ɧ}_0 + \sum_{i=1}^{n} \omega^{n-i}(1-\omega)\text{ɧ}_{Mi} \tag{12}$$

where $n = 1, 2, 3, \ldots, i$.

4.3. Punitive Module

The punitive module comprises the punishment scheme and the path administrator. These two modules ensure that nodes with total reputation values lower than the set threshold are dealt with as required.

4.3.1. Punishment Scheme

After evaluating the total reputation value of monitored nodes in our network, the values are stored in a node table and updated at regular intervals. After a period of time, it is expected that the total reputation value of a monitored node should increase if the node is transmitting data and routing control packets for other nodes. We defined a threshold value of 0.75, which is just a 25% increase in the initial default reputation value (0.6) assigned to all nodes at the onset of the network operations. The statuses of all monitored nodes are checked at regular intervals. The computed total reputation value of a node is mapped with a grading criterion, which helps to determine the status of a node.

Table 3 gives an overview of how the grading of the computed total reputation values is carried out by the nodes. When the status of a node is checked based on the computed total direct reputation value after a defined time interval, for example every 60 s, if the node status is flagged as "undecided", the node-ID of that node is placed on a watch-list within the punishment scheme. If subsequent node status checks still flag the node's status as "undecided", such that after two subsequent checks, the node status is changed to "bad node", the node is moved into a black-list within the punishment scheme. A node that is blacklisted will be denied network resources; all route requests that originate from it will be ignored. The node details are then passed on to the path coordinator, which checks the route cache and ensures that paths that contain that node are deleted, and an alternative route will be sourced for when needed. On the other hand, if a node is flagged as a "good node" or a "very good node", the node-ID is moved to a "white-list". Every node on the white-list is allowed to carry on with its normal network activities. Finally, when a node is flagged once as a bad node, the node is immediately blacklisted and its details passed to the path coordinator for immediate action.

Table 3. Grading criteria for the computed total reputation values.

Computed Reputation Value (R)	Grading Criteria	Node Status
1.000–2.000	Very good reputation	Very reliable node
0.750–0.999	Good reputation	Reliable node
0.500–0.749	Initial/normal/expected reputation	Undecided
0.000–0.499	Poor reputation	Unreliable node/bad node

4.3.2. Path Administrator

As already mentioned in Section 4.3, the path administrator ensures that nodes that are flagged as bad nodes are removed from the route cache. Its actions are based on the information it receives from the punishment scheme. The path administrator is integrated into the routing protocol, such that whenever a path is being sourced for sending a packet, it checks to ensure that the packet will not be sent via a path that contains a node that has been black-listed.

5. IMPLEMENTATION AND SIMULATIONS

We designed and programmed the modules described above using C++ and implemented the various classes to work with existing NS-2.34 modules [45]. Several modifications were also carried out on existing NS-2.34 modules to incorporate the various required node behaviours and the overall functionality of the proposed reputation management model. Dynamic source routing was used as the routing protocol to verify the functionalities of the proposed model. Exhaustive simulations were also carried out, averaging 10 simulations for each specified scenario. Other general parameters used are mentioned inTable 4.

5.1. The Implemented Behaviours

The simulated nodes were programmed to exhibit three different behaviours during the course of the simulations. The behaviours exhibited by these nodes are briefly described below:

- Good nodes: A good node in our model responds to all route requests and ensures that all of the data and routing control packets that are meant for other nodes are forwarded to the next hop node or the recipient node if they are the last hop in the path.

- Selfish nodes: These nodes do not respond to any route requests received from other nodes, this ensures that they do not forward data and routing control packets for other nodes. Their existence is only known to other nodes when they need to send their own packets.

- Deceitful nodes: Deceitful nodes sporadically reply to the route requests from other nodes, but ensure that all of the data packets that are meant for forwarding are dropped. For instance, a deceitful node drops one out of every three routing control packets that it receives and ensures that every data packet it receives for forwarding is dropped.

Table 4. Parameters of the simulations. CBR, constant bitrate.

Parameters	Values
Topographical area	900 m × 900 m
Simulation time	900 s
Channel type	WirelessChannel
Radio-propagation mode	TwoRayGround
Antenna type	Antenna/OmniAntenna
Interface queue type	CMUPriQueue
Maximum packet in queue	50
Network interface type	Phy/WirelessPhy
Link layer type	LL
MAC type	802.11
Number of connections	12
Traffic type	CBR
Data packet size	512 bytes
Number of mobile nodes	20
λ,ρ,ω	0.8, 0.2, 0.1
Behaviour Types	Good, selfish, deceitful nodes

5.2. Network Performance Evaluation

For the purpose of evaluation, we use the following network metrics in our study:

- Packet delivery ratio: This is the ratio between the amount of data packets received and the amount of data packets sent. The packet delivery ratio can also be interpreted as the ratio of the number of packets received at the constant bitrate (CBR) sink to the number of packet sent by the CBR source.
- Routing overhead: This is defined as the total number of routing control packets transmitted.
- Throughput: Network throughput refers to the average data rate of successful data or message delivery over a specific communications link.
- End to end delay: The end to end delay of a packet is defined as the time a packet takes to travel from the source to the destination.

6. RESULTS AND ANALYSIS

This section presents the simulation results that show the effects of an increase in the presence of selfish and deceitful nodes in networks. Furthermore, it also analyses how the deployment of the proposed reputation model is able to curb and mitigate the negative effects of the increased presence of these nodes in the network.

6.1. Packet Delivery Ratio

Figures 6 and 7, present the packet delivery ratio for the networks experiencing a gradual increase in the number of selfish and deceitful nodes with and without the deployed reputation model. When the performance of the networks shown inFigure 6 is analysed, a gradual increase in the number of selfish nodes operating in the networks led to a decrease in the packet delivery ratio of the networks. As observed in Figure 6, selfish nodes do not participate in route discovery processes, which exempts them from being presented packets for forwarding to other nodes in the network. Hence, there will be a high demand on the good nodes to forward packets for other nodes, such that the good nodes will be heavily relied on to deliver more and more data packets to the required destinations. This constitutes a huge task for the services these good nodes can offer to other nodes in the network. Thus, there is a possibility that some packets may be lost, and packet collision may also increase, which could also lead to further decline in the packet delivery ratio. The slightly improved packet delivery ratio recorded by the deployed reputation model is a result of the punishment module, which eliminates and isolates the detected selfish nodes and ensures that only reliable nodes (good nodes) use the network resources to transmit packets, which are delivered to the required destinations.

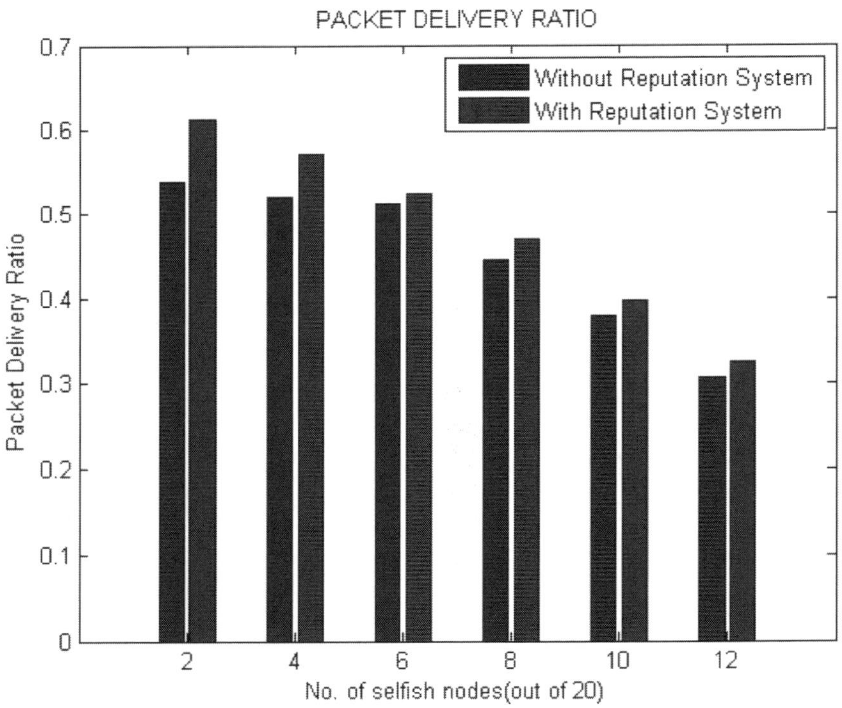

Figure 6. Packet delivery ratio for networks experiencing an increase in selfish nodes.

Similarly, from Figure 7, it is observed that as the number of deceitful nodes continues to increase in the network (2, 4, 6, 8, ..., 12), the packet delivery ratio of the network gradually decreases. This is expected as a result of the smaller number of good nodes forwarding data packets and more data packets being dropped by these deceitful nodes.

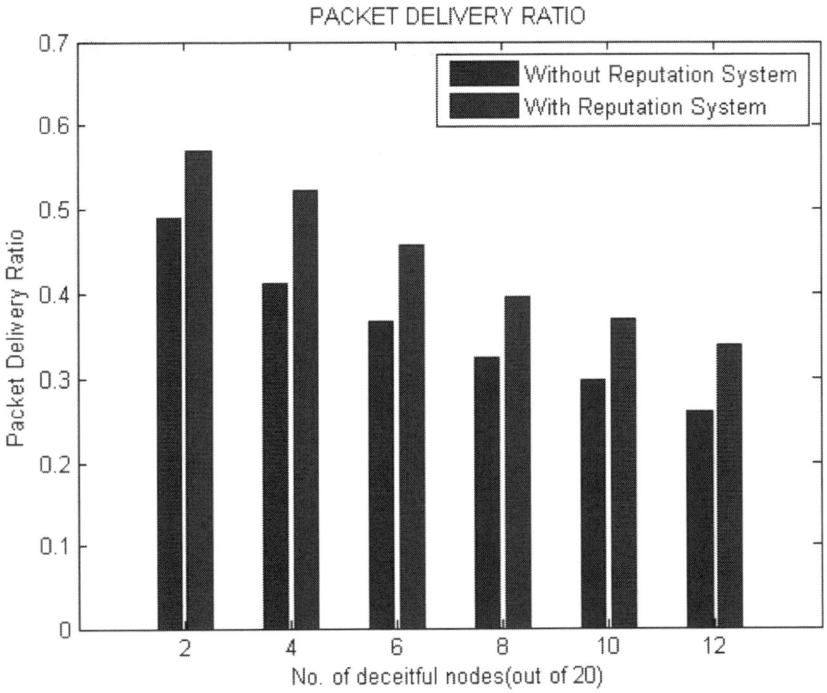

Figure 7. Packet delivery ratio for networks experiencing an increase in selfish nodes.

It is also observed from Figure 7 that the deployment of the reputation model improved the packet delivery ratio of the network. For all of the cases whereby a decline in the packet delivery ratio occurred as a result of more deceitful nodes, the networks with the reputation model registered a much improved packet delivery ratio, which is from 15%–20% in some cases. This improved packet delivery ratio recorded by the reputation model is mostly a result of more data packets being delivered due to the isolation and prevention of these deceitful nodes accessing the limited resources. Furthermore, the improved packet delivery ratio may also be a result of reduced packet collision in the network due to a few good nodes contending for limited bandwidth.

6.2. Routing Overhead

As shown in Figure 8, a downward trend could be observed as regards the amount of routing control packets in circulation in both networks as the number of selfish nodes in the networks increases. This is most likely due to fewer good nodes participating in the route discovery and route management processes for other nodes. As mentioned earlier, these selfish nodes do not participate in the route discovery processes for other nodes in the network. The number of routing control packets circulating in the network when the proposed reputation model was deployed is less compared to the network without the reputation model. This is expected, because when the selfish nodes are detected in the reputation model, they are deleted from the routing path and are denied network access, such that route requests from these nodes are ignored. This means that fewer route requests, route replies and route error packets will always be in circulation due to the isolation.

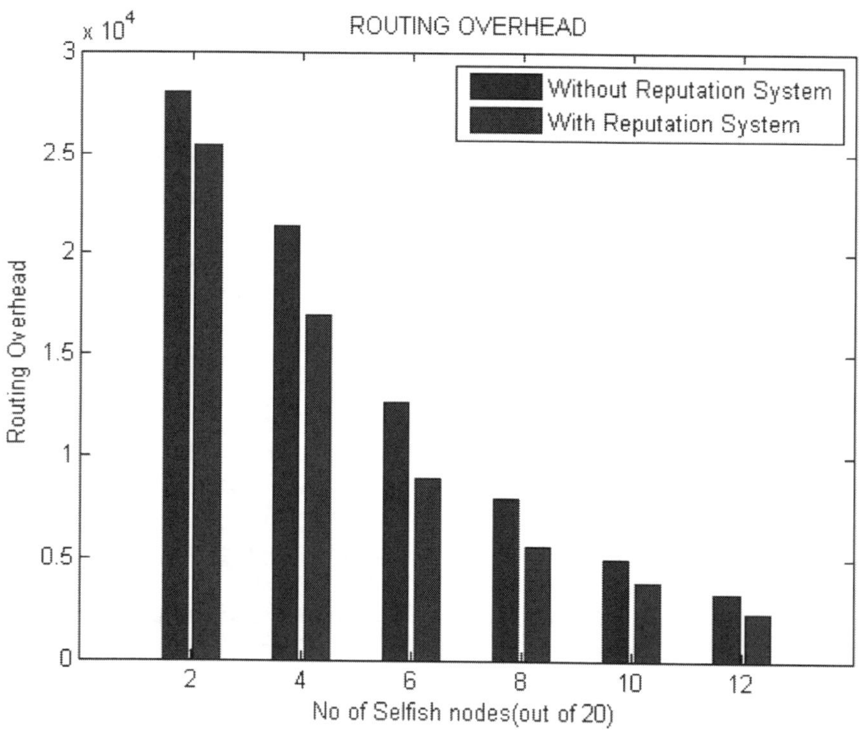

Figure 8. Routing overhead for networks experiencing an increase in selfish nodes.

Similarly, it is observed in Figure 9 that there is also a gradual decrease in the number of routing control packets circulating in the networks as the number of selfish nodes increased from two to 12 gradually. One significant difference between Figures 8 and 9 is in the amount of routing control packets in circulation as the number of selfish and deceitful nodes increases in the networks with and without the reputation model, respectively. This difference is due to the un-identical behaviour patterns, such that selfish nodes do not participate in route discovery or the route management process for other nodes. On the other hand, the deceitful nodes periodically participate in route discovery and management processes for other nodes. Hence, for the network with deceitful nodes, more routing control packets are in circulation compared to the network with selfish nodes.

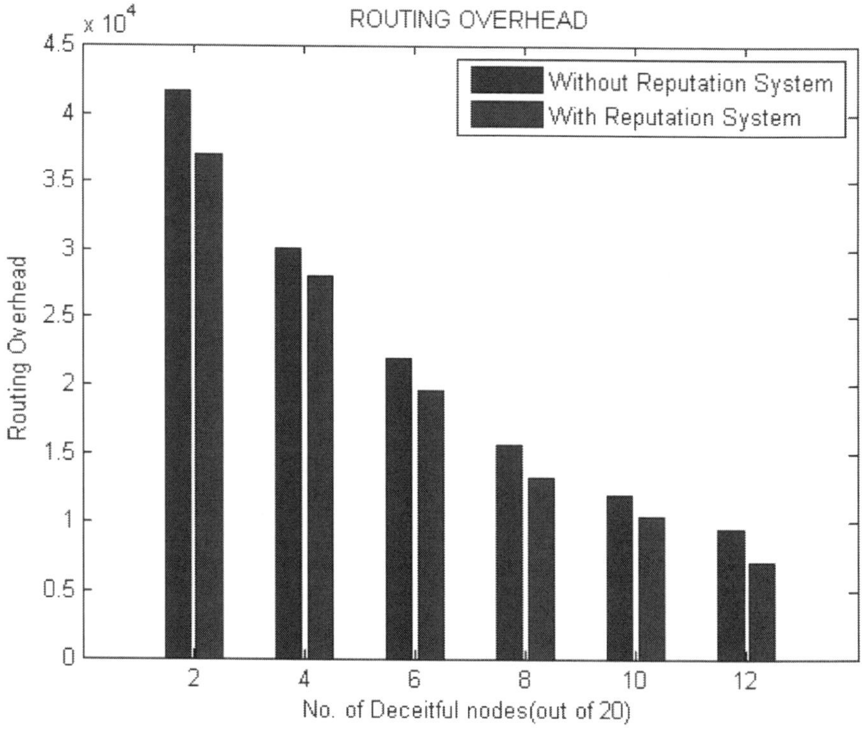

Figure 9. Routing overhead for networks experiencing an increase in deceitful nodes.

6.3. Throughput

As observed in Figure 10, an increase in the number of selfish nodes in the network results in a gradual decrease in the network throughput. This is a result of fewer data packets being delivered to the desired destination. When comparing the networks without the reputation model to the networks with the reputation model, the same trend of a reduction in the network throughputs is observed. However, the networks with the reputation model have a better network throughput performance. The improved network throughputs could be a result of fewer nodes utilizing the available bandwidth after the selfish nodes are blacklisted.

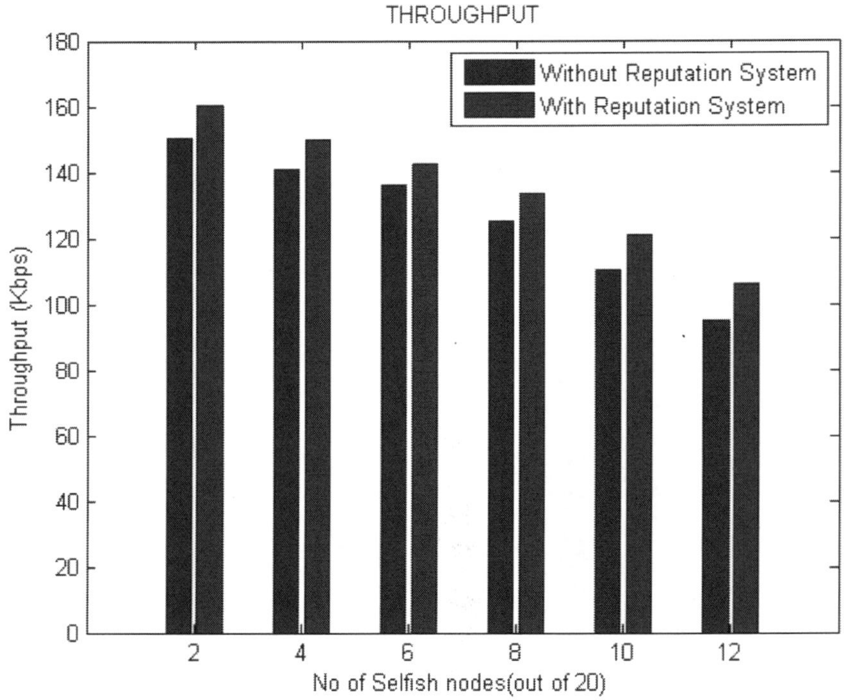

Figure 10. Throughput for networks experiencing an increase in selfish nodes.

The reputation model also increases the proportion of packets that reach the final destination by re-routing the packets to avoid blacklisted nodes. Additionally, since selfish nodes are blacklisted when detected through the computed reputation values, the act of ignoring their route requests means that they are not able to send their own data packets. Thus, a possible reduction in packet collision may most likely improve the network throughput.

Similarly, when the throughput of the networks with the reputation model and the networks without the reputation model are compared in the presence of an increased number of deceitful nodes, as observed in Figure 11, as the number of the deceitful nodes increases, the network throughputs decrease due to many fewer data packets being delivered to their respective destinations. Similarly, the improved network throughput observed in the network with the reputation model may also be a result of the ability of the network to isolate the deceitful nodes. The reputation model ensures that only nodes in the white-list and watch-list participate in network activities and results in reduced packet collision. It is also observed that the deceitful nodes reduce that network throughput more than the selfish nodes due to the behaviours, *i.e.*, continuously dropping data packets presented for forwarding.

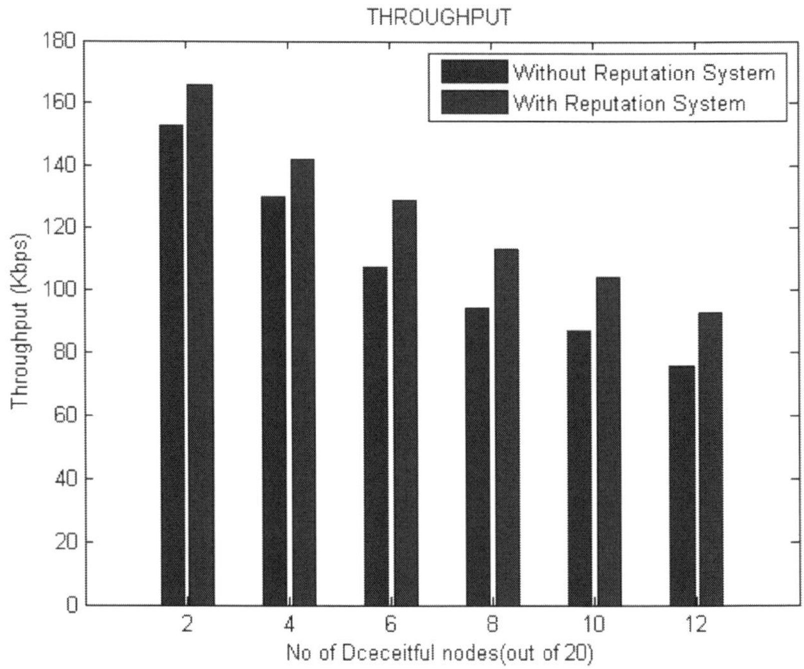

Figure 11. Throughput for networks experiencing an increase in deceitful nodes.

6.4. End to End Delay

In the networks without the reputation model, as shown in Figure 12, as the presence of selfish nodes gradually increased from 2 → 8, the network end to end delay decreased gradually. A slight increase in the delay was also observed when the number of selfish nodes increased from 8 → 12. The decrease in the end to end delay is due to fewer good nodes participating in packet routing activities. Since the selfish nodes do not participate in route discovery processes, their increased presence may partition the network, which, in turn, reduces the amount of time it takes to send and receive packets between the good nodes that remain in the various partitions. Increased presence of selfish nodes also means that there is a possibility of experiencing reduced packet collisions in the network. Their non-participation in route discovery processes may ensure that data transfer between established genuine links (between two good nodes) may be quicker due to fewer packets competing for bandwidth.

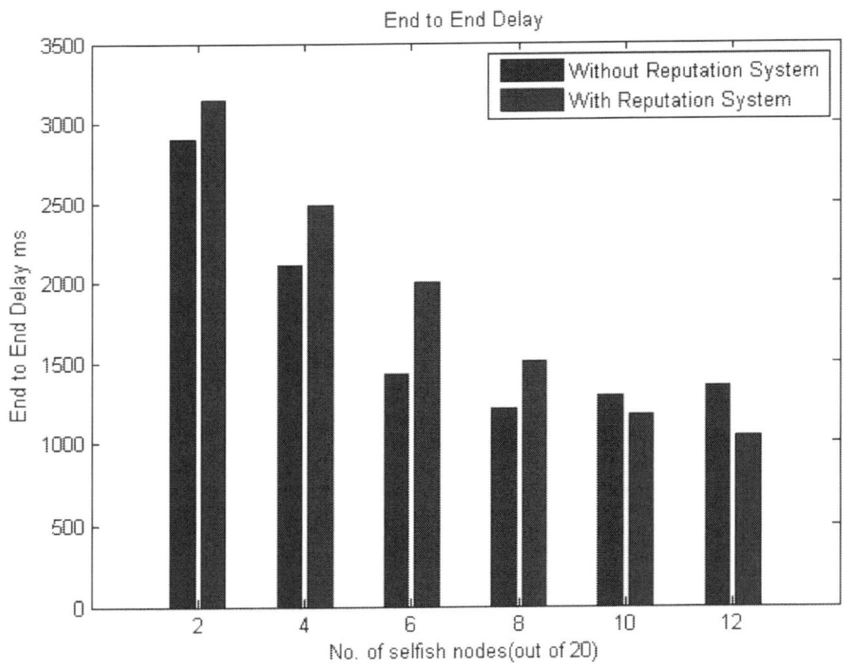

Figure 12. Overall end to end delay for networks experiencing an increase in selfish nodes.

On the other hand, the slight increase in the delay experienced by the networks when the number of selfish nodes increase from 8 → 12 could be a result of different factors. As observed in Figure 12, the registered increase in the delay is minimal and could be a result of increased hop counts from the source to the destination when data are being transferred between good nodes in disjoint partitions.

When compared to the networks with the deployed reputation model, the end to end delays are higher than the networks without the reputation model as the number of selfish nodes increased from $2 \rightarrow 8$. As the number of selfish nodes increases from $10 \rightarrow 12$, the end to end delays of the network slightly decrease when compared to the network without the reputation model. The higher end to end delay in the reputation model may be a result of the additional time it takes to check if a node is on the white-list, watch-list or blacklist before responding to the route request from that node. It may also be a result of the activities of the path coordinator to source paths without bad nodes before routing a packet.

When comparing the performance of the networks in Figures 12 and 13, a trend toward a decrease in the network delays as both sets of misbehaving nodes increase is observed. The networks with deceitful nodes had a much lower end to end delay when compared to the networks with selfish nodes. Deceitful nodes periodically respond to route requests and drop the corresponding data packets. This may lead to decreased end to end delays due to less queuing at the interface queue and buffering during route discovery latency.

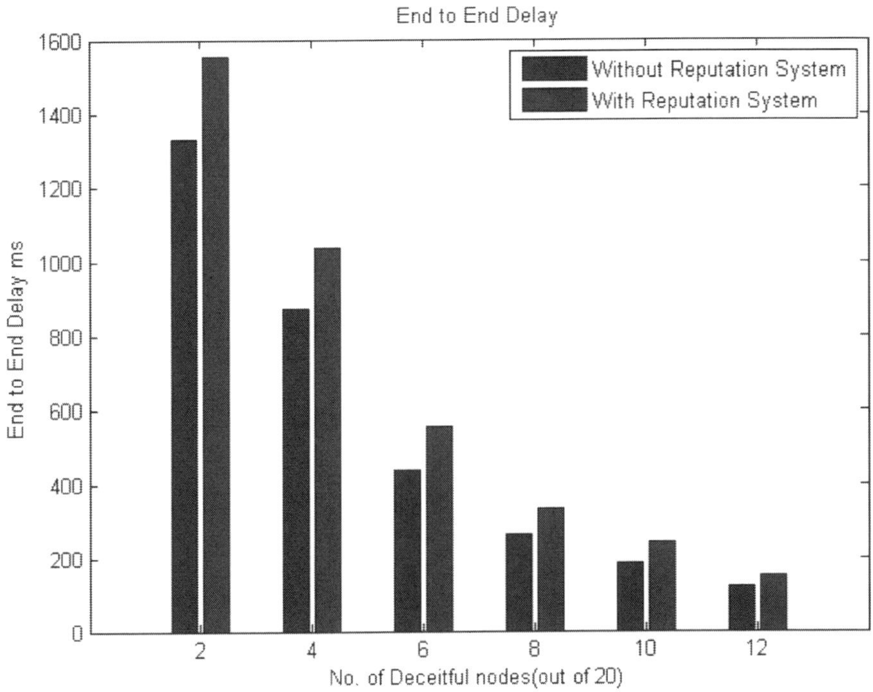

Figure 13. End to end delay for networks experiencing an increase in deceitful nodes.

6.5. Discussion

Simulation results show that the deployed reputation model is effective at detecting and isolating misbehaving nodes. The analysis of the results of the simulated networks shows that the network with the reputation model experiences a slightly higher end to end delay than the networks without the model. However, the network with the reputation model has a much better performance in terms of the throughputs, packet delivery ratios and lower routing overheads. This suggests that the deployed reputation model is beneficial to MANETs.

The registered network end to end delays with the deployed reputation model means that packets may take longer to get to their desired destination, which demonstrates that to accomplish a reliable MANET using the deployed reputation model, the possible increase in the average end to end of a network serves as the compromise. However, the trade-off between average end to end network delays and the other network metrics, that is better network throughput, packet delivery ratio and lower routing overhead, confirms that deployment of the proposed reputation model could lead to an improvement of the overall performance of a MANET.

The effectiveness of the proposed dynamic reputation management system could be further established by comparing the improved network metrics recorded with the deployed reputation model with another proposed reputation model. However, the main motivation for the monitoring and detection technique proposed in this paper is to monitor, detect and curb the negative effects of selective existence attacks carried out by selfish nodes that do not participate in route discovery processes for other nodes in a MANET, as described in Subsection 3.1. This attack has not been addressed by most existing reputation managements systems.

7. CONCLUSIONS

The proposed dynamic reputation management system describes a novel technique of observing the packet transmission activities of mobile nodes in the network. Although existing monitoring techniques have been successful in observing several misbehaviours of nodes in MANETs, selective existence attacks carried out by a special type of selfish node will go undetected with the deployment of the existing monitoring schemes. This paper further describes a unique way of observing and analysing the packet transmission activities of such behaviours and other selfish behaviours. The proposed reputation model is capable of mitigating the adverse effects in the presence of these types of misbehaving nodes (selfish and deceitful behaviours) on the scarce network resources. The presence of these misbehaving nodes in a mobile network is detrimental to good nodes. These good nodes consume their limited energy by participating in all network activities as required in a MANET. Future research work will focus on how to compensate the good nodes for consuming their limited energy in forwarding packets for other nodes in the network.

AUTHOR CONTRIBUTIONS

This paper was the result of collaboration among the three authors. The research theme and idea were proposed by Eric Chiejina and further refined by Hannan Xiao. Eric Chiejina and Hannan Xiao were mainly involved in developing the reputation model. Extensive simulations for testing and verifying the developed reputation model were carried out by Eric Chiejina. The result analyses were carried out by Bruce Christianson, Hannan Xiao and Eric Chiejina. All authors contributed to the writing of the paper, the literature review and the discussion of the obtained results. The three authors have read and approved the final version of the manuscript.

CONFLICTS OF INTEREST

The authors declare no conflict of interest.

REFERENCES

1. Giordano, S. Mobile ad hoc networks. In *Handbook of Wireless Networks and Mobile Computing*; Wiley: River Street Hoboken, NJ, USA, 2002; pp. 325–346.

2. Papadimitratos, P.; Haas, Z.J. Secure Routing for Mobile Ad Hoc Networks, Proceedings of the SCS Commnication Networks and Distributed Systems Modeling and Simulation Conference (CNDS), San Antonio, TX, USA, 27–31 January 2002; pp. 193–204.

3. Senthilkumar, S.; William, J. A Survey on Reputation Based Selfish Node Detection Techniques In Mobile Ad Hoc Network. *J. Theor. Appl. Inf. Technol.* **2014**, *60*, 208–215.

4. Cho, J.H.; Swami, A.; Chen, I.R. *Mission-Dependent Trust Management in Heterogeneous Military Mobile Ad Hoc Networks*; Technical Report, DTIC Document; Defense Technical Information Center: Fort Belvoir, VA, USA, 2010.

5. Velloso, P.B.; Laufer, R.P.; de O. Cunha, D.; Duarte, O.C.M.B.; Pujolle, G. Trust management in mobile ad hoc networks using a scalable maturity-based model. *IEEE Trans. Netw. Serv. Manag.* **2010**, *7*, 172–185.

6. McQuillan, J.M.; Richer, I.; Rosen, E. The new routing algorithm for the ARPANET. *IEEE Trans. Commun.* **1980**, *28*, 711–719.

7. Marti, S.; Giuli, T.J.; Lai, K.; Baker, M. Mitigating routing misbehavior in mobile ad hoc networks, Proceedings of the 6th Annual International Conference on Mobile Computing and Networking, Boston, MA, USA, 6–11 August 2000; pp. 255–265.

8. Banerjee, A.; Neogy, S.; Chowdhury, C. Reputation based trust management system for MANET, Proceedings of the 2012 Third International Conference on Emerging Applications of Information Technology (EAIT), West Bengal, India, 30 November–1 December 2012; pp. 376–381.

9. Sun, Y.L.; Han, Z.; Yu, W.; Liu, K.R. Attacks on trust evaluation in distributed networks, Proceedings of the 2006 40th Annual Conference on Information Sciences and Systems, Princeton, NJ, USA, 22–24 March 2006; pp. 1461–1466.

10. Liu, J.; Fu, F.; Xiao, J.; Lu, Y. Secure routing for mobile ad hoc networks, Proceedings of the Eighth ACIS International Conference on Software Engineering, Artificial Intelligence, Networking, and Parallel/Distributed Computing, 2007 (SNPD 2007), 30 July–1 August 2007; 3, pp. 314–318.

11. Denko, M.K. Detection and prevention of Denial of Service (DoS) attacks in mobile ad hoc networks using reputation-based incentive scheme. *J. Syst. Cybern. Inform.* **2005**, *3*, 1–9.

12. Yan, Z.; Zhang, P.; Virtanen, T. Trust evaluation based security solution in ad hoc networks, Proceedings of the Seventh Nordic Workshop on Secure IT Systems, Gjøvik, Norway, 15–17 October 2003; 14.

13. Theodorakopoulos, G.; Baras, J.S. Malicious users in unstructured networks, Proceedings of the 26th IEEE International Conference on Computer Communications (INFOCOM 2007), Anchorage, AK, USA, 6–12 May 2007; pp. 884–891.

14. Shabut, A.M.; Dahal, K.; Awan, I. Enhancing Dynamic Recommender Selection Using Multiple Rules for Trust and Reputation Models in MANETs, Proceedings of the 2013 IEEE 25th International Conference on Tools with Artificial Intelligence (ICTAI), Herndon, VA, USA, 4–6 November 2013; pp. 654–660.

15. Ayday, E.; Fekri, F. An iterative algorithm for trust management and adversary detection for delay-tolerant networks.*IEEE Trans. Mob. Comput.* **2012**, *11*, 1514–1531.

16. Ayday, E.; Lee, H.; Fekri, F. Trust management and adversary detection for delay tolerant networks, Proceedings of the IEEE Military Communications Conference (2010-MILCOM), San Jose, CA, USA, 31 October–3 November 2010; pp. 1788–1793.

17. Ayday, E.; Fekri, F. BP-P2P: Belief propagation-based trust and reputation management for P2P networks, Proceedings of the 2012 9th Annual IEEE Communications Society Conference on Sensor, Mesh and Ad Hoc Communications and Networks (SECON), Seoul, Korea, 18–21 June 2012; pp. 578–586.

18. Buttyán, L.; Hubaux, J.P. Enforcing service availability in mobile ad-hoc WANs, Proceedings of the 1st ACM International Symposium on Mobile Ad Hoc Networking & Computing, Boston, MA, USA, 2000; IEEE Press: Hoboken, NJ, USA, 2000; pp. 87–96.

19. Buttyán, L.; Hubaux, J.P. Stimulating cooperation in self-organizing mobile ad hoc networks. *Mob. Netw. Appl.* **2003**, *8*, 579–592.

20. Jakobsson, M.; Hubaux, J.P.; Buttyán, L. A micro-payment scheme encouraging collaboration in multi-hop cellular networks. In *Financial Cryptography*; Springer: Berlin, Germany, 2003; pp. 15–33.

21. Zhong, S.; Chen, J.; Yang, Y.R. Sprite: A simple, cheat-proof, credit-based system for mobile ad-hoc networks, Proceedings of the IEEE Societies Twenty-Second Annual Joint Conference of the IEEE Computer and Communications (INFOCOM 2003), San Francisco, CA, USA, 30 March–3 April 2003; 3, pp. 1987–1997.

22. Félegyházi, M.; Buttyán, L.; Hubaux, J.P. Equilibrium analysis of packet forwarding strategies in wireless ad hoc networks–the static case.

In *Personal Wireless Communications*; Springer: Berlin, Germany, 2003; pp. 776–789.

23. Cai, J.; Pooch, U. Allocate fair payoff for cooperation in wireless ad hoc networks using shapley value, Proceedings of the 18th International Parallel and Distributed Processing Symposium, Santa Fe, NM, USA, 26–30 April 2004; p. 219.

24. Chiejina, E.; Xiao, H.; Christianson, B. A Candour-based Trust and Reputation Management System for Mobile Ad Hoc Networks, Proceedings of the 6th York Doctoral Symposium on Computer Science & Electronics, York, UK, 29 October 2013; University of York: York, UK, 2013.

25. Michiardi, P.; Molva, R. Core: A collaborative reputation mechanism to enforce node cooperation in mobile ad hoc networks. In *Advanced Communications and Multimedia Security*; Springer: Berlin, Germany, 2002; pp. 107–121.

26. Buchegger, S.; Le Boudec, J.Y. Nodes bearing grudges: Towards routing security, fairness, and robustness in mobile ad hoc networks, Proceedings of the 10th Euromicro Workshop on Parallel, Distributed and Network-based Processing, Canary Islands, Spain, 9–11 January 2002; pp. 403–410.

27. Bansal, S.; Baker, M. *Observation-Based Cooperation Enforcement in Ad Hoc Networks*; Cornell University: Ithaca, NY, USA, 2003.

28. Virendra, M.; Jadliwala, M.; Chandrasekaran, M.; Upadhyaya, S. Quantifying trust in mobile ad-hoc networks, Proceedings of the IEEE International Conference of Integration of Knowledge Intensive Multi-Agent Systems (KIMAS), Waltham, MA, USA, 18–21 April 2005.

29. He, Q.; Wu, D.; Khosla, P. A secure incentive architecture for ad hoc networks. *Wirel. Commun. Mob. Comput.* **2006**, *6*, 333–346.

30. Li, J.; Li, R.; Kato, J. Future trust management framework for mobile ad hoc networks. *IEEE Commun. Mag.* **2008**, *46*, 108–114.

31. Buchegger, S.; Le Boudec, J.Y. Performance analysis of the CONFIDANT protocol, Proceedings of the 3rd ACM International Symposium on Mobile Ad Hoc Networking & Computing, Lausanne, Switzerland, 9–11 June 2002; ACM: New York, NY, USA; pp. 226–236.

32. Hu, J.; Burmester, M. Cooperation in mobile ad hoc networks. In *Guide to Wireless Ad Hoc Networks*; Springer: Berlin, Germany, 2009; pp. 43–57.

33. Buchegger, S.; Le Boudec, J.Y. *A Robust Reputation System for Peer-to-Peer and Mobile Ad-Hoc Networks*; P2PEcon 2004, No. LCA-CONF-2004-009; Harvard University: Cambridge, MA, USA, 2004.

34. Zouridaki, C.; Mark, B.L.; Hejmo, M.; Thomas, R.K. A quantitative trust establishment framework for reliable data packet delivery in MANETs, Proceedings of the 3rd ACM Workshop on Security of Ad Hoc and Sensor Networks, Alexandria, VA, USA, 7 November 2005; ACM: New York, NY, USA, 2005; pp. 1–10.

35. Zouridaki, C.; Mark, B.L.; Hejmo, M.; Thomas, R.K. Robust cooperative trust establishment for MANETs, Proceedings of the Fourth ACM Workshop on Security of Ad Hoc and Sensor Networks, Alexandria, VA, USA, 30 October–3 November 2006; ACM: New York, NY, USA; pp. 23–34.

36. Pirzada, A.A.; McDonald, C. Trust establishment in pure ad-hoc networks. *Wirel. Pers. Commun.* **2006**, *37*, 139–168.

37. Boukerche, A.; Ren, Y. A security management scheme using a novel computational reputation model for wireless and mobile ad hoc networks, Proceedings of the 5th ACM Symposium on Performance Evaluation of Wireless Ad Hoc, Sensor, and Ubiquitous Networks, Vancouver, BC, Canada, 27–28 October 2008; ACM: New York, NY, USA; pp. 88–95.

38. Li, N.; Das, S.K. A trust-based framework for data forwarding in opportunistic networks. *Ad Hoc Netw.* **2013**, *11*, 1497–1509.

39. Kumar, S.G.C. A Novel Routing Strategy for Ad Hoc Networks with Selfish Nodes. *J. Telecommun.* **2010**, *3*, 23–28.

40. Gong, W.; You, Z.; Chen, D.; Zhao, X.; Gu, M.; Lam, K.Y. Trust based routing for misbehavior detection in ad hoc networks. *J. Netw.* **2010**, *5*, 551–558.

41. Gong, W.; You, Z.; Chen, D.; Zhao, X.; Gu, M.; Lam, K.Y. Trust based malicious nodes detection in MANET, Proceedings of the International Conference on IEEE E-Business and Information System Security, 2009 (EBISS'09), Wuhan, China, 23–24 May 2009; pp. 1–4.

42. Bakar, K.A.A.; Irvine, J. A Scheme for Detecting Selfish Nodes in MANETs using OMNET++, Proceedings of the 2010 6th International

Conference on Wireless and Mobile Communications (ICWMC), Valencia, Spain, 20–25 September 2010; pp. 410–414.

43. Tamilarasi, M.; Sundararajan, T. Secure Enhancement Scheme for Detecting Selfish Nodes in Manet, Proceedings of the 2012 International Conference on Computing, Communication and Applications (ICCCA), Tamilnadu, India, 22–24 February 2012; pp. 1–5.

44. Vigna, G.; Gwalani, S.; Srinivasan, K.; Belding-Royer, E.M.; Kemmerer, R.A. An intrusion detection tool for AODV-based ad hoc wireless networks, Proceedings of the 20th Annual Computer Security Applications Conference, Tucson, AZ, USA, 6–10 December 2004; pp. 16–27.

45. Fall, K.; Varadhan, K. *The ns Manual (2011)*, Available online: http://www.isi.edu/nsnam/ns/doc/nsdoc.pdf accessed on 16 April 2015.

CHAPTER 5

An ant colony-based multi objective quality of service routing for mobile *Ad Hoc* networks

ABSTRACT

Routing, the act of moving information from a source node to a destination node across any kind of network is one of the major issues in computer network literature. *Ad hoc* wireless networks are increasing in popularity, because of the spread of laptops, sensor devices, personal digital assistants, and other mobile electronic devices. These devices will eventually need to communicate with each other, without an adequate infrastructure to rely on. For mobile *ad hoc* networks, the complexity of routing increases because of its characteristics such as dynamic topology, absence of centralized authority, time varying quality of service (QoS) requirements, etc. The biggest challenge in this kind of networks is to find a path between communication end points satisfying user's QoS requirement in spite of frequent path failures because of node mobility. Recent advances in wireless technology and availability of mobile computing devices with networking capabilities have generated a lot of interest in wireless *ad hoc* networks for QoS-based real-time multimedia applications. In this article, we are proposing AMQR, an ant-based multiobjective on demand QoS routing algorithm for mobile *ad hoc* network which will be highly adaptive, efficient, scalable, and mainly reduces end-to-end delay in high mobility cases.

KEYWORDS

MANET, quality of service (QoS) routing, ant colony optimization

1. INTRODUCTION

Mobile *Ad hoc* NETwork (MANET) [1] is a collection of wireless mobile nodes, which dynamically form a temporary network, without using any existing network infrastructure or centralized administration making these mobile nodes to dynamically establish routing paths between themselves. In recent years, a large number of MANET routing algorithms have been proposed which deal with dynamic aspects of MANETs using reactive or proactive approach or a combination of both. However, features such as multi-hop relaying, dynamic topology because of the random movement of mobile nodes, absence of centralized authority which is unique to MANET lead to massive overheads for route discovery and maintenance. This fact is further provoked by resource constraints in energy, computational capacities, and restricted bandwidth with variable capacity links.

To address these routing challenges in MANETs, myriad number of approaches is provided in literatures which can be classified as proactive and reactive. The proactive category [2, 3] continuously maintains routing information about every node in the network. The main idea behind this behavior is to have always a path available on which to send an eventual flow of data packets. The reactive category otherwise referred as on-demand [4–6] will find routes whenever required, that is, they establish a multihop path between a pair of nodes only if there are packets to be transmitted. Thus, saving bandwidth and reducing overhead is achieved. Also, reactive algorithms are efficient if routes are used at irregular intervals. All these previous works provide a basic "best effort" routing functionality which is sufficient only for applications where data to be transmitted is just a text file or an email message.

Since the demand for real time and quality of services (QoSs) has been increased as the Internet expands, provision of QoS is necessary in addition to basic routing functionality. The goal of QoS provisioning is to achieve a more deterministic network behavior, so that information carried by network can be better delivered and network resources can be better utilized. Lack of central coordination and imprecise state information about network links and flows makes the job tough. Link-specific state information includes bandwidth, delay, delay jitter, loss rate, error rate, stability cost, and distance value of each link whereas flow-specific information includes maximum and minimum bandwidth requirements, maximum delay and maximum delay jitters.

With the growth in potential use of MANETs, a lot of research is being focused on providing QoS [7–15]. For the current Internet, there are two different models to obtain a QoS guarantee, namely, Integrated Services (IntServ) [9] and Differentiated Services (DiffServ) [16]. Using resource reservation protocol, RSVP [17, 18] IntServ carries QoS parameters from senders to receivers to make resource reservations along a path and hence provides a rich end-to-end QoS solution, by the way of end-to-end signaling, state-maintenance for each RSVP-flow as well as reservation and admission control at each network element. As an alternate, DiffServ works on a service level agreement between providers and users. All packets from a user carry service levels and are treated accordingly. Multiple flows in DiffServ model are mapped to a single service level and state information about every flow need not be maintained along the paths. The IntServ-based model on per-flow resource reservation is not particularly suitable for MANETs because of its frequently changing topology and limited resources. This results more signaling overhead and unaffordable storage and computing power for mobile nodes. However, DiffServ-based approach is a lightweight model using a relative-priority scheme to soften the requirements of hard QoS models like IntServ. Since service differentiation is based on per-hop behaviors no flow states need to be maintained and making DiffServ as a potential QoS model in MANETs.

The role of a QoS routing strategy is to compute paths that are suitable for different types of traffics generated by various applications while maximizing the utilizations of network resources. Since QoS routing is a multiobjective problem with high computational complexity, heuristics algorithms can be used for QoS routing to reduce this complexity but at the expense of not attaining optimal solution finding just a feasible solution.

Recently swarm intelligence has been offered as a novel computational approach that replaces traditional emphasis on control, preprogramming and centralization, with designs featuring autonomy, emergence, and distributed functioning. Swarm Intelligence systems [19] are typically made up of a population of simple agents interacting locally with one another and also with their environment. Usually, there is no centralized control structure dictating how individual agents should behave, but local interactions between such agents often lead to emergence of a global behavior. Examples of systems like this can be found in nature, including ant colonies, bird flocking, bee swarming, animal herding, bacteria molding, and fish schooling.

The ant colony optimization (ACO) metaheuristic [20] is based on generic problem representation and definition of ant's food foraging behavior. The

ACO metaheuristic has successfully been applied to a number of different combinatorial optimization problems such as Vehicle Routing Problem [21], traveling salesman [22], and routing in communication networks such as AntNet [23], Mobile Ants Based Routing (MABR) algorithm [24], ARA [25], ARAMA [26], and AntHocNet [27].

In this article, we have attempted to design a QoS-based routing algorithm for mobile *ad hoc* networks using ACO metaheuristic. The rest of the article is organized as follows. In Section 2, we discuss about basics of ACO and its suitability to network routing. In Section 3, similar works related to proposed work are discussed. The proposed work, AMQR, is discussed in Section 4 and subsequently simulation and results are discussed in Section 5.

2. ANT COLONY OPTIMIZATION

A metaheuristic is a set of algorithmic concepts that can be used to define heuristic methods applicable to a wide set of different problems. ACO has been formalized into a metaheuristic for combinatorial optimization problems by Dorigo et al. [28, 29]. ACO takes inspiration from the foraging behavior of ant species which deposit pheromone on ground in order to mark some favorable paths that should be followed by other members of the colony. ACO exploits a similar mechanism for solving optimization problems. An individual ant is a simple insect with limited memory and capable of performing simple actions. Though a single ant has no global knowledge about the task it is performing and its actions are based on local decisions and are usually unpredictable, an ant colony expresses a complex collective behavior providing intelligent solutions to problems such as carrying large items, forming bridges and finding shortest routes from nest to a food source. This intelligent behavior naturally emerges as a consequence of self-organization and indirect communication among ants which can be termed as emergent behavior or swarm intelligence.

In basic ACO, after initialization, the metaheuristic iterates over three phases, namely, ConstructAntSolutions, ApplyLocalSearch, and UpdatePheromones. A number of solutions are constructed by ants which are optionally improved through a local search and finally the pheromone is updated. Given this formulation, ants in ACO build solutions to the problem being solved by moving concurrently and asynchronously on an appropriately defined construction graph which represents any given problem domain. It defines the way of solution construction, pheromone updating, and possible interactions in the solution process. ACO's constructive population based metaheuristic [28, 29] which exploits an indirect form of memory of prior performance makes it a unique approach to solve optimization problems.

Mobile *ad hoc* network routing is a difficult problem because network characteristics such as traffic load and network topology may vary stochastically and in a time-varying nature. The distributed nature of network routing is well matched by the multiagent nature of ACO algorithms. The set of core properties [20] that characterizes ACO instances for routing problems provides traffic-adaptive and multipath routing, relying on both passive and active information monitoring and gathering, making use of stochastic components, not allowing local estimates to have global impact, setting up paths in a less selfish way than in pure shortest path schemes favoring load balancing and showing limited sensitivity to parameter settings.

3. RELATED WORKS

A network or service provider can offer different kinds of services [30] to users which can be categorized a set of measurable prespecified service requirements such as minimum bandwidth, maximum delay, maximum delay variance (jitter), and maximum packet loss rate. After accepting a service request from user, network has to ensure that service requirements of user's flow are met, as per the agreement, throughout the duration of flow.

As discussed in [31], several researchers [32–37] addressed general problem of QoS in MANETs, providing overviews and insights on the work being done in this area. To achieve QoS provisioning, QoS routing algorithms normally integrate QoS provisioning into routing protocols. The QoS version of AODV (QoS-AODV) [37], Core-Extraction Distributed Ad Hoc Routing (CEDAR) protocol [38], and Multimedia Support for Mobile Wireless Networks (MMWN) protocol [39] are some of the examples of QoS routing algorithms proposed for MANETs. However, QoS signaling techniques are independent of underlying routing protocols. The In-band signaling for QoS in Ad-Hoc Mobile Networks (INSIGNIA) algorithm [40] is a typical signaling protocol designed exclusively for MANETs. The idea of CEDAR and MMWN is to broadcast link-state information across the network in order to enable other nodes to find routes that meet QoS criteria, like minimum bandwidth. On the other hand, INSIGNIA piggybacks resource reservations onto data packets, which can be modified by intermediate nodes to inform the communication endpoint nodes in case of lack of resources. These approaches are based on the idea that wireless links between mobile nodes have certain QoS-related properties, in particular a known amount of available bandwidth, and that nodes are able to give guarantees for traffic traversing these links.

4. PROPOSED ALGORITHM

The proposed algorithm ant-based multi-objective QoS routing, AMQR inspired by ant food foraging intelligence, is an on-demand QoS routing algorithm for MANETs to face requirements of various applications that may vary time to time. The proposed approach has two phases, namely, route exploration and route maintenance phases. When a source node has data for passing to a destination node with QoS requirements, it starts with route discovery phase. Data transfer will take place once the route is found. While data transmission is going on, it is also required to maintain paths during route maintenance phase which is desirable and required in mobile *ad hoc* networks.

The proposed algorithm incorporates positive feedback, negative feedback, and randomness into routing computation. Ant-like packets, analogous to ant foragers, are used to locally find new paths. Artificial pheromone is laid on communication links between adjacent nodes and route reply and data packets are inclined toward strong pheromone, whereas next hop is chosen probabilistically. Positive feedback is initiated from destination nodes to reinforce existing pheromone on recently learned good paths. To prevent old routing solutions from remaining in the current network status, exponential pheromone decay is adopted as negative feedback.

Each node running this algorithm contains three tables, namely, neighbor, path preference, and routing. In neighbor table, each neighbor is listed along with pheromone substance indicating goodness of outgoing link to various destinations and available bandwidth of outgoing link from that neighbor. In routing table, desired destinations for which source node has data will be listed with best next hop. While in path preference table, each entry for a destination is associated with a list of neighbor nodes. A probability value in the list expresses goodness of a neighbor node as next hop on the path to destination. The neighbor node which has a higher path preference value will be copied to routing table for the related destination on desire.

4.1. Message formats

To implement proposed algorithm AMQR, following four control messages are used.

4.1.1. Hello message

The hello packet shown in Figure 1 consists of its starting time at current node. When it is broadcast, neighbors who receive it will advertise hello packet receiving time back to the actual sender. Based on starting time and receiving time of hello packet and also size of hello packet, current node will calculate available bandwidth of outgoing links. For each node from which hello packet receiving time has been reported, an entry is created in neighbor table along with calculated available bandwidth and initial pheromone of the neighborhood links. For subsequent hello messages, available bandwidth as well as pheromone will be updated to indicate current status of outgoing links.

0	2	17
Pkt_Type = HELLO	Starting Time	

Figure 1. Hello packet format.

4.1.2. Route request message

The route request message, RREQ_ANT of AMQR, is shown in Figure 2. In addition to exploring shortest path from source to destination, RREQ_ANT additionally senses the network environment-related factors like nodes visited, end-to-end delay from source to destination, and available bandwidth of the path through which it is propagated.

4.1.3. Route reply message

The route reply message, RREP_ANT of AMQR, is shown in Figure 3. From Req_Starting_Time and RREQ_ANT's arrival time, end-to-end delay experienced by RREQ_ANT is found and converted as the parameter, delay. RREP_ANT will bring route availability information in addition to parameters sensed by RREQ_ANT through the same path taken by RREQ_ANT in reverse direction.

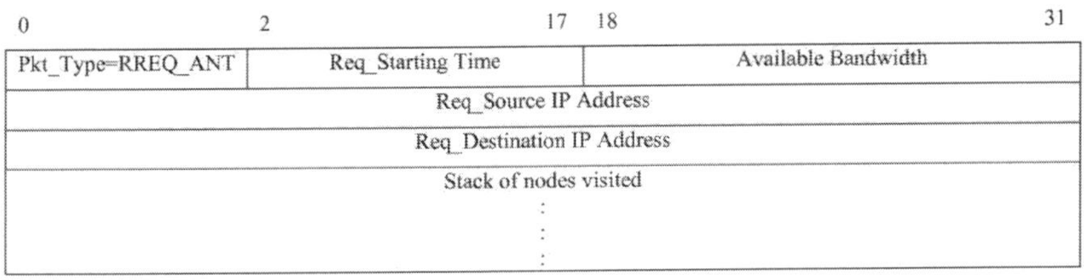

Figure 2. Route request packet format.

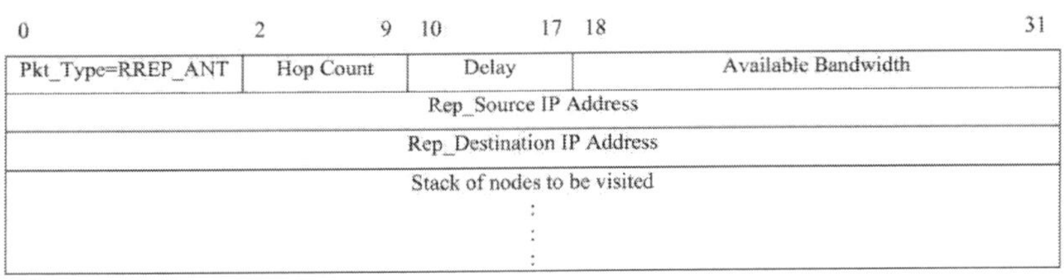

Figure 3. Route reply packet format.

4.1.4. Route error message

Whenever a node learns that it cannot reach a particular destination for which it has an entry in its routing table, the node updates its routing table and sends route error message, RERR in the format as shown in Figure 4. Upon receiving this message, intermediate nodes will update their routing table and path preference probability table for the unreachable destination.

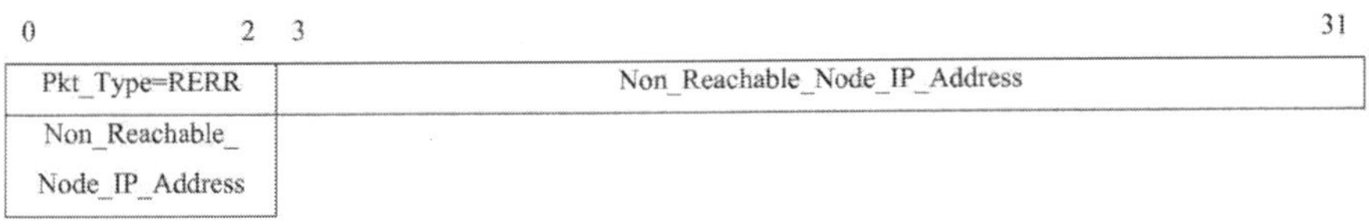

Figure 4. Route error packet format.

4.2. Mathematical model

The objective function of proposed work is to find a path from source to destination through a neighbor with maximum path preference probability. As in [41], path preference probability from source *i* to destination *d* through *i*'s neighbor *j* is calculated as

$$P_{ijd} = \frac{[\tau_{ij}]^{\alpha}[D_{ijd}]^{\beta}[\eta_{ijd}]^{\gamma}[B_{ijd}]^{\delta}}{\sum_{l \in N_i}[\tau_{il}]^{\alpha}[D_{ild}]^{\beta}[\eta_{ild}]^{\gamma}[B_{ild}]^{\delta}} \quad (1)$$

where N_i is a set of neighbor nodes of i, τ_{ij} relative weight of pheromone trail on link (i, j), D_{ijd} is relative metric for delay on the path from i to d through j, η_{ijd} Relative metric for number of nodes on the path from i to d through j, B_{ijd} available bandwidth of the path from I to d through j, α, β, γ, and δ tunable parameters which represent the importance of pheromone decay, delay, number of hops and available bandwidth on the path from i to d through j.

4.2.2. Calculation of relative metrics

For calculating relative metrics, the additive metrics delay, hop count, and non-additive concave metric bandwidth are considered. Since additive metrics have to be minimized for shortest paths, reciprocal values are used while calculating relative metrics. Owing to the desire of maximizing bandwidth, it is considered as in (1).

(i) Delay

The delay between source and destination is considered as

$$D_{ijd} = \frac{1}{\text{delay}(\text{path}_j(i, d))} \quad (2)$$

where delay($\text{path}_j(i\ d)$) is experienced end-to-end delay from source i to destination d through neighbor j by route request message at the time of route exploration.

(ii) Hop count

The measure hop count indicates the number of nodes visited by route request message from source to destination. A destination node finds this from route request message it receives in which first 96 bits indicate source, destination identity, and QoS measure information whereas remaining bits contain list of nodes' IP addresses through which request message has traveled. Hop count can be measured as

$$\text{Hopcount} = \frac{\text{size of (Received RREQ\_ANT)} - 96}{32} \qquad (3)$$

The relative metric for number of intermediate nodes between source and destination is found as

$$\eta_{ijd} = \frac{1}{\text{Hopcount}(\text{path}_j(i,d))} \qquad (4)$$

where Hopcount(path$_j$ (i, d)) is the number of hops seen by route request message along the path i to d through j and found using (3).

(iii) Bandwidth

The available bandwidth of the path from i to d is calculated as minimum of available bandwidth of all links along that path.

$$B_{ijd} = \min\{\text{available\_bandwidth}\,(l)\} \quad \forall\, l \in \text{path}_j(i,d) \qquad (5)$$

whereas available bandwidth of a link is calculated as

$$\text{available\_ bandwidth (link)} = \frac{\text{HPS}}{\text{HPST} - \text{HPRT}} \qquad (6)$$

where HPS is hello packet size, HPST is hello packet starting time, and HPRT is hello packet receiving time. Because hello messages are frequently transmitted to keep neighborhood alive connectivity, they can better reflect current available bandwidth of outgoing links rather than route exploration messages.

(iv) Pheromone

Initially when there is no neighborhood relation between i and j, pheromone on link (i, j) is made as $\tau_{ij} = 0.0$. When j is detected as neighbor of i through hello message, an initial pheromone is deposited as $\tau_{ij} = 0.1$. Whenever a route reply message is received from j to i, it is considered that link (i, j) contributes to a possible path from source i to destination d. So it is positively reinforced as

$$\tau_{ij} = \tau_{ij} + \Delta\tau_{ij} \tag{7}$$

where $\Delta\tau_{ij} = 0.05$.

Though link (i, j) contributes for a possible path from i to d, if no data transmission is detected on that path, it is considered as a path with insufficient QoS requirements. In such case, pheromone on link (i, j) is decreased by a factor ρ as follows.

$$\tau_{ij} = \begin{cases} 1 & if \\ (1-\rho)\tau_{ij} & if \\ 0.1 & i \,\&\, j \text{ are still neighbors} \end{cases} \quad \forall i \in V, j \in N_i \tag{8}$$

where V is set of nodes in mobile network and N_i is set of neighbors of i.

4.3 Route exploration

When source node i has data to forward to a destination d, it searches its routing table for next best hop to reach destination. Since network follows on-demand routing approach, off the rack route will not be available in all cases. So node i initiates a route request message RREQ_ANT through all its neighbors about which it has learned from periodic hello messages. While traveling to destination, RREQ_ANT checks available capacity of each link, identity of hops it has visited. If available capacity of link visited is lower than that of in RREQ_ANT message, the available bandwidth field in RREQ_ANT message is updated by recently visited link's capacity. This will make request message to carry minimum available bandwidth of a link along the path it has traveled. Finally, when RRREQ_ANT reaches the destination, it will be converted as route reply message called RREP_ANT. The RREP_ANT will take same path of corresponding RREQ_ANT, but in reverse direction. For this, RREP_ANT replicates and converts stack of nodes visited by RREQ_ANT as stack of nodes to be visited. At every node from RREP_ANT's starting point, stack is popped to see next hop to forward RREP_ANT. At intermediate nodes and at source i, information coming along with RREP_ANT such as delay, bandwidth, and hop count are used to calculate path preference probability to reach destination. Source node i updates path preference probability to destination d through its entire neighbors provided, it has received RREP_ANT through these neighbors. The neighbor node which contributes a higher path preference probability over all neighbors of node i is selected as best next hop to reach destination d. Once routing table is updated with best next hop for desired destination d, data transmission starts through that best next hop.

4.4. Route maintenance

When data transmission is going on, paths are reinforced positively making it more desirable for further selection. Also when session is going on, load on selected paths may increase causing more delay and less available bandwidth which can be detected using periodic hello and route request messages. Also, nodes might have moved causing link failures. In such cases, path preference probability will automatically decrease and hence alternate routes can be used which are found during route discovery phase. In our proposed scheme, each node maintains an updated view of its immediate neighbors by periodically sensing neighbors. Hence, link failures can be detected as early as possible before they can lead to heavy transmission errors and subsequent packet loss. The presence of neighbor is envisioned by periodic hello message exchanges or sending and receiving unicast data messages. The desertion of neighbor node is detected when neighbor's presence is not sensed by hello messages for a predefined amount of period. When a neighbor desertion is detected, the node removes lost neighbor from its neighbor table, path preference probability table and also from routing table according to necessity. If data transmission was taking place through that failed link, alternate route with next best updated path preference probability will be selected for further transmission. In worst case, all available routes to destination might be lost and reinitialization of route exploration phase might be required.

5. SIMULATION AND RESULT ANALYSIS

5.1. Experimental setup

Performance of proposed algorithm, AMQR, existing *ad hoc* on demand distance vector algorithm, AODV, and AntHocNet [29] are tested in a number of simulated scenarios. Diverse simulation scenarios have been created by varying number of nodes, number of constant bit rate (CBR) sessions in the entire network referred as flow count, and amount of pause time. Implementation of proposed algorithm, AMQR, is done in C++ and checked with NS-2.34 TCL simulation scripts [42]. In all scenarios, nodes are placed randomly in a 1500 m × 1500 m region. The maximum transmit range of each mobile node is 250 m. Normally, nodes move according to random way mobility model with a speed in the range [0,10] m/s and for certain scenarios, node mobility is varied from [10, 80] m/s to find the effect of node mobility in latency and throughput. All nodes move toward a new destination position in the region and stay there for a specified time called pause time and again proceed toward a new direction as previously described. The channel capacity is 2 Mbps and at MAC layer IEEE 802.11 DCF is used. Each simulation is run for 900 s each time. The data traffic was generated by a number of CBR sources with repeated sources and repeated destinations. Various timers used in AMQR for periodic control messages and tunable parameter values that can control the relative weight of pheromone trail are specified in Table 1.

Table 1. AMQR Parameter settings

Parameters	Values
Pheromone decay factor, ρ	0.05
Pheromone positive reinforcement, $\Delta\tau_{ij}$	0.05
Pheromone decay weight, α	1.0
Delay weight, β	1.0
Shortest hop weight, γ	1.0
Bandwidth weight, δ	1.0
Hello Interval	1 sec
Hello Retry times	3
Upper pheromone bound	1.0
Lower pheromone bound	0.1

The value for relative weight parameters α, β, γ, and δ is kept as 1.0 for the sake of initial study. Later values for these parameters are refined to check their influence on path preference probability.

5.2 Result analysis

Figures 5 and 6 show the effect of end-to-end average delay with various flow counts for 50 and 100 nodes scenario. In case of AODV, there are possibilities that some links might be shared by more than one shortest path. This will increase traffic on selected links which may lead to congestion and hence data packets transmitted through these links may face additional delay. The situation is further aggravated if many traffic connections start sharing these links. In case of AMQR, a path is considered as good not only based on number of hops, but also on other parameters like available bandwidth along the links on that path. So, when a link contributes itself on a shortest path of a particular traffic, available bandwidth of that link will get reduced. Since bandwidth is a kind of property to be maximized, this leads to a reduction in path preference probability of the paths which have this link as one of their intermediate links. This will lead to the selection of other possible paths which may have higher path preference probability. Though alternate paths may not be shortest in number of hops, they may have less traffic. Hence, data may be transmitted as they are received and not making them to wait in the queues. This can be realized well when number of flow count is increasing. AntHocNet considers pheromone, prespecified delay bound at receiver and number of hops to determine path probability and randomly select a path for data transmission. This offers good load balance in the entire network and may not offer shorter delay and wider bandwidth paths for a specific data flow. In all our experiments, we have seen that AntHocNet has close performance with proposed work, AMQR. From Figures 5 and 6, it is seen that proposed the algorithm has lesser delay especially in increased flow counts compared to AODV and AntHocNet.

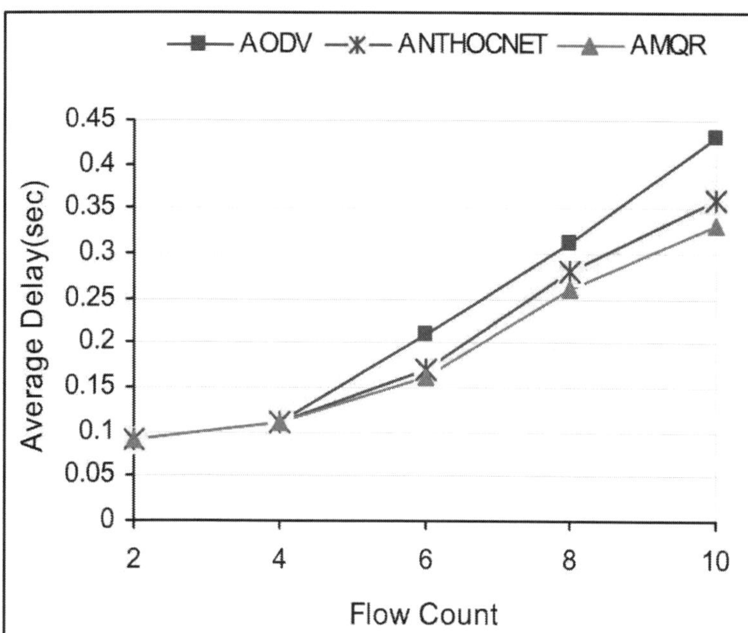

Figure 5. Average delay for various flow counts in a 50-node network.

Also, in case of high number of CBR connections, many numbers of links are used by multiple traffic flows and hence probability of occurrence of congestion is high. In AODV, local repair of link breaks in routes some times results in increased path lengths to destinations. This introduces heavy end-to-end delay for data packets. Since AMQR as well as AntHocNet maintains multiple paths to destinations based on current status of network, alternate paths with less traffic can be selected with better path preference. When such paths are selected for data transmission, delay faced will be less than AODV using shortest paths.

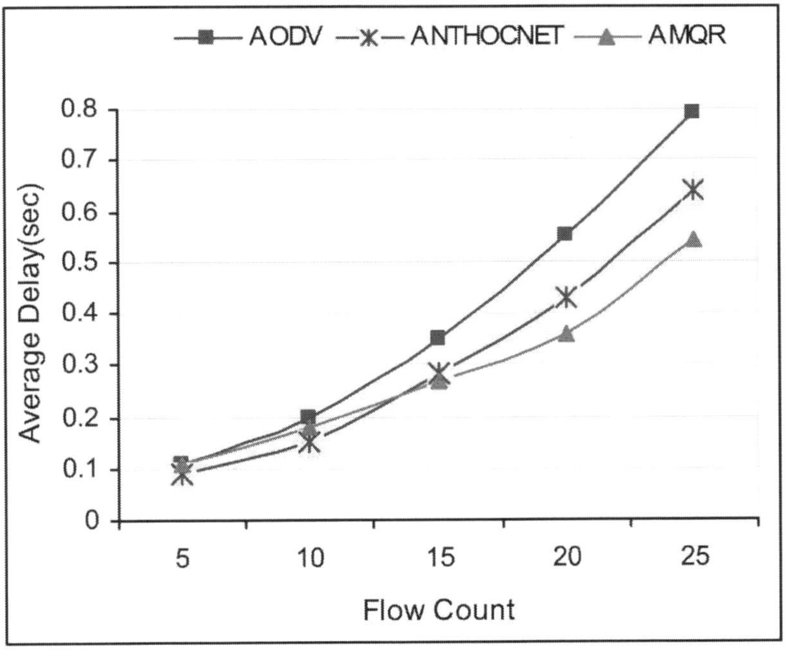

Figure 6. Average delay for various flow counts in a 100-node network.

Figure 7 shows the packet delivery ratio for 100 nodes network with 25CBR connections by varying node mobility. Between AODV and AMQR, performance difference is very much visible at all mobility levels. Also, AMQR performs better than AntHocNet. Figure 8 indicates performance difference between AODV, AntHocNet, and AMQR for average delay with increasing node mobility for the same 100 nodes network with 25 as flow count. AMQR performs well compared to AODV in case of low node mobility because as mobility increases, paths between communication end points will be broken frequently. Owing to subsequent path repairing and new path exploration, average delay is getting increased for all three algorithms. However, AMQR depends upon alternate available paths and in worst case in which all identified paths are broken, it can go for new path exploration mechanism. Figure 9compares average jitter, the inter packet arrival time for various node mobility. At high node mobility, jitter increases because of path breaks and subsequent alternate path selection or new path identification.

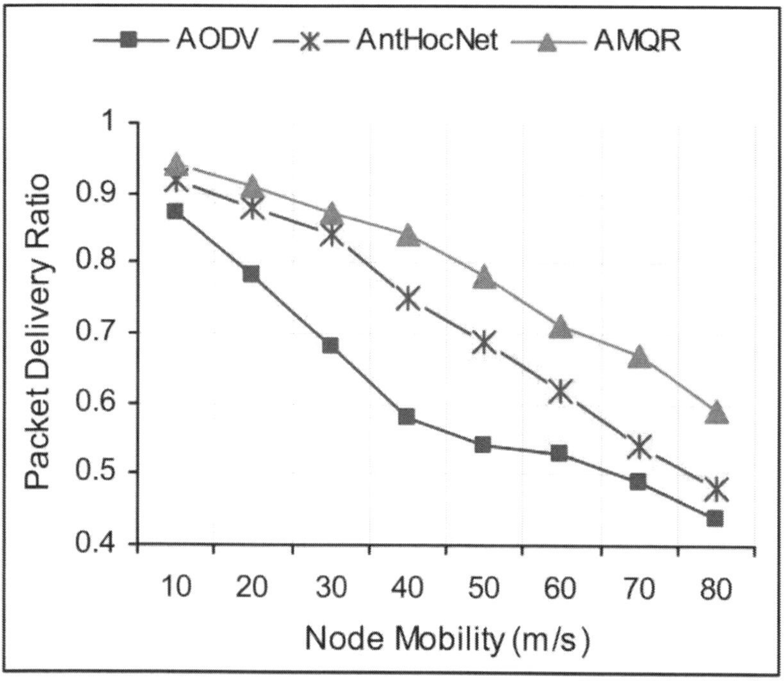

Figure 7. Packet delivery ratio under increasing node mobility for 100 nodes network with flow count as 25.

Normally at higher pause time, nodes may stick on to the terrain boundaries for longer time making itself to be invisible for others. This leads to path breaks for longer time causing a reduced amount of packet delivery ratio at higher pause times as shown in Figure 10. But, if number of nodes in network increases and different nodes start moving at different timings, network connectivity can be maintained well. In case of shorter pause time, nodes will not stay in one place and keep on moving frequently. This creates path breaks but connectivity among network nodes will be maintained well. Owing to multiple path maintenance, AMQR and AntHocNet can achieve good packet delivery ratio at shorter pause time. As pause time increases, delivery ratio decreases whereas jitter increases. Average delay variation, jitter, has been analyzed in Figure 11 for increasing pause time. In AODV, when a link breaks, if possible route repair is done or otherwise new paths are explored. So, in case of path breaks, a time gap is introduced while data are transmitted causing increase in jitter.

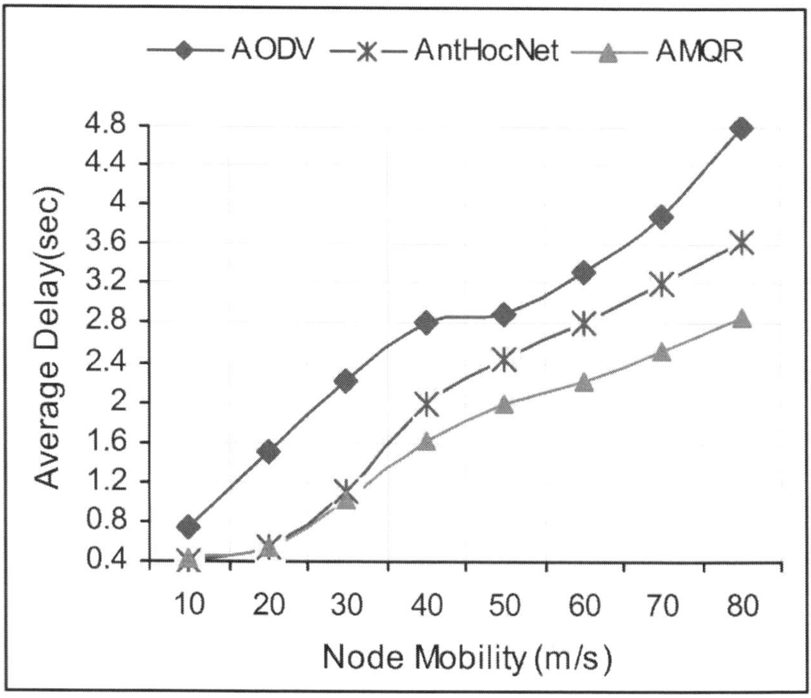

Figure 8. Average delay under increasing node mobility for 100 nodes network with flow count as 25.

The improved performance we have achieved in AMQR is at a cost of routing control overhead compared to AODV and AntHocNet. In AMQR, four kinds of control messages are used to keep neighborhood connectivity, to search for routes using request messages, to reply for routes requests, and to inform route errors. The size of request message will dynamically increase as it moves through network toward destination whereas reply message's size will decrease as it move toward source node. AMQR satisfies QoS requirements and achieves better performance by maintaining multiple paths to destinations through these dynamically size varying ant messages. Figures 12 and13 show routing overhead in terms of packets for increasing pause time and increasing node mobility. AODV has least control overhead and AntHocNet has moderate routing overhead. Since proposed algorithm, AMQR, shares nodes visited and delay information through request and reply messages periodically to maintain multiple paths, it has highest control overhead.

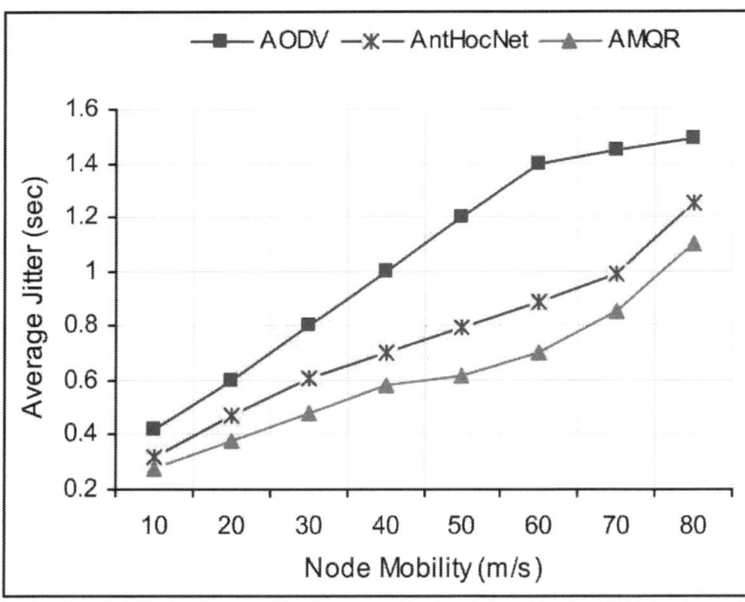

Figure 9. Average jitter (delay variance) under increasing node mobility for 100 nodes network with flow count as 25.

In all simulations carried out previously, equal weight is given to the parameters α, β, γ, and δ which represent the importance of pheromone decay, delay, number of hops, and available bandwidth, respectively. We have carried additional simulations by varying β and δ values to find their effect on path preference probability and subsequently on delay and packet delivery ratio. To learn the importance of considering delay in case of selecting best paths, value of β alone is varied as 0.25, 0.5, 0.75, and 1 and results are expressed in Figure 14.

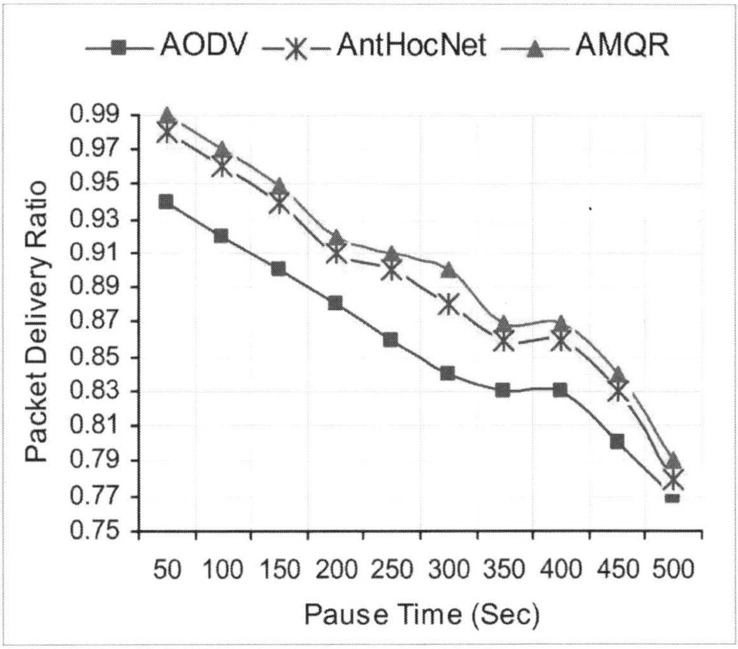

Figure 10. Effect of pause time on packet delivery ratio.

It is also observed that as β value is decreasing, average delay is increasing. The reason is, as β decreases, importance to paths with shorter delay are given less preference than paths with higher delays which may have least hop count, less available bandwidth. This may increase path preference probability of paths with higher delays. So when these paths are selected for data transmission, higher delays are introduced. Similarly, to know the importance of considering available bandwidth of paths while calculating path preference probability, value of δ is varied as 1, 0.75, 0.5, and 0.25, and the analysis is shown in Figure 15 in which packet delivery ratio is compared for various values of δ. Clearly proposed algorithm performs well for higher values of δ and the packet delivery ratio gets decreased as the value of δ decreases.

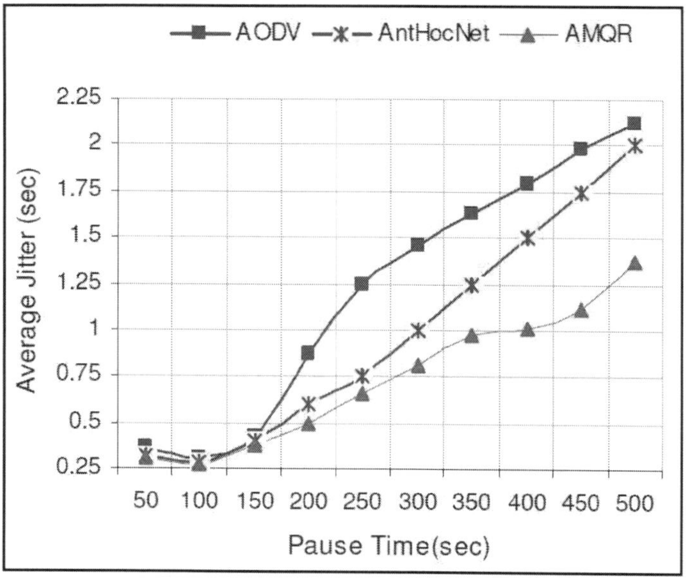

Figure 11. Effect of pause time on average jitter.

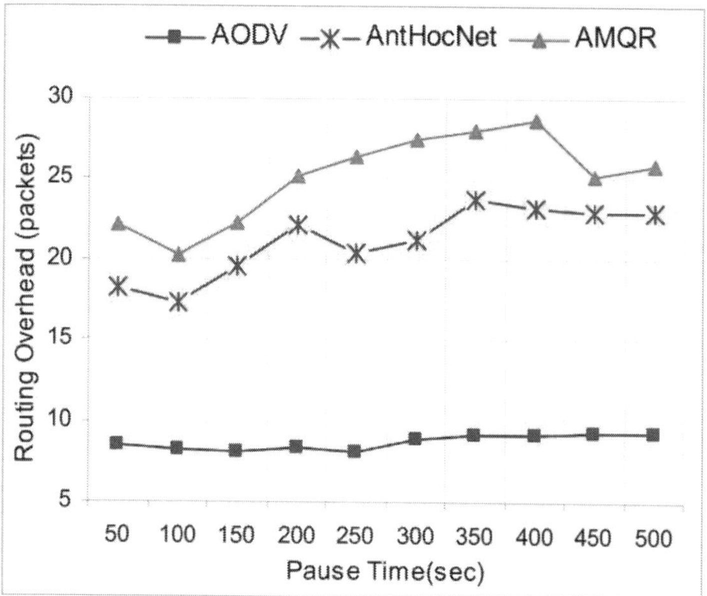

Figure 12. Routing overhead in terms of control packets for each successfully delivered data packet for various node pause time.

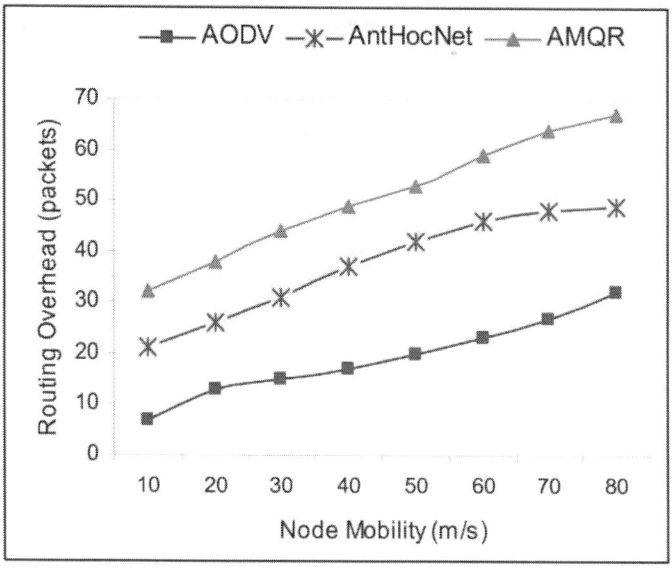

Figure 13. Routing overhead in terms of control packets for each successfully delivered data packet for various node mobility.

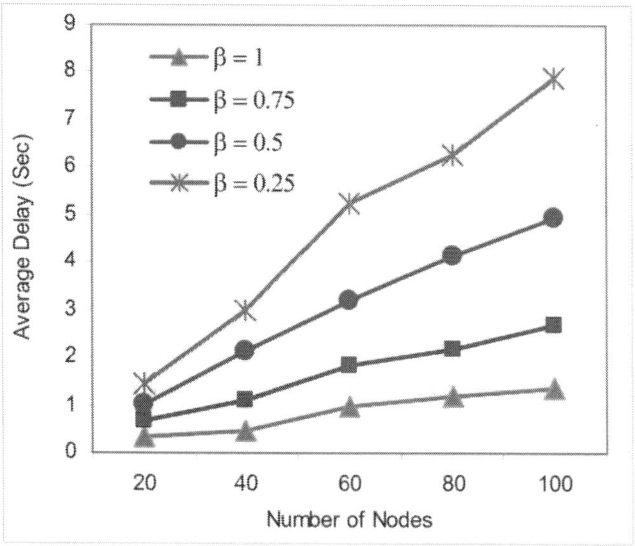

Figure 14. AMQR: average delay for various β values under increasing network size.

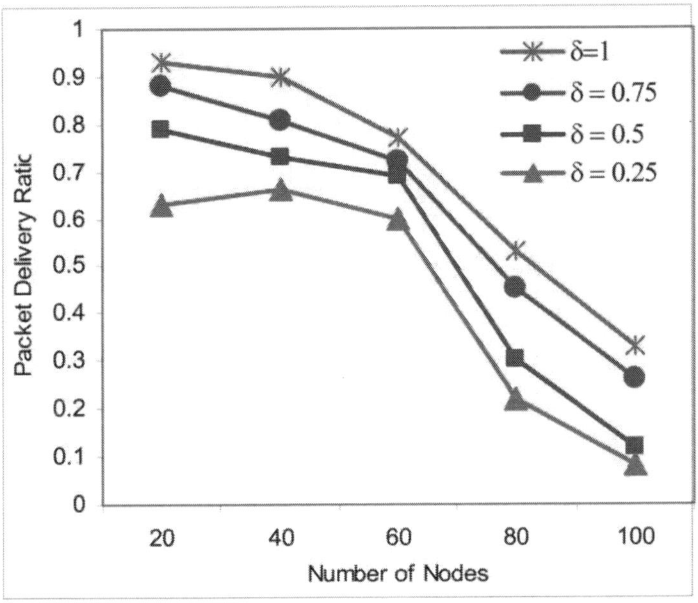

Figure 15. Packet delivery ratio for various δ values under increasing network size.

6. CONCLUSION AND FUTURE WORK

Mobile *ad hoc* networks grant a wide range of challenges in routing and network management because of their dynamic and distributed natures. Several protocols have been proposed to address the challenges. In this article, we have proposed AMQR, an ant-based routing protocol to meet the QoS requirement of mobile *ad hoc* networks to support real-time traffic. In addition to considering only presence of links or connectivity between nodes, network-related status of links like delay experienced through that links, available bandwidth in links, and a link's suitability for data transmission are also collected and measured. These measures provide an indication of how much a link is suitable while deciding about paths for providing QoS routing. From a given source to destination, multiple paths have been found and their path preference probability is calculated based on the above said measures. Apparently, the path with higher path preference probability offers an optimized consideration of multiple QoS metrics delay, bandwidth, and shortest hop count. Initially, data are sent over the path with higher path preference probability which can provide lesser delay, higher bandwidth, and shorter path in terms of number of hops. In case of any link failure leading to path breaks, alternate possible paths with next higher path preference probability are immediately considered and data transmission will be continued. The proposed algorithm, AMQR, has been compared with AODV and AntHocNet in terms of delay, throughput, jitter with various flow counts, node mobility, and various pause times. It is also observed that proposed algorithm provides good packet delivery ratio and shorter delay and jitter compared to AODV and AntHocNet in all cases but at cost of increased routing overhead.

Future work may include testing the performance of our algorithm, AMQR for various MANET applications with variety of topologies and varying load situations. Also, values for tunable parameters α, β, γ, and δ can be experimented for various applications of *ad hoc* network and also can be optimized.

COMPETING INTERESTS

The authors declare that they have no competing interests.

REFERENCES

1. Macker J, Corson S: Mobile Ad Hoc Networks (MANET). *IETF WG Charter* 1997. [http://www.ietf.org/dyn/wg/charter/manet-charter.html]

2. Jacquet P, Muhlethaler P, Clausen T, Laouiti A, Qayyum A, Viennot L: Optimized link state routing protocol for ad hoc networks. In *Proceedings of the 5th IEEE International Multi Topic Conference (INMTC 2001)*. Le Chesnay, France; 2001.

3. Perkins CE, Bhagwat P: Highly dynamic destination sequenced distance-vector routing (DSDV) for mobile computers. *Comput Commun Rev* 1994, 10(4):234-244.

4. Perkins CE, Royer EM, Das SR: Ad hoc on demand distance vector (AODV) routing. In *Proceedings of IEEE Workshop on Mobile Computing Systems and Applications(WMCSA'99)*. New Orleans, LA, USA; 1999.

5. Johnson DB, Maltz DA: Dynamic source routing in Adhoc wireless networks. In *Mobile Computing*. Edited by: Imelinsky T, Korth H. Kluwer Academic Publishers; 1996:153-181.

6. Park VD, Corson MS: A highly adaptive distributed routing algorithm for mobile wireless networks. In*Proceedings of IEEE Conference on Computer Communications (INFOCOM)*. Kobe, Japan; 1997.

7. Chakrabarti S, Mishra A: QoS issues in ad hoc wireless networks. *IEEE Commun Mag* 2001, 39(2):142-148.

8. Mohapatra P, Li J, Gui C: QoS in mobile ad hoc networks. *IEEE Wirel Commun Mag* 2003, 10(3):44-52.

9. Braden R, Clark D, Shenker S: Integrated services in the internet architecture--an overview. In *Request For Comments 1663*. Internet Engineering Task Force; 1994.

10. Perkins DD, Hughes HD: A survey on quality-of-service routing in ad hoc networks. *Wirel Commun Mobile Comput* 1999, 17(8):503-513.

11. Chalmers D, Sloman M: A survey of QoS in mobile computing environments. *IEEE Commun Surv* 1999, 2(2):2-10.

12. Corson MS, Campbell AT: Toward supporting quality of service in mobile ad hoc networks. In *Proceedings of the 1st Conference on Open Architecture and Network Programming*. San Francisco, USA; 1998.

13. Nikaein N, Bonnet C: A glance at quality of services in mobile ad hoc networks. In *Proceedings of 16th conference of New Architectures for Communications (DNAC'02)*. Paris, France; 2002.

14. Ge Y, Kunz T, Lamont L: Quality of service routing in ad hoc networks using OLSR. In *Proceedings of 36th Annual Hawaii International Conference on System Sciences (HICSS'03)*. Hawaii, USA; 2003.

15. Chen S, Nahrstedt K: Distributed quality-of-service routing in ad hoc networks. *IEEE J Sel Areas Commun* 1999, 17(8):1488-1505.

16. Blake S: An architecture for differentiated services. In *Request for Comments 2475*. Internet Engineering Task Force; 1998.

17. Braden R, Zhang L, Berson S, Herzog S, Jamin S: Resource reservation protocol (RSVP)--version 1 functional specification. In *Request For Comments 2205*. Internet Engineering Task Force; 1997.

18. Wroclawski J: The use of RSVP with IETF integrated services. In *Request for Comments (Standard Track) 2210*. Internet Engineering Task Force; 1997.

19. Bonabeau E, Dorigo M, Theraulaz G: *Swarm Intelligence: from Natural to Artificial Systems*. Oxford University Press, Oxford, USA; 1999.

20. Dorigo M, Birattari M, Stutzle T: Ant colony optimization: artificial ants as a computational intelligence technique.*IEEE Comput Intell* 2006, 1(4):28-39.

21. Bell JE, Mcmullen PR: Ant colony optimization techniques for the vehicle routing problem. *Adv Eng Inf* 2004, 18(1):41-48.

22. Dorigo M, Gambardella LM: Ant colony system: a cooperative learning approach to the traveling salesman problem. *IEEE Trans Evol Comput* 1997, 1(1):53-66.

23. Di Caro G, Dorigo M: AntNet: distributed stigmergetic control for communications networks. *J Artif Intell Res*1998, 9: 317-365.

24. Heissenbu M, Braun T: Ants-based routing in large scale mobile ad hoc networks. In *Proceedings of Kommunikation in Verteilten Systemen(KiVS03)*. Leipzig; 2003.

25. Gunes M, Sorges U, Bouazzi I: ARA--the ant-colony based routing algorithm for MANETs. In *Proceedings of the International Conference on Parallel Processing Workshops (ICPPW'02)*. Vancouver, BC; 2002.

26. Hussein O, Saadawi T: Ant routing algorithm for mobile ad hoc networks (ARAMA). In *Proceedings of the International Performance Computing and Communications Conference(IPCCC 2004)*. Phoenix, Arizona; 2004.

27. Di Caro G, Ducatelle F, Gambardella LM: AntHocNet: an adaptive nature inspired algorithm for routing in mobile ad hoc networks. *Eur Trans Telecommun* 2005, 16(2):443-455.

28. Dorigo M, Di Caro G: The ant colony meta-heuristic. In *New Ideas in Optimization*. Edited by: Corne D, Dorigo M, Golver F. McGraw-Hill; 1999:11-32.

29. Dorigo M, Di Caro G, Gambardella LM: Ant algorithms for discrete optimization. *Artif Life* 1999, 5(2):137-172.

30. Siva Ram Murthy C, Manoj BS: *Ad Hoc Wireless Networks: Architectures and Protocols*. Prentice Hall: Upper Saddle River: NJ; 2004.

31. Liu Z, Kwiatkowska MZ, Constantinou C: A biologically inspired QoS routing algorithm for mobile ad hoc networks. *Int J Wirel Mobile Comput* 2010, 4(2):64-75.

32. Mohapatra P, Li J, Gui C: QoS in mobile ad hoc networks. *IEEE Wirel Commun* 2003, 10(3):44-52.

33. Zhu H, Li M, Chlamtac I, Prabhakaran B: A survey of quality of service in IEEE 802.11 networks. *IEEE Wirel Commun* 2004, 11(4):6-14.

34. Bheemarjuna Reddy T, Karthigeyan I, Manoj BS, Siva Ram Murthy C: Quality of service provisioning in ad hoc wireless networks: a survey of issue and solutions. *Ad Hoc Netw* 2006, 4(1):83-124.

35. Chen L, Heinzelman WB: A survey of routing protocols that support QoS in mobile ad hoc networks. *IEEE Netw*2007, 21(6):30-38.

36. Hanzo L II, Tafazolli R: A survey of QoS routing solutions for mobile ad hoc networks. *IEEE Commun Surv Tutor*2007, 9(2):50-70.

37. Royer EM, Perkins CE: Quality of service for ad hoc on demand distance vector (AODV) routing. *IETF Internet Draft, draft-ietf-manet-aodvqos-00.txt* 2000.

38. Sivakumar R, Sinha P, Bharghavan V: CEDAR: a core-extraction distributed ad hoc routing algorithm. *IEEE J Sel Areas Commun* 1999, 17(8):1454-1465.

39. Ramanathan R, Steenstrup M: Hierarchically-organized, multihop mobile wireless networks for quality-of-service support. *ACM/Baltzer Mobile Netw Appl* 1998, 3(1):101-119.

40. Lee SJ, Ahn GS, Campbell AT: Improving UDP and TCP performance in mobile ad hoc networks with insignia.*IEEE Commun Mag* 2001, 36(6):156-165.

41. Deepalakshmi P, Radhakrishnan S: Ant colony based QoS routing algorithm for mobile ad hoc networks. *Int J Recent Trends Eng* 2009, 1(1):459-462.

42. Ros FJ, Ruiz PM: *Implementing a new MANET unicast routing protocol in ns2.* Technical Report, University of Murcia; 2004.

CHAPTER 6

Effective Route Maintenance and Restoration Schemes in Mobile *Ad Hoc* Networks

Byung-Seok Kang * **and In-Young Ko**

Department of Computer Science, Korea Advanced Institute of Science and Technology (KAIST), 335 Gwahangno, Yuseong-gu, Daejeon, 305-701, Korea

ABSTRACT

This study proposes a location-based hybrid routing protocol to improve data packet delivery and to reduce control message overhead in mobile *ad hoc* networks. In mobile environments, where nodes move continuously at a high speed, it is generally difficult to maintain and restore route paths. Therefore, this study suggests a new flooding mechanism to control route paths. The essence of the proposed scheme is its effective tracking of the destination's location based on the beacon messages of the main route nodes. Through experiments based on an NS-2 simulator, the proposed scheme shows improvements in the data packet delivery ratio and reduces the amount of routing control message overhead compared with existing routing protocols such as AODV, LAR, ZRP and AODV-DFR.

KEYWORDS

route maintenance; route restoration; mobile *ad hoc* network

1. INTRODUCTION

A mobile *ad hoc* network (MANET) is a self-configuring network of mobile devices connected by wireless links. In a MANET, each node acts as a router to establish end-to-end connections, and because the network topology between sources and destinations frequently changes, it is difficult to maintain and restore a route. To deal with these issues, several routing protocols for MANETs have been proposed. However, these protocols are simulated with low numbers of network nodes with low node mobility. Moreover, to track mobile destination, they require large a number of control messages.

This study suggests a location-based hybrid routing protocol for a large number of high-mobility nodes. The proposed routing scheme effectively manages the maintenance and restoration of a route. The basic operation of the scheme is similar to the *Ad Hoc* On-demand Distance Vector (AODV) algorithm [1], as the suggested scheme adds a greedy forwarding algorithm, the location information of a Global Positioning System (GPS), and directional forwarding [2] to the AODV algorithm. In addition, the proposed algorithm can reduce routing overhead. The main route nodes broadcast beacon messages, which have the location of the destination, to their one-hop neighbors. This approach provides efficient tracking of a mobile destination and reduces messages for routing.

To evaluate the performance of the proposed scheme, the data packet delivery ratio and routing control overhead messages are analyzed and compared with existing routing protocols of AODV, Location-Aided Routing (LAR) [3], Zone Routing Protocol (ZRP) [4], and AODV-DFR [5].

The remainder of this paper is organized as follows: Section 2 reviews the previously known MANET and related algorithms. Section 3 develops the proposed routing scheme. In Section 4, the proposal is verified by simulation. Finally, Section 5 summarizes the contributions of this study.

2. RELATED WORKS

In a MANET, routing protocols can be divided into two major categories - proactive routing and reactive routing. Proactive routing protocols, also known as table-driven routing protocols, contain information on every node and update the routing table information periodically. In DSDV [6], OLSR [7], and WRP [8], typical proactive routing protocols, the source node is equipped beforehand with information appertaining to the pathway of the destination node before it send data packets there. As a fatal drawback of the proactive routing approach, however, a mass of route-updating messages flood the entire network periodically to maintain the route information fresh. Furthermore, each node unnecessarily stores the full set of route information, especially in a highly mobile environment where the routing table of a node is updated frequently for dynamic topology. Each node must find the latest broadcast routing path information periodically. Such periodic updates cause unnecessary network overhead.

Reactive routing protocols, also known as on-demand routing protocols, do not conserve the routing table information; instead, they execute a route discovery procedure to determine a route to the destination only when the source node requires a path to the destination node. Once a route has been discovered, the route is maintained until the destination becomes inaccessible or the route is no longer desired. AODV, DSR [9] and the Temporally Ordered Routing Algorithm (TORA) [10] are representative examples of reactive protocols. Particularly with a large number of nodes, reactive routing protocols are more appropriate than a proactive routing approach.

In the following subsections, existing routing protocols that aim to improve the data packet delivery ratio and reduce routing overhead are explained.

2.1. Algorithms to improve the data packet delivery ratio

Hybrid routing strategies, which draw upon the most advantageous features of both proactive and reactive mechanisms, are designed to improve the communication quality for active routes with lower overhead. As a hybrid routing strategy, ZRP has been proposed to provide a hybrid routing framework for a locally proactive and globally reactive approach so as to minimize the sum of the proactive and reactive control overhead. For the zone radius, the main idea of ZRP, each node proactively advertises its link state over a fixed number of hops. These local advertisements over nodes offer an updated view of the routing zone collection of all nodes (or links) that are reachable within the zone radius. The nodes, termed peripheral nodes, are located on the boundary of the routing zone and play an important intermediate role in reactive zone-based route discovery.

The other means of improving the data packet delivery ratio is via a Clustering algorithm [11–13]. Cluster head-Gateway Switch Routing (CGSR) is a typical cluster-based hierarchical routing method. A stable clustering algorithm, Least Cluster head Change (LCC), is used to partition the entire network into several clusters with the selection of a cluster head for each cluster. A mobile node that belongs to two or more clusters is a gateway connecting them, and data packets are routed through paths with the format of a "Cluster head-Gateway" between every source and destination pair.

Integrated Services (IntServ) [14] and Differentiated Services (DiffServ) [15] also guarantee a good quality of packet delivery ratio. An IntServ protocol such as the Bandwidth Reservation over *Ad Hoc* Wireless Networks (BRAWN) [16] mechanism not only guarantees certain QoS levels but also naturally distributes the traffic more evenly among network nodes, similar to load balancing through a rich end-to-end QoS solution mechanism. On the other hand, DiffServ such as a Stateless Wireless *Ad Hoc* Network (SWAN) [17] can be used to classify network traffic into different priority levels and apply priority scheduling and queuing management mechanisms to obtain QoS guarantees.

2.2. Algorithms to reduce routing overhead

Compared to the proactive approach, the reactive approach is high-powered at a lower network overhead and has less data transmission delay and no periodical routing update. The LAR protocol has been presented as an On-Demand protocol based on source routing. The protocol utilizes location information to limit the area when seeking to discover a new route to a smaller "request zone". As a consequence, the number of route request messages is reduced.

The Greedy Perimeter Stateless Routing (GPSR) protocol [18], another Geo-routing protocol, holds only neighbor location information for delivering data packets. This approach is appropriate for dense wireless networks due to its small number of per-node routing states and low routing message complexity.

The Fisheye technique, another algorithm to reduce routing message overhead, is used for Fisheye State Routing (FSR) [19] and AODV-DFR.

First, FSR exchanges all of the link state information with closer neighbors instead of flooding the information over the network. Regarding link state table management, FSR uses an up-to-date technique. Secondly, in FSR, the link state information is swapped periodically instead of being event-triggered as a method to prevent frequent link state updates which cause link breaks and unreliable wireless links. Moreover, periodic broadcasts of the link state information are operated using different frequencies on different entries that depend on their hop distances to the current node.

Finally, protocols similar to the improved original AODV routing protocol were presented in other studies [20,21]. In these two protocols, the originating node can estimate the distance to the destination node and set the initial value of the TTL field in the RREQ message based on that estimated value. This is done using a simple modification of TTL field technique, which may result in an unnecessarily large number of control packets traveling through the network.

3. PROPOSED ALGORITHM

As explained in the previous section, many studies that sought to improve the data packet delivery ratio have been done, but these works leave a considerable number of routing overhead messages. This section describes a detailed scheme to improve the data packet delivery ratio while reducing the number of routing overhead messages via one-hop neighbor beaconing of the main route nodes.

3.1. Directional forwarding

Figure 1 shows the proposed directional forwarding algorithm. Each node recognizes its location through GPS. A one-hop neighbor node, which is at a distance of one hop from the main route, recognizes the location of the main route node through a beacon message. In the figure, node A contains information about its location (Xa, Ya). In this situation, node A broadcasts its location information using a beacon message. Nodes B and C store the location of node A in each routing table. Four-directional forwarding, directions 1 to 4, is then applied. Direction 1 is (+, +), Direction 2 is (+, –), Direction 3 is (–, –), and Direction 4 is (–, +). In Figure 1, Node B locates direction 1 from node A, and node A sets the position of direction 3 from node B. In the same manner, node C locates direction 2 from node A and node A locates direction 4 from node C. Though two-, four-, eight-, and 16-

way directions can be applied, four-way direction shows the best performance with the least routing overhead. Using two-way direction, it causes many routing overhead as similar data packet delivery ratio. Furthermore, using eight- and 16-way direction, they result very low data packet delivery ratio because there are not enough control messages to trace the destination's location.

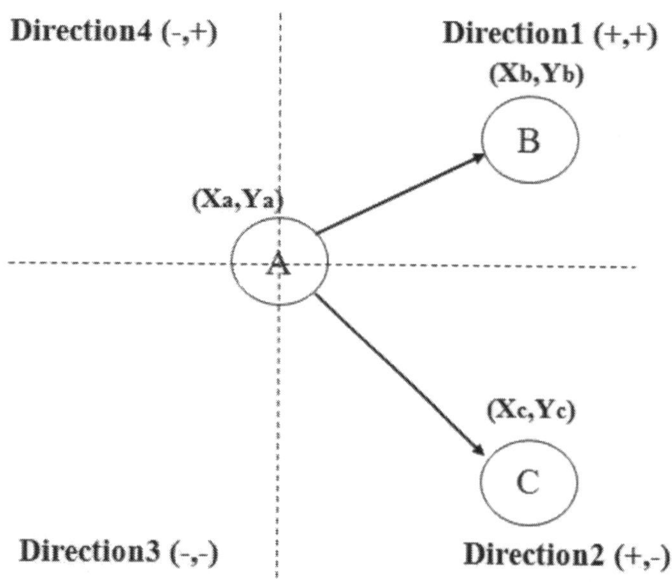

Figure 1. Four-way directional forwarding.

3.2. Basic operation of the algorithm

The proposed algorithm uses four message types: beacon, Route Request (RREQ), Route Reply (RREP), and Route Error (RERR). Originally, any node can broadcast beacon messages but in the proposed scheme, only the main route nodes send beacon message to one-hop neighbor nodes by setting the TTL value of the beacon message to 1. RREQ and RREP are used in the route discovery process. RERR is used in the route maintenance and restoration process. Figure 2 depicts the basic operations of the proposed algorithm.

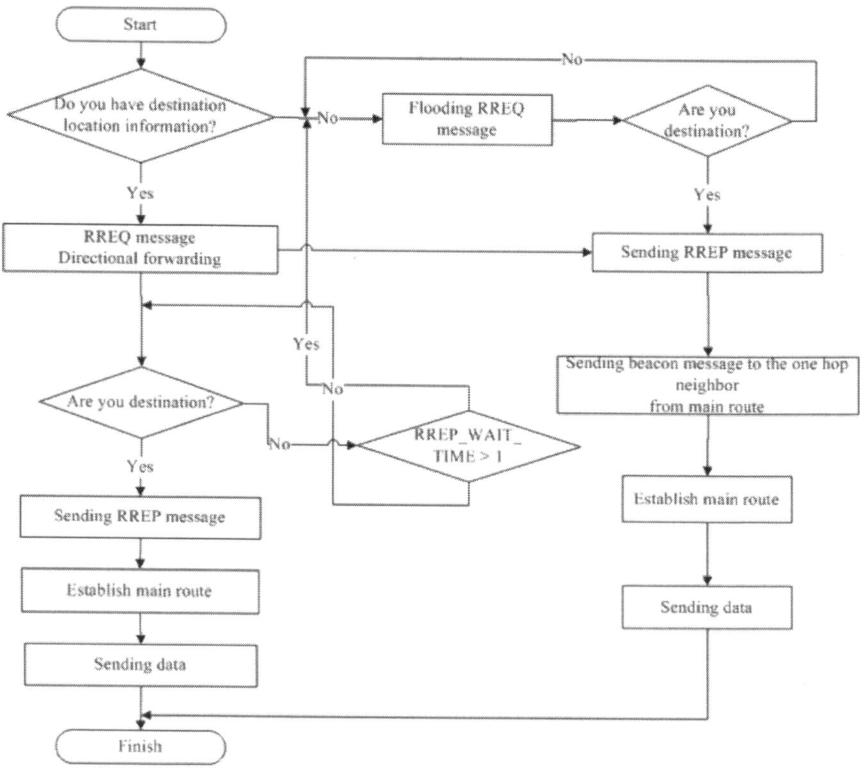

Figure 2. Basic operational flow chart.

3.2.1. Local routing table

As reactive routing protocols typically operate based on a routing table, the proposed protocol also has a local routing table. The local routing table is updated whenever it receives RREQ, RREP, and RERR messages. Table 1 shows the proposed local routing table, which has more fields than the AODV routing table. The function of each field is described below. The DestID field stores the destination node ID using direction values that range from 1 to 4. The distance field stores the distance value between two neighbor nodes, from 1 to 250, as the transmission range of the node. The HopCnt field indicates the hop count information to the destination node. SeqNo is given automatic sequential numbers, which specify a larger sequence number as newer route information. Lifetime is the lifetime of the route information; the information with a higher lifetime value remains in the routing table longer. Finally, the state field determines whether or not the route information is valid. If the lifetime field is 0 or if the state field reads INVALID, the routing tab entry is deleted.

Table 1. Local routing table.

DestID	Direction to Destination	Next Node	Distance	HopCnt	SeqNo	Lifetime	State
Node 14	1	Node 17	220	4	341	10	VALID
Node 46	3	Node 54	160	5	268	0	INVALID
Node 75	4	Node 32	130	5	342	5	VALID

3.2.2. Route maintenance and restoration

Route maintenance and restoration are important factors in MANETs. In this subsection, the proposed route maintenance and restoration schemes are discussed.

Figure 3 illustrates the route maintenance method between the source node and the destination node. The black nodes are the main route nodes, the gray nodes are one-hop distance nodes from the main route node, and white nodes are two hops or more from the main route nodes. For instance, if a white node moves to a one-hop distance from the main nodes, it will then change its status to a gray node. Under the same approach, if a gray node moves away from the main route node by more than two hops, it will change its status to a white node. The difference between gray and white nodes is whether or not the node receives a beacon message from the one of the main route nodes.

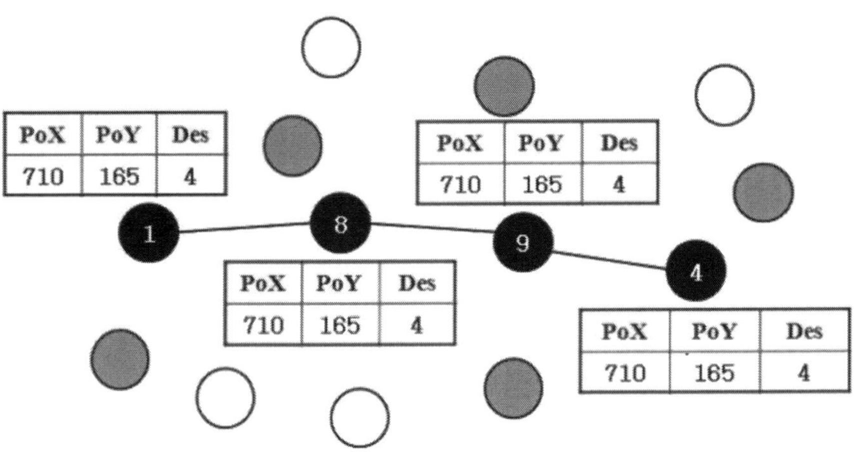

Figure 3. Route maintenance.

In Figure 3, node 1 transmits the information of the location of the destination node to its one-hop neighbor node 8. This information is broadcast with a beacon message every second to its one-hop neighbor nodes by setting the TTL of beacon message to 1. Similarly, nodes 8, 9, and 4 broadcast beacon messages to their neighbors that have the location information and address of the destination node. Next, the one-hop-distant neighbor nodes from the main route nodes write the routing information on each routing table. The purpose of beaconing is to find the location of the destination immediately when route failure occurs along the main route nodes. This procedure is used as an effective type of local repair.

Regarding the local repair procedure of an AODV, it broadcasts an RREQ message to find the destination node set as TTL field = 2 when a node finds a link failure. If no destination node is found, it then sends an RERR message back to all active nodes that are dependent on the broken link. When every node receives the RERR message, those nodes delete the route of the broken link. Particularly for a source that receives such an RERR message, it can restart the route discovery procedure; a stale route is expired according to a timer-based technique in what is known as an AODV local repair procedure.

In the present scheme, when an upstream node detects a link failure, the node sends an RREQ message toward only the direction of the destination. These procedures contribute toward reducing the routing message overhead. Figure 4 shows a flow chart of the proposed local repair procedure.

3.3. Packet forwarding

Once a source node recognizes the location of the destination, the source node selects one node from the routing table toward the destination direction. If many candidate nodes are selected, the source node selects the node of the minimum hop count and the highest sequence number. Nevertheless, if it still has two or more candidate nodes, it finally selects the one node with the longest distance value. The distance is determined from the distance field value of the routing table. If there is no suitable node for packet forwarding, local repair procedures are executed.

Figure 5 depicts source node S selecting one of the forwarding packets among nodes which locate in its transmission range. First, node S selects A and B nodes having the same direction (direction = 2) to the destination from its routing table. Subsequently, if they have the same hop count value and sequence number, node S then compares the distance field value of each one. As described in Figure 5, node A is finally selected as the packet forwarding node that has a larger distance value than node B.

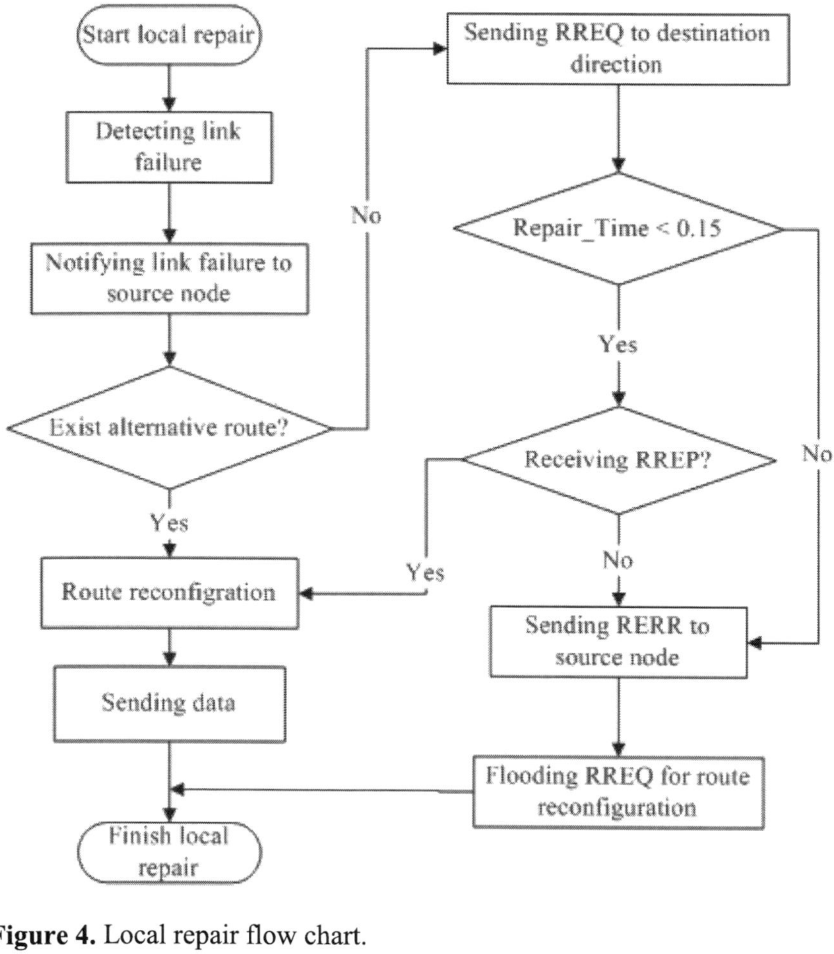

Figure 4. Local repair flow chart.

3.4. Control routing overhead

Ad Hoc On-demand Distance Vector with Controlled Flooding (AODV-CF) [22] uses two new messages to determine an alternative route in order to prepare for link failure. The first is a Controlled message, and the second is a Controlled-ACK message. Once the alternative node is set, there is no periodical update until a link failure occurs. This can cause critical problems when nodes are moving fast. In such an environment, the alternative nodes no longer perform their function as alternative nodes. In this circumstance, in the suggested scheme the main nodes send a beacon message containing information pertaining to the location of the destination to their one-hop neighbor nodes periodically every second.

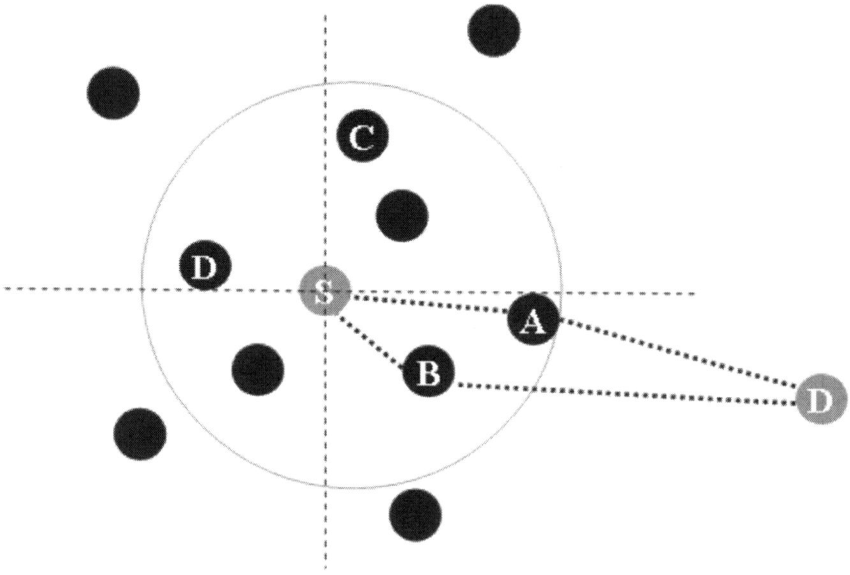

Figure 5. Packet forwarding.

The black node is the main route node described in Figure 6. The gray node, the one-hop neighbor from the main node, receives information regarding the location of the destination as periodically transmitted from the main route nodes. The main route nodes continue to send location information to their new one-hop neighbors unless gray nodes move far away from the main route nodes. This mechanism works effectively with a large network. In existing hybrid algorithms, every node sends a beacon to its one-hop neighbor, which creates a tremendous amount of routing message overhead. Although the proposed scheme has some routing message overhead, it has small number of messages compared to the previous hybrid routing protocols.

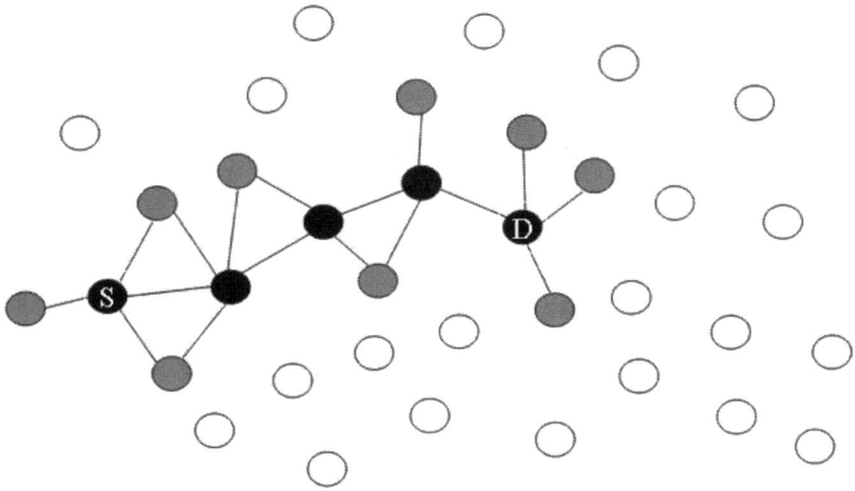

Figure 6. Limitation in sending beacon messages.

4. SIMULATION ANALYSIS

In this section, the experimental results of the proposed routing algorithm as evaluated with the NS-2 simulator are explained. The simulation results prove that the proposed scheme outperforms traditional routing protocols.

4.1. Network model and performance metrics

The superiority of the proposed algorithm was verified with the environment settings shown in Table 2. In particular, simulations were run for 200 simulated seconds in a 10 km × 10 km large rectangular network space.

Three metrics were used to evaluate the performance: the percentage of data packets that were received at the destination node, the control messages overhead, and the average number of control messages being used to deliver a message to a destination. The data packet delivery ratio refers to the percentage of the number of packets that are received at the destination to the number of packet sent by the source. The larger this metric is, the more efficient the MANET will be. The control message overhead metric represents the total number of control message packets per second in the experiment network. By combining the two metrics, the average number of control messages being used to deliver a message to a destination, can be calculated and finally used to present the performance of each algorithm. The simulation results of the proposed scheme are compared with the results of AODV, LAR, ZRP and AODV-DFR.

Table 2. Simulation environments.

Environments	Value
Simulation time	200 sec.
Area size	10 km × 10 km
Transmission range	250m
Movement speed	5 m/s, 20 m/s
Packet size	512 Bytes
Number of nodes	50~200
Number of UDP connection	5~20
MAC	IEEE 802.11 WLAN DCF
Data sending rate	4 kBps

4.2. Data packet delivery ratio

The simulation results describe the data packet delivery ratios of the AODV, LAR, ZRP, AODV-DFR schemes and the proposed routing algorithm. In the simulations, 5 m/s and 20 m/s node movements are considered.

In Figure 7(a), as the node count increases, the packet delivery ratio is decreased. When 50 nodes exist in the network, all protocols show a data packet delivery ratio greater than 75%. They show different success ratios as the number of nodes increases. However, the proposed scheme results in a data packet delivery ratio of 72% even in case of 200 nodes used because each node efficiently stores the node information of its surrounding neighbors. In contrast, the performance degradations in AODV and LAR are significant as the number of nodes increases. This results because there are frequent route changes and reconfigurations in a densely populated environment. When the number of nodes is small, AODV-DFR, LAR and ZRP work well and provide high delivery ratios, while the delivery ratio of AODV quickly falls to less than 70%. The AODV routing protocol is not efficient when numerous nodes exist in a large network.

The performance levels of AODV, LAR, ZRP, AODV-DFR and the proposed routing protocols are also investigated at high speeds of 20 m/s (72 km/hour) and while varying the number of nodes. The increased speed of node movement stresses the routing protocols and introduces several new problems, as shown in Figure 7(b). As Figure 7(b) shows, every routing protocol experiences large-scale degradation compared to the 5 m/s node movement except for AODV-DFR and the proposed algorithm. At a node movement speed of 20 m/s, the data packet delivery ratios of the AODV and LAR falls to less than 30% with more than 150 nodes. The simulation results prove that AODV and LAR are not appropriate in high-mobility environments.

In both cases of different node movement speeds, even though the proposed algorithm results in a higher data packet delivery ratio, the AODV-DFR and proposed algorithms show similar delivery ratios. This occurs because AODV-DFR creates more routing control messages than the proposed protocol as the following subsection shows.

4.3. Control message overhead

The simulation results of the control message overhead are presented in Figures 8(a,b). At a node speed of 5 m/s, the proposed scheme shows results that are better than AODV-DFR and ZRP and similar to AODV, whereas at a node speed of 20 m/s, the proposed scheme shows results that are better than those of AODV, AODV-DFR and ZRP. The proposed protocol uses slightly more control messages than LAR due to its use of an additive one-hop beacon message from the main route nodes.

4.4. Number of control messages per delivered message

The results of previous subsections 4.2 and 4.3 can be combined into a graph that represents number of control messages being used to deliver a message. In case of 5 m/s of node movement, as Figure 9(a) and Table 3 show, the proposed algorithm uses less control messages of 11.7% on average than AODV-DFR and 38.7%, 42.6%, and 65.1% than ZRP, LAR, and AODV respectively. And in case of 20 m/s of node movement, the proposed algorithm shows better result in reducing control messages of 9.5% on average compared with AODV-DFR and 33.9%, 43.4%, and 82.4% compared with ZRP, LAR, and AODV respectively as shown in Figure 9(b) and Table 3. These results clearly show that the suggested algorithm effectively reduces the number of control messages to deliver a message than other existing algorithms especially on the high speed of node movement.

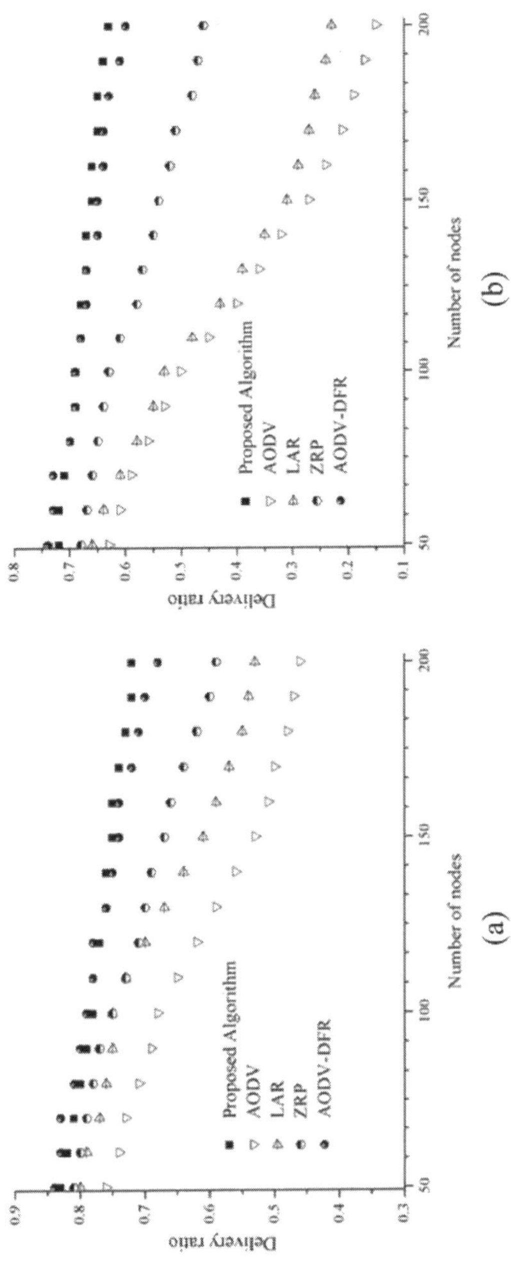

Figure 7. Data packet delivery ratio. (a) 5 m/s node movement; (b) 20 m/s node movement.

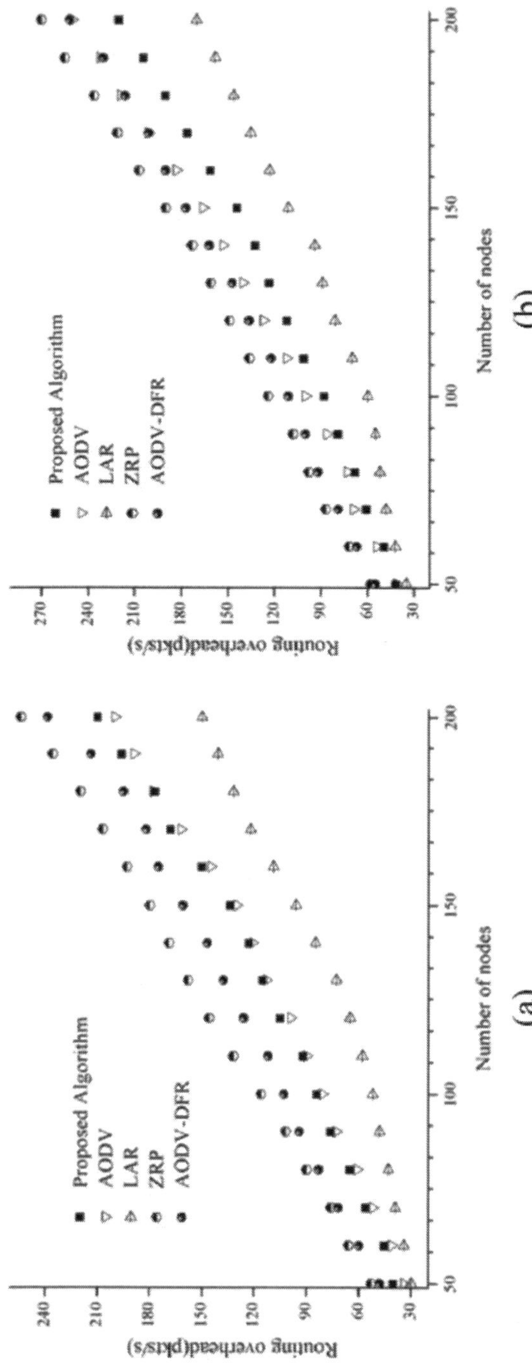

Figure 8. Control message overhead. (a) 5 m/s node movement; (b) 20 m/s node movement.

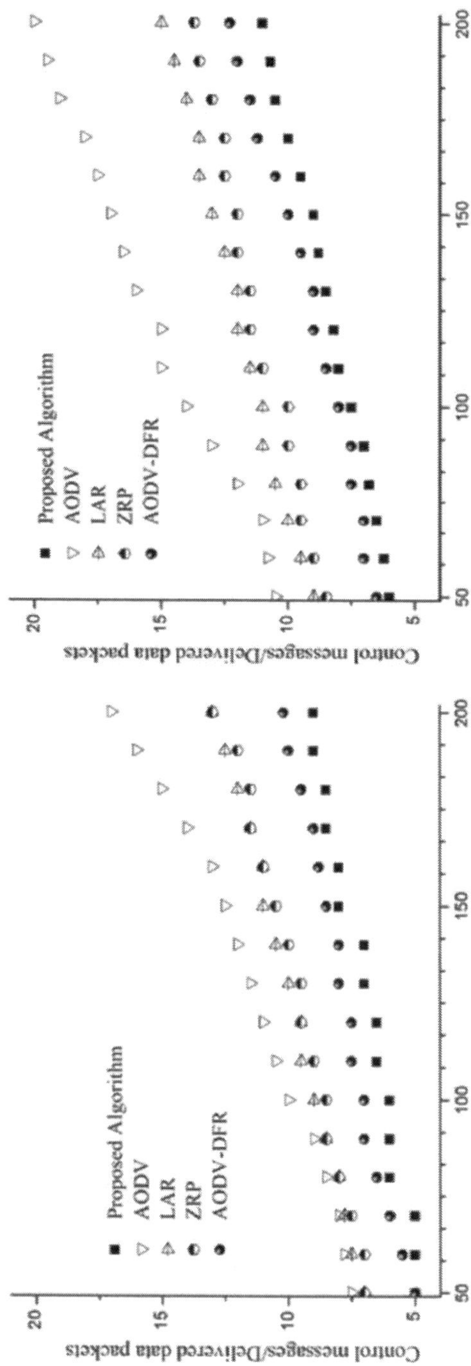

Figure 9. Number of control messages per delivered message. (a) 5 m/s node movement; (b) 20 m/s node movement.

Table 3. Average number of control messages per delivered message.

Node speed	Proposed	AODV-DFR	ZRP	LAR	AODV
5 m/s	6.94	7.75	9.63	9.89	11.46
20 m/s	8.39	9.19	11.23	12.03	15.3

5. CONCLUSIONS

Several routing protocols for MANETs have been studied recently. This research, including simulations of different routing protocols, is limited to illustrating the performance levels as evaluated using a relatively small number of nodes, leaving the manner of scaling the protocols to populations with larger nodes as a future line of research. As the number of users over wireless environments has increased, wireless protocols are also required to scale-up before they can fit increasingly larger populations of nodes.

In this study, an effective MANET routing protocol suitable for larger and faster node mobility network environments is presented. To establish the routing protocol, we applied directional forwarding with one-hop beaconing from the main route nodes for route maintenance and restoration, a routing algorithm operating based on GPS location information, and greedy packet forwarding.

The NS-2 simulator was used to evaluate the proposed protocol. The evaluations showed that the proposed scheme increases the data packet delivery ratio over that of industrialized MANET routing protocols. A reduction of the control message overhead in large and high-node mobility networks was also obtained.

ACKNOWLEDGMENTS

This work was supported by the IT R&D program of MKE/IITA Development of Urban Computing Middleware [2008-F-047-02] and Development of Open-IPTV Technologies for Wired and Wireless Networks [A1100-0801-3015].

REFERENCES AND NOTES

1. Perkins, C.E.; Royer, E.M. *Ad hoc* on demand Distance Vector routing, mobile computing systems and applications. Proceedings of 2nd IEEE Workshop on Mobile Computer Systems and Applications, New Orleans, LA, USA, Feburary 1999; pp. 90–100.

2. Lee, Y.; Gerla, M.; Chen, J.; Zhou, B.; Caruso, A. Direction forward routing for highly mobile *ad hoc* networks. In *Ad Hoc and Sensor Wireless Networks*; Old City Publishing: Philadelphia, PA, USA, 2006; pp. 101–118.

3. Ko, Y.B.; Vaidya, N.H. Location Aid Routing (LAR) in mobile *ad hoc* networks. Proceedings of ACM/IEEE MOBICOM, Dallas, TX, USA, October 1998; pp. 66–75.

4. Hass, Z.J.; Pearman, M.R. The zone routing protocol (ZRP) for *Ad hoc* networks. Proceedings of 6th International Conference on Universal Personal Communications, San Diego, CA, USA, October 1997; pp. 562–566.

5. Chen, J.; Zheou, H. AODV-DFR: Improving *ad hoc* routing scalability to mobility and load. Proceedings of Mobile Ad Hoc and Sensor Systems, Vancouver, Canada, October 2006; pp. 550–553.

6. Perkins, C.; Bhagwat, P. Highly dynamic destination sequenced distance-vector routing (DSDV) for mobile computers. Proceedings of ACM SIGCOMM, London, UK, August 1994; pp. 234–244.

7. Jacquet, P.; Muhlethaler, P.; Qayyum, A. *Optimized Link State Routing Protocol*; IETF Manet; IETF: Fremont, CA, USA; November; 1998. [

8. Murthy, S.; Garcia-Luna-Aceves, J.J. An efficient routing protocol for wireless networks. *Mobile Netw. Appl* **1996**, *1*, 183–197.

9. Johnson, D.B.; Maltz, D.B. Dynamic source routing in *ad hoc* wireless networks. In *Mobile Computing*; Springer US: New York, NY, USA, 1996; pp. 153–181.

10. Weiss, E.; Hiertz, G.R.; Bangnan, Xu. Performance analysis of temporally ordered routing algorithm based on IEEE 802.11a. Proceedings of 62nd IEEE Vehicular Technology Conference, Dallas, TX, USA, September 2005; pp. 2565–2569.

11. Chiang, C.C.; Tsai, T.C.; Liu, W.; Gerla, M. Routing in clustered multihop, mobile wireless networks with fading channel. Proceedings of the IEEE Singapore International Conference on Networks, Singapore, April 1997; pp. 197–211.

12. Liliana, M.; Arboleda, C. Cluster-based routing protocol for mobile sensor networks. Proceedings of the 3rd International Conference on Quality of Service in Heterogeneous Wired/wireless Networks, Waterloo, Ontario, Canada, August 2006.

13. Sinha, P.; Sivakumar, R.; Bharghaven, V. CEDAR: A core-extraction distributed *ad hoc* routing algorithm. Proceedings of the IEEE Conference on Computer Communications, New York, NY, USA, March 1999; pp. 202–209.

14. Braden, R.; Clark, D.; Shenker, S. *Integrated Services in the Internet Architecture—An Overview*; IETF RFC1663; IETF: Fremont, CA, USA; June; 1994.

15. Blake, S. *An Architecture for Differentiated Services*; IETF RFC2475; IETF: Fremont, CA, USA; December; 1998.

16. Guimaraes, R.; Cerda, L. *BRAWN: Bandwidth Reservation over Ad Hoc Wireless Networks*; Technical Report (UPC-DAC-RR-XCSD-2008-3); UPC: Barcelona, Spain; March; 2008.

17. Veres, A.; Ahn, G.; Campbell, A.T.; Sun, L. SWAN: Service differentiation in stateless wireless *ad hoc* network. Proceedings of Conference on Computer Communications (IEEE Infocom), New York, NY, USA, June 2002; pp. 457–466.

18. Karp, B.; Kung, H.T. GPSR: Greedy perimeter stateless routing for wireless networks. Proceedings of ACM/IEEE MOBICOM, Boston, MA, USA, August 2000; pp. 243–254.

19. Pei, G.; Gerla, M.; Chen, T.W. Fisheye state routing in mobile *ad hoc* networks. Proceedings of International Conference on Distributed Computing Systems, Taipei, Taiwan, April 2000; pp. 71–78.

20. Espes, D.; Mammeri, Z. Adaptive expanding search methods to improve AODV Protocol. Proceedings of IST Mobile and Wireless Communications Summit, Budapest, Hungary, July 2007; pp. 1–5.

21. Asenov, H.; Hnatyshin, V. GPS-Enhanced AODV routing. Proceedings of the International Conference on Wireless Networks (ICWN'09), Las Vegas, NV, USA, July 2009.

22. Costa, L.H.; De Amorim, M.D.; Fdida, S. Reducing latency and overhead of route repair with controlled flooding. *Wirel. Netw* **2004**, *10*, 347–358.

CHAPTER 7

Efficient Public Key Certificate Management for Mobile Ad Hoc Networks

P. Caballero-Gil and C. Hern´andez-Goya

Department of Statistics, Operations Research and Computing, University of La Laguna, 38271 Tenerife, Spain

ABSTRACT

Mobile ad hoc networks involve communications over a shared wireless channel without any centralized infrastructure. Consequently, in an optimal solution, management and security services depend exclusively on network members. The main contribution of this paper is an efficient public key management scheme that is suitable for fully self-organized mobile ad hoc networks where all nodes play identical roles. Our approach implies that the operations of creating, storing, distributing, and revoking nodes' public keys are carried out locally by the nodes themselves. The goal of the presented methods is the improvement in the process of building local certificate repositories of nodes. In order to do it, an authentication solution based on the web of trust concept is combined with an element of routing based on the multipoint relay concept introduced in the optimized link state routing protocol. Our proposal leads to a good tradeoff among security, overhead, and flexibility. Experimental results show a considerable decrease in resource consumption while carrying out the certificate verification process.

1. INTRODUCTION

A Mobile Ad hoc NETwork (MANET) is a highly dynamic wireless network with no fixed infrastructure and heavy constraints in node capabilities. Such characteristics unable the use of the classical public key management paradigm based on a centralized Certification Authority (CA).

Research on the deployment of a Public Key Infrastructure (PKI) in MANETs has been mainly two tiered so far. In particular, the two main approaches we can find in the bibliography are a distributed certification model and a self-organized scheme.

The methods here described and evaluated are aimed at improving the process of building the local certificate repository associated to each node in the self-organized model, which leads to a significant improvement in the efficiency of the whole model. Particularly, a considerable decrease in resource consumption while undertaking the verification process associated to authentication is obtained from the experiments. In order to achieve such improvement, we face the problem by combining typical authentication elements with common ideas used in routing protocols in MANETs. In particular, the Optimised Link State Routing (OLSR) protocol from which some ideas regarding the use of the MultiPoint Relay (MPR) technique have been borrowed to design the proposed algorithm for updating repositories.

The structure of this paper is as follows. Section 2 is devoted to the description of the background, including the description of the MPR technique. Since our proposal is specifically designed to be deployed in the self-organized public-key management model, Section 3 deals with the details of the graph-based version of such an approach. A complete algorithmic description of the proposed method is provided in Section 4. Section 5 describes the results of several computational experiments while several conclusions are included in the last section.

2. BACKGROUND

In order to improve the construction of certificate repositories for the key management scheme when adopting the web of trust model and the self-organized approach to implement a PKI, we use certain elements of the routing protocol known as OLSR. This section contains an introductory description of such a protocol, paying special attention to the MPR technique embedded in it.

Routing in MANETs has been one of the research areas with more activity [1]. A first basic classification used when talking about routing protocols distinguishes between proactive and reactive protocols. Protocols in the first category are characterized by the fact that each node stores a route for each reachable member of the network, although such a path may not be required at that precise moment; while in reactive protocols only when a request for communication between two nodes is required, a route discovery procedure is initiated. Due to this feature, reactive protocols are referred to as on-demand routing protocols. Proactive algorithms are also known as table-driven routing protocols since local routing information defining the different paths is organized according to a table stored by each node. The information contained in such a table defines an entry associated to each reachable node containing the next node in the path to the destination, and a metric or distance, among other data. The metric can be defined in function of several criteria such as the hop distance, the total delay, or the cost of sending messages.

In general, when comparing proactive and reactive protocols, we have that in the first case certain overload is originated in the network due to the continuous updates produced in routing information, while in the second case, certain delay is produced by the execution of routing discovery procedures any time a new path is defined. In networks with high mobility, reactive routing protocols have a better behaviour since the paths are recalculated as soon as a link state change is detected. Building an accurate topological map of the network requires exchange of information among nodes on a regular basis, which can lead to certain network overloading on the network, unless network traffic is sporadic. On the other hand, when dealing with delay-sensitive networks (such as Vehicular Ad hoc NETworks or VANETs) proactive protocols outperform better [2].

In this work, we use certain elements of the Optimized Link State Routing protocol (OLSR) [3], which is one of the four basic protocols adopted for MANETs. OLSR is a proactive protocol because local routing information defining the different paths is organized according to a table stored by each node.

The OLSR routing procedure has been extensively analyzed in the bibliography, and currently OLSRv2 is under consideration [4]. Some works devoted to improve it by integrating security tools [5] have been also developed. In the OLSR proactive routing two stages can be clearly differentiated. Firstly, a reliable map of the network is built. In order to obtain such an accurate map, all the network nodes must exchange messages regarding the state of their connections links. In the second stage, and based on the built map, the optimum route among the nodes is generated. The main obstacle this protocol has to skip is the high number of messages to be exchanged among nodes. However, thanks to these messages the network configuration is known by all its members.

In order to reduce the overhead and message redundancy and to avoid the storm problem [6], a specific technique, named the MultiPoint Relay technique, was defined in OLSR. In this technique each node selects a particular neighbour subset (nodes at one-hop distance with bidirectional links) whose members will be in charge of broadcasting the information. By doing so, the number of messages exchanged is considerably reduced [7].

The MPR technique was originally deployed for reducing the duplicity of messages at local level when broadcasting information in a proactive MANET. In general, the number of redundant packets received by a node may be equal to the number of neighbours a node has. Roughly speaking, it can be said that the MPR allows determining the minimum number of nodes needed for reaching the whole network when it is recursively applied. This approach obtains better results regarding optimization in large and dense networks. The way we use the basics of the MPR in the proposed key management for MANETs, as well as its relationship with Graph Theory problems is included below.

2.1. OLSR Description and Notation

In the OLSR protocol only a subset of nodes will be in charge of retransmitting the received packets. In this way, every node u must define among its direct neighbours a set of transmitters (here denoted by $MPR(u)$) that will be the only ones in charge of retransmitting the messages emitted by the initial node. This means that control packets are retransmitted by a node belonging to $MPR(u)$ only when the packet was sent by u and it is the first time it is received. According to this method, each router chooses independently the set MPR among its symmetric 1-hop neighbours such that all symmetric 2-hop neighbours are reachable via at least one symmetric 1-hop neighbour belonging to $MPR(u)$.

In routing models, the network is usually represented with a graph whose vertex set $V = \{u_1, u_2, \dots, u_n\}$ symbolizes the set of nodes of the network. In this way, for any node u, $N^i(u)$ denotes the set of u's symmetric neighbours in an i-hop distance from u. It is assumed that $u \notin N^1(u)$. Consequently, $N^1(u)$ stands for u's direct neighbours and the cardinality $|N^1(u)|$ corresponds to u's degree. These sets are defined by using the shortest path and in such a way that $N^i(u)$ and $N^{i+1}(u)$ are disjoint sets. Computation of these shortest paths may be accomplished as stated in [8].

Following the notation defined in [9] jointly with the one previously introduced in this paper, it is feasible to formally define the set MPR for a vertex u as $MPR(u) \subseteq N^1(u) \mid \forall w \in N^2(u) \exists v \in MPR(u) \mid w \in N^1(v)$.

Through this definition, decision and optimization problems associated to the MPR construction may be defined. According to the Computational Complexity hierarchy the associated decision problem may be reduced in polynomial time to the Dominating Set problem, which belongs to the NP-complete class. Therefore a heuristic approach is adequate for computing the MPR set. The description of OLSR [3] includes a particular heuristic for solving this problem (although in [4] it is stated that "Routers can freely interoperate whether they use the same or different MPR selection algorithms") as example. The heuristic defined there uses a greedy approach handling, among other parameters, the willingness of nodes to participate in the routing process and the vertex degree. A complete description and analysis of this heuristic may be found in [10]. Next we include a brief description of such a heuristic.

Step 1.Begin with an empty MPR set.

Step 2.Select those one-hop neighbour nodes of u that are the only neighbour of some two-hop neighbours of u, and add them to $MPR(u)$.

Step 3.Add to $MPR(u)$ the neighbour node of u that covers the largest number of two-hop neighbours of u that are not yet covered by the current $MPR(u)$ set.

Repeat Step 3 until all two-hop neighbours are covered.

Using the notation introduced so far we may describe the greedy heuristic distinguishing two main stages as follows. In the first one those vertices w in $N^2(u)$ with a unique neighbour v in $N^1(u)$ are examined in order to include in $MPR(u)$ the vertex v. If there are remaining nodes without covering in $N^2(u)$, in the second stage, those vertices in $N^1(u)$ covering more vertices in that situation are also included in $MPR(u)$. A graphic explanation of how the algorithm works is included in Figure 2.

In order to clarify the proposal we need to define several vertex subsets that are specified below. First, for each node v in a one-hop distance from u it is required to consider a new vertex subset $W_u(v)$ formed by those vertices that simultaneously belong to the order 2 u's neighbourhood and are direct neighbours of v (see Figure 1(a)). This set may be calculated by the following intersection $W_u(v) = N^2(u) \cap N^1(v)$. Vertices in this set have in common the fact that they are candidates to be covered by vertex v.

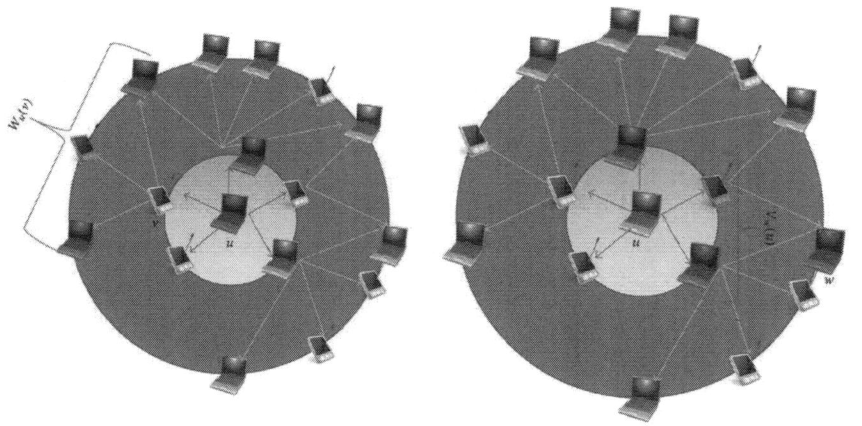

Figure 1. Defining some vertex subsets. $W_u(v)$ $V_w(u)$

A second vertex subset $V_w(u)$ is defined for each vertex w belonging to u's two-hop neighbourhood. In this case, such a subset may be obtained through the intersection $V_w(u) = N^1(w) \cap N^1(u)$ (Figure 1(b)). This new set gathers those vertices in $N^1(u)$ that may cover vertex w. When transferring this computation to the self-organized PKI model, $V_w(u)$ is computed by using the set of predecessors of vertex w denoted by $N_1(w)$.

3. PKI APPROACHES IN MANETS

In this section the main characteristics of the public-key infrastructure models used in MANETs are described before introducing some new ideas that conform our proposal. We may find two main alternatives for the deployment of PKIs in MANETs in the bibliography: distributed certification authorities, and self-organized public-key management.

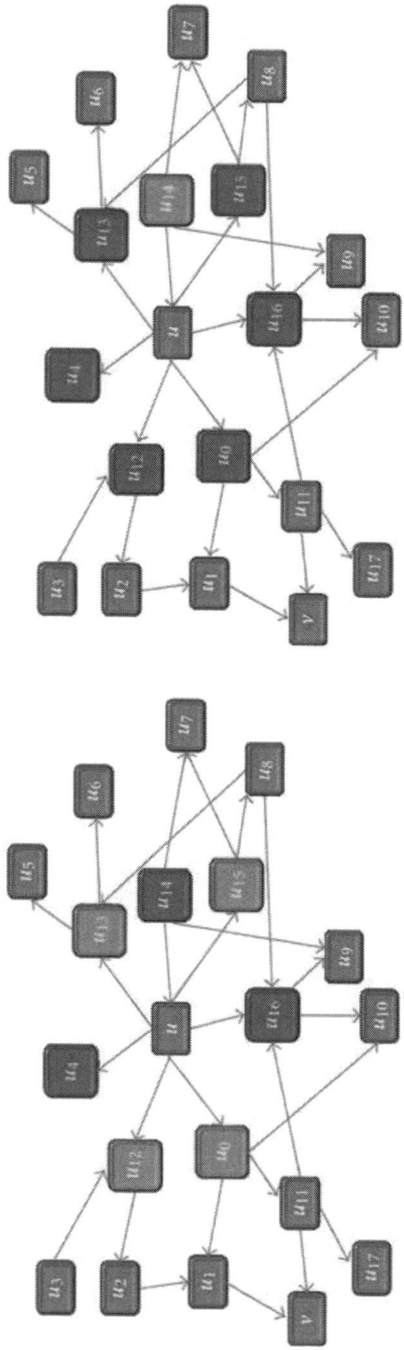

Figure 2. Stages in MPR-OLSR. Stage 1: Isolated nodes in $N^2(u)$ are analyzedStage 2: Nodes of maximum degree are included in $MPR(u)$

In the first case, the certification process is underpinned by distributed CAs, which use a threshold digital signature scheme and are in charge of issuing and renewing certificates of nodes [11–13]. One of the first schemes following this approach was proposed in [14], where a group of special nodes, acting as a coalition, are responsible for certification tasks. There the authors put forward that the CA's functions should be the responsibility of a set of special servers set included in the network. These servers will sign the public key of the nodes trough a (t,n)threshold signature scheme [15]. Therefore, each time a node in the network B wishes to communicate with one of his peers A, he should contact with $t+1$ servers in advance in order to obtain A's public key signed with the CA's secret key. One of the servers included in the previous coalition will be in charge of playing the combiner's role. This means that once he receives the shares from its peers in the coalition, he generates the signature of the requested public key. However, there are some general drawbacks associated to this alternative. First, the combiner figure and the servers acting as certification authorities produce system overload as all the communications requesting certification issuance and validation should be attended for them. Additionally, introducing special servers does not guarantee the elimination of vulnerabilities to DoS attacks. Another question to take into account is the need for additional storage requirements since the public keys of all the members of the network must be stored by the servers. When the network is sparse or during its first deployment stages finding $t+1$ servers available in its transmission range may become a handicap.

The methods included in [16, 17] solve some of the previous problems by establishing that any node may act as a member of a distributed CA. Consequently in both references any group of $t+1$ nodes without distinction may act as servers at the moment of issuing certificates. Hence, one of the mayor advantages of this strategy is the balance reached in the distribution of the computational load. Even though this characteristic is truly important in the scenario of MANETs, there are still disadvantages associated to this proposal. For instance, a distributor in charge of providing credentials to the first nodes should be considered during the bootstrapping stage. Also finding a valid coalition each time a certificate needs to be verified may result infeasible depending on the network actual topology and conditions. Besides, the methods in [16] do not provide any instrument to protect against malicious nodes when they send fake shares.

A general drawback of those methods based on distributed CA's is the computational intensive operations required by the threshold application when signing a certificate, and the definition of additional procedures such as share refreshing [18].

Other proposals related to this paradigm may be found in the more recent bibliography, but in this work we have opted by the second type of solutions, based on the self-organized paradigm, which has been also used for node authentication [19].

Such a self-organized version of public-key management was chosen as base for this paper in order to guarantee identical roles for all MANET nodes. This approach involves the relocation of the responsibility for creating, storing, distributing, and revoking public keys among the members of the network.

3.1. Describing the Self-Organized Approach

The self-organized model in MANETs was initially described in [20]. Its authors put forward the substitution of the centralized certification authority by a self-organized scenario where certification is carried out through chains of certificates which are issued by the nodes themselves. Such a scheme is based on the information stored by each node and the trust relationship among neighbour nodes.

In this work we decided to follow the self-organized key management model based on the web of trust approach. Several are the reasons that justify the choice of this option. First, this model demands less maintenance overhead. Secondly, it is well worth remarking that on the one hand the self-organized approach eases the use of a simple bootstrap mechanism, and on the other hand all the nodes perform equal roles.

In this model, public keys and certificates are represented as a directed graph $G=(V,A)$, known as certificate graph. Each vertex u in this graph defines a public key of a node, and each arc (u,v) denotes a certificate associated to v's public key, signed with u's private key. Each node u has a public key, a private key, and two certificate repositories, the updated and the nonupdated repositories, denoted, respectively, G_u and G_u^N. Initially the updated certificate repository contains the list of certificates on which each node trusts (out-bound list) and the list of certificates of all the nodes that trust on u (in-bound list). A sequence $P_{uv}=\{(u,u_0),(u_0,u_1),\ldots,(u_m,v)\}$ of certificates where the vertices are all different is called a certificate chain from u to v.

The tasks that any member of the network has to develop in this public-key management scheme are:

Certificate Management:

1) Key generation: the node generates its keys by itself.

a) Certificate issuance: each node issues certificates that bind public keys of other nodes to their identities.

b) Certificate exchange: each node exchanges certificates with other nodes and builds its non-updated repository.

c) Updated certificate repository construction: the node builds its updated repository

2) Public-Key Verification:

a) Finding a certificate chain.

b) Verifying the certificates in the chain.

Although the self-organized methodology for PKI deployment has been extensively analyzed [21–23], there are still open questions that needs further research. One of this pending questions is how to encourage node's participation in the tasks related to certification issuance or certification exchange. Since many resources are limited in MANETs the cooperation issue is a major issue when dealing with many node tasks, and PKI management is one of the crucial ones.

In the following we describe how certificate management and public-key verification are carried out in the self-organized model.

Each node u generates by itself the pair formed by its public key and its secret key. Then a request for signing the generated public key is sent to u 's neighbours. Since these nodes are in a one-hop distance from u , they can use any trusted mechanisms such as side channels in order to assure the binding established between the corresponding public key and the node's identity.

Apart from that, in order to ease certificate revocation, each certificate issued will be valid for a certain period of time. This parameter may be chosen depending on the mobility characteristics of the underlying MANET.

Since the certificates issued by a node are stored in its local repository, one of the tasks that a node may perform during idle periods is the renewal of certificates issued by it to those nodes that might still be considered as trusted. Otherwise, certificate renewal may be developed on demand. It means that when an expired certificate is included in the non-updated repository of a node, such a node should request a renewal for that certificate. When a certificate for a node u is issued by a node v the edge (v, u) is added to the certificate graph and each node u and v stores it in its in-bound and outbound list, respectively.

Note that the speed in the creation of the certificate graph and its density depend on the willingness of users for distributing certificates, and on nodes' mobility. In particular, the more mobility the nodes have, the more complete the repositories will be. The same happens with other aspects related to MANET cooperation.

As in any PKI-based system, certificate revocation should be also taken into account. When revocation is initiated due to key compromise or misbehaviour of the corresponding node, the certificate issuer sends a message to all nodes stating that such a certificate has been revoked. This can be accomplished because each node maintains a list containing the members of the network that have contacted it to request updates of the certificates it had issued. Hence, in fact it is not necessary to send the revocation message to all the members of the network. The last proposals related to revocation policies in MANETs defend the creation of schemes based in reputation systems [24, 25]. When revocation is due to the fact that the expiration time has been reached, such a revocation can be deduced directly by all nodes since the expiration date is contained in the certificate. The work in [26] describes a method to update expired certificates by using probabilistic multicast. The importance of this method is that nodes different from the actual issuer of the certificate can update it once it has expired.

Certificate exchange can be considered a low-cost procedure because it only involves one-hop distance nodes. It allows to share and to distribute the issued and stored certificates. A description of this procedure is as follows.

1) Every node u retransmits the hash values of the certificates stored in the repositories G_u and G_u^N to its neighbours. The recipient nodes answer with the hash values of the certificates contained in their repositories.

2) Every node compares the received value with the one it already has and requests to its neighbours only the certificates that are new.

3) If the local memory of a node is not large enough, the expired certificates are deleted from the non-updated repository, starting by the oldest ones.

4) In this way, after a short period of time the non-updated repository G_u^N contains almost all the certificate graph G. Afterwards, the only task to be carried out by the nodes is to exchange the new certificates.

In the original proposal two ways of building the updated certificate repository G_u of a node u were described.

1) Node u communicates with its neighbours in the certificate graph.

2) Node u applies over G_u^N an appropriate algorithm in order to generate G_u after checking the validity of every single certificate.

One of the crucial issues in the self-organized scheme that may influence the correct behaviour of the whole scheme is the selection of the certificates stored by each node in its repository. The method specified with this objective should satisfy two requirements at the same time: limitation in storing requirements, and performance of the updated repository in terms of ability to find chains for the largest possible number of nodes. This problem, known as certification chain discovery problem, has received particular attention in the bibliography related to MANETs [21–23, 27].

Since the algorithm used in the construction of the updated repositories will influence the efficiency of the scheme, it should be carefully designed. The simplest algorithm for that construction is the so-called Maximum Degree Algorithm (MDA) [20] (see Algorithm 1), where the criterion followed in the selection of certificates is mainly the degree of the vertices in the certificate graph.

There is another more sophisticated algorithm, called Shortcut Hunter Algorithm, in which certificates are chosen taking into account that when they are deleted, the length of the minimum path between the nodes connected through that certificate is increased in more than 2.

When using the MDA, every node u builds two subgraphs, the out-bound subgraph and the inbound subgraph, which when joined generate the updated certificate repository G_u. The outbound subgraph is formed by several disjoint paths with the same origin vertex u while in the in-bound subgraph u is the final vertex. In the description of the MDA algorithm, the starting node is u and $deg_{out}(u)$, $deg_{in}(u)$ stands for the in-degree and the out-degree of node u, respectively. The number of paths to be found is represented by c.

A bound on the number of disjoint paths starting at u as well as a bound on the number of disjoint paths to be built with u as final node are given by e_{out} and e_{in}, respectively.

Another important input parameter is s, which represents the maximum number of vertices to be included in the subgraph generated when the in-bound and the out-bound subgraphs are combined. This parameter may be also controlled by defining as $l_{out} = \lceil s / (2e_{out}) \rceil$ the length of the chains generated when building the out-bound subgraph and $l_{in} = \lceil s / (2e_{in}) \rceil$ for the in-bound one.

```
input: G, u, l_out, c
Output: MDA − G_out
//Initialization
V_out ← ∅, A_out ← ∅, D_out ← ∅
e_out = min{deg_out(u), c}
l ← deg_out(u)
N^1(u) = S_out(N^1(u)) = {v_1, v_2, ..., v_l}
D_out = {v_1, v_2, ..., v_{e_out}}
V_out = V_out ∪ {u} ∪ D_out
A_out = A_out ∪ {(u, v_i)}, i = 1, 2, ..., e_out
i ← 1, l_i ← 1
while i < e_out do
    while D_out ≠ ∅ do
        if l_i = l_out then
            i ← i + 1
        end
        else
            v_i = get(D_out)
            N^1(v_i) = S_out(N^1(v_i))
            w_i = get(N^1(v_i))
            while w_i ∈ D_out and N^1(v_i) ≠ ∅ do
                w_i = get(N^1(v_i))
                if N^1(v_i) = ∅ then
                    i ← i + 1
                end
                else
                    if w_i ∉ D_out then
                        put(w_i, D_out)
                        A_out = A_out ∪ {(v_i, w_i)}
                        V_out = V_out ∪ {w_i}
                        l_i = l_i + 1
                        i ← i + 1
                    end
                end
            end
        end
        if i mod e_out = 0 then
            i ← 0
        end
    end
end
```

Algorithm 1: $\mathrm{MDA} - G_{\mathrm{out}}$ heuristic.

In order to apply the greedy criterion, $S_{out}(N)$ and $S_{in}(N)$, where N consists of a set of vertices, include the sorted vertices of N into descending order according to $deg_{out}(u)$ and $deg_{in}(u)$, respectively.

Note that the process to build the in-bound subgraph is equivalent to it except for the fact that in this case the edges to be chosen are always incoming edges.

In the first stage of the MDA, $deg_{out}(u)$ outgoing arcs from u are included. The final vertices of these arcs are then included in D_{out}. This set is implemented as a typical queue where the insertion (put) and the extraction (get)operations are used. Henceforth, e_{out} arcs are chosen in such a way that the formed paths are disjoint. This is accomplished by selecting their origin belonging to D_{out} and checking that neither the origin nor the final vertices were previously used in another path.

4. PROPOSED ALGORITHM

The main contribution of this paper consists in substituting the MDA algorithm proposed for the updated repository construction by a new algorithm that uses the MPR technique described in Section 2 (see Algorithm 2). In this way, for each vertex in the certificate graph we have to define a re-transmitter set.

The MPR heuristic adapted to the certificate graph is described below. First, node u starts by calculating $MPR(u) = \{v_1, v_2, \dots, v_k\}$. Then, these vertices are included in G_{out} together with the edges $(u, v_i),\ i = 1, 2, \dots, k$. Henceforth, nodes v_i in $MPR(u)$ apply recursively the same procedure of retransmitting backwards the result $MPR(v_i)$.

In order to extend the notation used in the introduction of the MPR greedy heuristic described in Section 2, which is required to be used in the certificate graph, we denote by $N_i(u)$ the set of predecessors of node u that may be found in an i-hop distance. This means that the smallest number of certificate chains required in order to reach the remaining nodes will be obtained as well. The algorithm proposed is an iterative scheme that may be described in the following way.

```
input: G, u
output: MPR - G_{out}(u)
//Initialization
MPR - G_{out}(u) = \emptyset
//Stage 0
N^1(u) = \{v_1^0, v_2^0, ..., v_l^0\}
for i <- 1 to l do
    N^1(v_i^0)
    if N^1(v_i^0) = \emptyset then
        MPR - G_{out}(u) = MPR - G_{out}(u) \cup \{v_i^0\}
    end
end
l = l - |MPR - G_{out}(u)|
N(u) = N(u) \ MPR - G_{out}(u) = \{v_1^1, v_2^1, ..., v_l^1\}
//Stage 1
for i <- 1 to l do
    W_{v_i^1}(u) = N^1(v_i^1) \cap N^2(u) = \{w_1, w_2, ..., w_k\}
    if k \neq 0 then
        for j = 1 to k do
            N_1(w_j)
            V_{w_j}(u) = N^1(u) \cap N_1(w_j)
            if |V_{w_j}(u)| = 1 then
                MPR - G_{out}(u) = MPR - G_{out}(u) \cup \{v_i^1\}
                N^2(u) = N^2(u) \ W_{v_i^1}(u)
            end
        end
    end
end
l = l - |MPR - G_{out}(u)|
N(u) = N(u) \ MPR - G_{out}(u)) = \{v_1^2, v_2^2, ..., v_l^2\}
//Stage 2
While N^2(u) \neq \emptyset do
    for i = 1 to l do
        N^1(v_i^2)
        W_{v_i^2}(u) = N^1(v_i^2) \cap N^2(u)
        d_u(v_i^2) = |W_{v_i^2}(u)|
    end
    d_{max}(u) = max d_u^+(v_i^2), i = 1,2,...,l
    for i = 1 to l do
        if d_u^+(v_i^2) = d_{max}(u) then
            MPR - G_{out}(u) = MPR(u) - G_{out}(u) \cup \{v_i^2\}
            N^2(u) = N^2(u) \ W_{v_i^2}(u)
        end
    end
    N^1(u) = N^1(u) \ MPR - G_{out}(u)
end
```

Algorithm 2: $MPR - G_{out}$ heuristic.

1) Every vertex $u \in G$ locally determines its re-transmitter set ($MPR(u)$), which include the certificates associated to the corresponding edges.

2) This vertex contacts all the nodes in $MPR(u)$. At this stage, every node $v \in MPR(u)$ has previously obtained its retransmitters set $MPR(u)$, and consequently it may send to node u the certificates associated to such a set.

Since each node knows from whom is a re-transmitter, the G_{in} subgraph is generated by applying first the reverse process and then adding in-going arcs. The certificate chains required in the authentication are built by using the arcs $(u, MPR(u))$. After that, for all $v \in MPR(u)$ and for all $w \in MPR(v)$ the arcs (v, w) are also added after having checked that they have not been added in previous updates.

Note that the procedure every node $u \in G$ has to develop in order to build $MPR(u)$ takes $1 + \ln(N^2(u))$ steps when no bound is defined on the length of the chains to be built. Otherwise, the number of iterations to be carried out is given by the number of hops to explore in the certificate graph. As for the definition of the aforementioned bound, it has to be remarked that such a parameter may be dynamically adjusted in function of the changes experienced by the certificate graph. This may be justified by the fact that as the network evolves, the information contained in each node's repository is more complete. Thanks to this substitution the generated procedure is easier and more efficient, guaranteeing in this way that each node has a set of neighbours that allows it to reach the biggest number of public keys.

One of the main advantages of the proposal is that all the information gathered for the construction of the chains is locally obtained by each node. After obtaining the in-bound and out-bound subgraphs, both subgraphs are merged and the initial repository is generated so that the authentication process may start. When a node u needs to check the validity of the public key of another node v, it has to find a certificate chain P_{uv} from itself to v in the graph that results from combining its own repository with v's repository. If this chain is not found there, the search is extended to $G_u \cup G_u^N$, what implies the inclusion of u's nonupdated repository in the search. If this second exploration is successful, u should request the update of those certificates that belong exclusively to G_u^N. When no path is found, the authentication fails. Once the path P_{uv} is determined, u should validate every certificate included in it. This is done as follows.

1) The first certificate in the chain (u, u_0) is directly checked by u since it was signed by u himself.

2) Each one of the remaining certificates (u_i, u_{i+1}) in the chain may be checked using the public key of the previous node u_{i-1}.

3) The last arc (u_m, v) corresponds to the certificate issued by u_m that binds v with its public key.

The proposal described in this work will allow us to integrate information obtained and used by the routing process into the PKI management tasks. This approach will simplify the certification procedures. This idea of combining routing information within authentication procedures was also put forward in [21]. One of the main differences between our proposal and the scheme described there is the routing scheme used as base. We make use of the OLSR proactive scheme (more specifically we use the MPR technique used there), while the reactive AODV routing protocol is used by the other proposal. The main idea behind this alternative is to build a binary tree of trust connecting all the nodes in the network claiming that this structure will simplify certificate path discovery and certificate issuance. The main difficulties behind the use of such a global structure is that network partition may occur easily since each node only has direct trusted connections with its parent and two-child nodes. Depending on the mobility pattern associate to member nodes this number of connections may be inadequate.

There is a characteristic in the designed algorithm that is shared with the proposal described at [22]. It is possible to adapt the number of certificate chains to be built as well as their length depending on the characteristics of the MANET where the proposal must be implemented.

5. EXPERIMENTAL RESULTS

This work proposes the application of the MPR technique in the computation of certificate repositories included in the self-organized public-key management model. Our proposal is supported by the good results obtained when using the MPR procedure in the OLSR routing algorithm in MANETs as well as computational experiments. A detailed description of the implementation and the results provided by it are presented in the current section. The main goal of the experiments was showing that applying the MPR technique when building certificate repositories in the self-organized approach instead of using the MDA heuristic provides the public-key management scheme with simplicity and efficiency.

5.1. Implementation Characteristics

The implementation has been carried out using Java and the open source library JUNG 2.0 (Java Universal Network/Graph Framework) which provides the basic tools for representing and dealing with graphs.

One of the reasons why JUNG was selected was having the possibility of working with random graphs with the small-world property. When a graph follows the small-world model, it is assumed that its paths have a small average length and a high Clustering Coefficient (CC). The CC corresponds with the average of the fraction of pairs of u's neighbours (taken over all the network nodes $u \in |V|$) which are at the same time direct neighbours of each other.

This characteristic is supported by certificate graphs as it was shown in [28]. When a graph holds this feature, most nodes may be reached by a small number of hops from any source node. This kind of graphs has received special attention in several scientific disciplines [29]. In [30], an extended small-world model with applications in different MANET scenarios was introduced.

The small-world model used in the simulation developed was proposed by Kleingberg [31]. When generating a graph with $|V| = n^2$ vertices according to this model, the first step is to create an $n \times n$ toroidal lattice. Then each node u is connected to four local neighbours, and in addition one long range connection to some node v, where v is chosen randomly, according to a probability proportional to $d^{-\alpha}$. d denotes the lattice distance between u and v and α stands for the CC. Generating the graphs following this model guarantees that the shortest paths may be determined using local information, what makes them particularly interesting for the networks we are dealing with.

5.2. Computational Results

Some of the data gathered from the first computational experience are shown below (see Table 1). The number of nodes in the graph (n), the rate of certificates contained in the repository (R_c), the clustering coefficient (α), the maximum length in the chains generated (C_l), and the time consumption while the execution (t) expressed in seconds are the parameters that have been measured. From this experience, it may be remarked that the certificate rate finally contained in the local repository increases as the size of the graph increases as well as the clustering coefficient increases. This phenomenon may be better appreciated in Figure 3. Additionally, the maximum lengths in the obtained chains are kept at reasonable values, that is what makes the chain verification process lighter. Finally, the rate of certificates stored in the repository surpasses 95% in more than 75% of the executions while time consumption corresponds to sensible values. These first experiments showed promising results.

Another computational experience consisted of generating random graphs according to the Kleingberg's model where the size of the graphs $|V|$ ranges in the interval [9,441], the Clustering Coefficient (CC) takes values between $[0,30]$. For these parameters, the Certificate Rate obtained by MPR (CR_{MPR}) jointly with time consumption (t_{MPR})expressed in seconds were measured.

For analyzing the MDA alternative, it is applied over the same input graphs using as specific parameters the maximum number of chains to built (n_{chains}) and their maximum length (c_l) is bounded by 7. In this case, the Certificate Rate in the repository (CR_{MDA}) and time consumption (t_{MDA}) were also obtained.

From this experience, there are some general conclusions that may be remarked. The certificate rate CR_{MPR} finally contained in the local repository increases as the size of the graph increases. However, the behaviour of the certificate rate is not affected by the growth of the Clustering Coefficient. This phenomena may be better appreciated in Figure 4. Additionally, the maximum length in the chains obtained by MPR are kept at reasonable values, what makes the chain verification process lighter.

The most important fact when comparing the certificate rates CR_{MDA} and CR_{MPR} is that only in the 3.95% of the executions the MDA algorithm outperforms MPR, and it only occurs when the input certificate graph is small. Although, in the previous figure it seems that the difference between both certificates rates is reduced as the size of the graph increases, it should be taken in mind that MANETs have a limited number of nodes. Furthermore, in the 45.83% percent of the problems the difference between the certificate rates CR_{MPR} and CR_{MDA} is in the interval [50%,75%] (see Figure 5).

Hence, it may be concluded that the repository built by MPR provides further information to facilitate the authentication process. Finally, another result that illustrates the positive characteristics of MPR to solve the problem of updating the certificate repository is that in the 82.45% of the executions the repository built by MPR contains more than the 75% of the whole certificate set.

Table 1. Computational Experience.

	$\alpha = 0.1$			$\alpha = 0.4$			$\alpha = 0.8$		
n	R_c	C_l	t	R_c	C_l	t	R_c	C_l	t
9	42.93	4	0.24	37.03	3	0.27	37.78	3	0.18
16	82.08	3	0.49	86.67	3	0.41	84.17	3	0.46
25	93.13	3	0.64	96.00	3	0.59	96.00	3	0.69
36	98.70	3	0.81	99.63	3	0.83	99.44	3	0.8
49	99.73	4	1.24	99.18	4	1.2	99.59	4	0.92
64	99.59	3	0.68	100.00	4	0.68	99.48	3	0.64
81	99.92	4	0.77	99.92	4	0.81	99.82	4	0.84
100	99.93	4	0.91	99.93	4	0.97	99.80	4	0.96

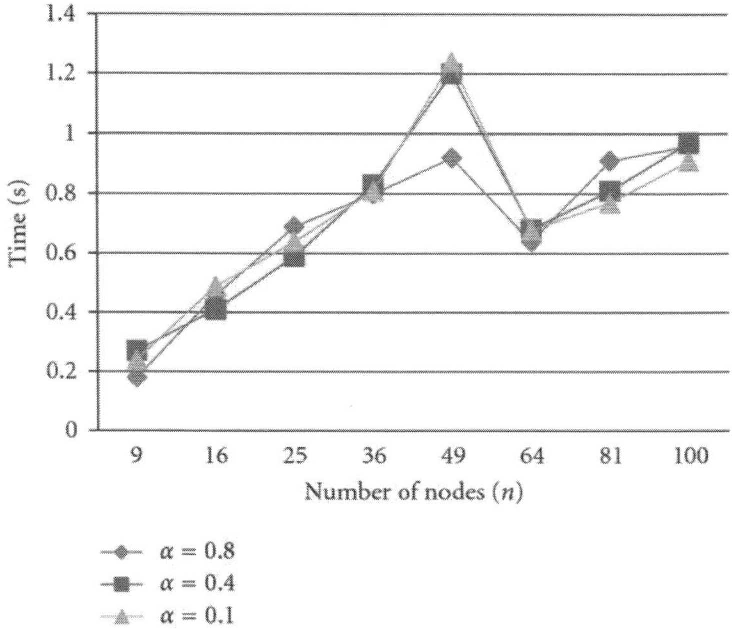

Figure 3. Time consumption.

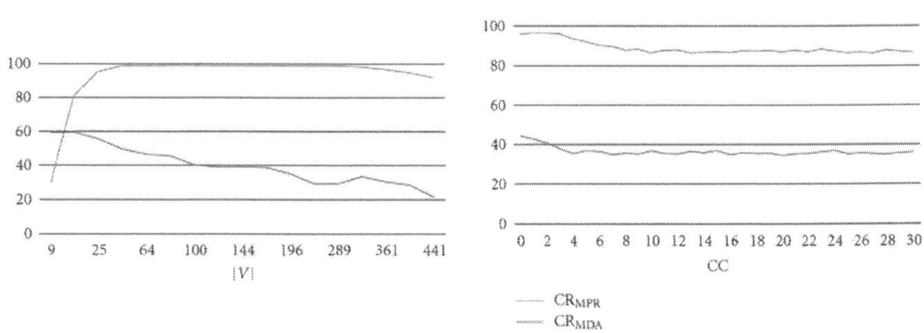

Figure 4. Comparing certificate rates.

6. CONCLUSION

The application of the Multipoint Relay Technique in the update process of public key certificate repositories in MANETs has been evaluated in this work. For the assessment of this proposal, several experiments with an implementation developed in JAVA have been carried out. According to these experiments the presented alternative outperforms the original graph-based and self-organized model in several aspects. The most relevant improvements of the proposed MPR-based method are a higher certificate rate included in the repository and the shorter generated certificate chains. They result in a less need of interaction among nodes during the building process of an authentication chain and lead to a more efficient verification procedure.

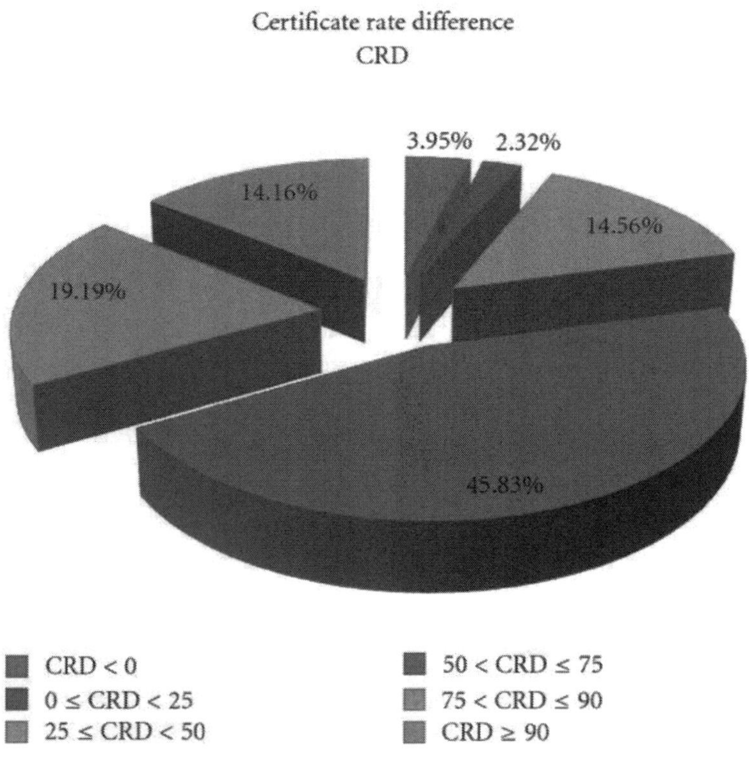

Figure 5. Certificate rate difference.

Our immediate goal is to adapt the developed implementation to a network simulator in order to evaluate the behaviour of the method with different mobility models.

ACKNOWLEDGMENTS

This research was supported by the Ministerio Español de Educación y Ciencia and the European FEDER Fund under TIN2008-02236/TSI project and by the Agencia Canaria de Investigación, Innovación y Sociedad de la Información under PI2007/005 project.

REFERENCES

1. Ilyas M (Ed): *The Handbook of Ad Hoc Wireless Networks*. CRC Press, Boca Raton, Fla, USA; 2003.

2. Haerri J, Filali F, Bonne C: Performance comparison of AODV and OLSR in VANETs urban environments under realistic mobility patterns. *Proceedings of the 5th IFIP Mediterranean Ad-Hoc Networking Workshop (Med-Hoc-Net '06), 2006, Lipari, Italy*

3. Clausen T, Jacquet P: RFC 3626: Optimized Link State Routing Protocol. (OLSR), 2003

4. Clausen T, Dearlove C, Jacquet P: The optimized link state routing protocol version 2 draft-ietf-manet-olsrv2-11. IETF Internet-Draft, April 2010

5. Vilela JP, Barros J: A feedback reputation mechanism to secure the optimized link state routing protocol. In*Proceedings of IEEE Communications Society/CreateNet International Conference on Security and Privacy for Emerging Areas in Communication Networks (Securecomm'07), 2007*. IEEE Computer Society;

6. Ni SY, Tseng YC, Chen YS, Sheu JP: The broadcast storm problem in a mobile ad hoc network. *Proceedings of the 5th Annual ACM/IEEE International Conference on Mobile Computing and Networking (MobiCom '99), 1999*151-162.

7. Laouti A, Mhlethaler P, Najid A, Plakoo E: Simulation results of the OLSR routing protocol for wireless network.*Proceedings of the 1st Mediterranean Ad-Hoc Networks workshop (Med-Hoc-Net '02), 2002, Sardegna, Italy*

8. Baccelli E, Jacquet P, Nguyen D, Clausen T: Ospf multipoint relay (mpr) extension for ad hoc networks. IETF Request for Comments: 5449, February

9. Mans B, Shrestha N: Performance evaluation of approximation algorithms for multipoint relay selection.*Proceedings of the 3rd Annual Mediterranean Ad Hoc Networking Workshop, 2004*

10. Härri J, Bonnet C, Filali F: OLSR and MPR: mutual dependences and performances. *IFIP International Federation for Information Processing* 2006, 197: 67-71.

11. Saxena N, Tsudik G, Yi JH: Threshold cryptography in P2P and MANETs: the case of access control. *Computer Networks* 2007, 51(12):3632-3649.

12. Wu B, Wu J, Fernandez EB, Ilyas M, Magliveras S: Secure and efficient key management in mobile ad hoc networks. *Journal of Network and Computer Applications* 2007, 30(3):937-954.

13. Joshi D, Namuduri K, Pendse R: Secure, redundant, and fully distributed key management scheme for mobile ad hoc networks: an analysis. *EURASIP Journal on Wireless Communications and Networking* 2005, 2005(4):579-589.

14. Zhou L, Haas ZJ: Securing ad hoc networks. *IEEE Network* 1999, 13(6):24-30.

15. Gennaro R, Jarecki S, Krawczyk H, Rabin T: Robust threshold DSS signatures. *Information and Computation*2001, 164(1):54-84.

16. Kong J, Zerfos P, Luo H, Lu S, Zhang L: Providing robust and ubiquitous security support for mobile ad-hoc networks. *Proceedings of the International Conference on Network Protocols (ICNP '01), November 2001* 251-260.

17. Kaliaperumal S: Securing authentication and privacy in ad hoc partitioned networks. In *Proceedings of the Symposium on Applications and the Internet Workshops (SAINT-W '03), 2003, Washington, DC, USA*. IEEE Computer Society; 354.

18. Narasimha M, Tsudik G, Yi J: On the utility of distributed cryptography in P2P and MANETs: the case of membership control. *Proceedings of the 11th IEEE International Conference on Network Protocols (ICNP '03), 2003* 336-345.

19. Caballero-Gil P, Hernández-Goya C: Self-organized authentication in mobile ad-hoc networks. *Journal of Communications and Networks* 2009, 11(5):509-517.

20. Capkun S, Buttyan L, Hubaux JP: Self-organized public key management for mobile ad hoc networks. *Mobile Computting and Communication Review* 2002., 6(4):

21. Kambourakis G, Konstantinou E, Douma A, Anagnostopoulos M, Fotiadis G: Efficient certification path discovery for MANET. *EURASIP Journal on Wireless Communications and Networking* 2010, 2010:-16.

22. Satizábal C, Hernández-Serrano J, Forné J, Pegueroles J: Building a virtual hierarchy to simplify certification path discovery in mobile ad-hoc networks. *Computer Communications* 2007, 30(7):1498-1512.

23. Li R, Li J, Liu P, Chen H-H: On-demand public-key management for mobile ad hoc networks. *Wireless Communications and Mobile Computing* 2006, 6(3):295-306.

24. Arboit G, Crépeau C, Davis CR, Maheswaran M: A localized certificate revocation scheme for mobile ad hoc networks. *Ad Hoc Networks* 2008, 6(1):17-31.

25. Moore T, Clulow J, Nagaraja S, Anderson R: New strategies for revocation in ad-hoc networks. *Proceedings of the 4th European Workshop on Security and Privacy in Adhoc and Sensor Networks (ESAS '07), 2007*

26. Xie D, Zhou H: A probabilistic certificate updating protocol for manet. *Proceedings of the 20th International Conference on Advanced Information Networking and Applications (AINA '06), 2006, Washington, DC, USA* 2: 147-154.

27. Jung E, Elmallah ES, Gouda MG: Optimal dispersal of certificate chains. *IEEE Transactions on Parallel and Distributed Systems* 2007, 18(4):474-484.

28. Capkun S, Buttyan L, Hubaux JP: Small worlds in security systems: an analysis of the PGP certificate graph.*Proceedings of the ACM New Security Paradigms Workshop, September 2002, Norfolk, Va, USA* 8.

29. Liu C, Wu J: Scalable routing in delay tolerant networks. *Proceedings of the 8th ACM International Symposium on Mobile Ad Hoc Networking and Computing (MobiHoc '07), September 2007* 51-60.

30. Wu J, Yang S-H: Small world model-based polylogarithmic routing using mobile nodes. *Journal of Computer Science and Technology* 2008, 23(3):327-342.

31. Kleinberg J: Small-world phenomenon: an algorithmic perspective. *Proceedings of the 32nd Annual ACM Symposium on Theory of Computing, May 2000* 163-170.

CHAPTER 8

Collision Avoidance in Mobile Wireless Ad-Hoc Networks with Enhanced MACAW Protocol Suite

Şadan Cambazoglu[1], Arif Sari[2]

[1]Department of Management Information Systems, European University of Lefke, Lefke, Cyprus

[2]Department of Management Information Systems, Girne American University, Kyrenia, Cyprus

ABSTRACT

Jamming attack is quite serious threat for Mobile networks that collapses all necessary communication infrastructure. Since mobile nodes in Mobile Ad Hoc Networks (MANET) communicate in a multi-hop mode, there is always a possibility for an intruder to launch a jamming attack in order to intercept communication among communication nodes. In this study, a network simulation has been carried out in order to explore and evaluate the possible impacts of jamming attack on MACAW protocol. Ad-hoc network modelling is used to provide communication infrastructure among mobile nodes in order to modelling the simulation scenarios. In simulation model, these nodes have used AODV routing protocol which is designed for MANET while second scenario contains simulated MACAW node models for comparison. On the other hand, this paper is the first study that addresses performance evaluation of MACAW protocol under a constant Jamming

Attack. The performance of MACAW protocol is simulated through OPNET Modeler 14.5 software.

KEYWORDS

OPNET, Simulation, MACAW, Mobile Ad-Hoc Networks, Collision, Jamming, AODV

1. INTRODUCTION

Wireless networks take important place in the world of communication. Today a great number of people such as businessmen, managers, students and employees can easily access to the internet or to the corporate networks through wireless connections. Although wireless technologies expand the limits of communication area, they are exposed to some problems due to their nature. These problems violate quality of wireless communication.

Collision, one of these problems occurs when two nodes in the same network, attempt to transmit data at the exact same time [1] -[4] . Corresponding problem results in loss of quality in communication. Especially in mobile wireless networks collision avoidance issue becomes more difficult due to transmission environment. Up to now, considerable solutions addressing to this problem have been proposed in variety of researches.

MACAW, one of these solutions provides effective collision avoidance mechanisms. MACAW protocol is generally used in mobile wireless networks [4] -[6] .

On the other hand, security attacks which are another reason for collision occurrence, result in loss of quality in communication as well. In this study, a network simulation has been carried out in order to evaluate performance of MACAW protocol. During this simulation, MACAW protocol has been exposed to a constant Jamming Attack which results high collision occurrence rate in the network. The entire network mechanisms are simulated through OPNET Modeler 14.5 simulation software which is widely used in the network industry to estimate behaviors of network component in a virtual environment. The importance of this study is the first simulation case that addresses performance evaluation of MACAW protocol under a Jamming Attack.

2. COLLISION IN MOBILE WIRELESS NETWORKS

In computer networks, there are many nodes and they have to transmit data packages over the same carrier. This carrier can be an optic cable in wired networks while it is a frequency in wireless networks. Owing to this networking principle, if two nodes in the same network attempt to send data packages to the communication line at the exact same time, a collision occurs. Collisions are important problems for networks because they violate data transmission and results in loss of information. When any collision occurs in the network, the communication stops; ultimately, data packages are dropped. Collisions always results in less throughput of the network, high network load, high delay and high data drop rate [7] -[9] .

2.1. Collision Avoidance Protocol in Mobile Wireless Networks

As mentioned previously, owing to collisions, network nodes face with loss of packet integrity. That means a proper communication cannot be established in the network. In seven layer OSI model [10] -[12] , Media Access Control (MAC) layer is responsible for avoidance of package collision. MAC sub layer performs this task through avoidance protocols. These protocols play a critical role in preventing data collision; they aim to rule situations out which multiple nodes access to the network at the exact same time and to provide packet transmission to any node without any collision. There are some protocols that mostly used and are developed to prevent collisions in the networks such as ALOHA, CSMA, MACA and MACAW.

MACAW Protocol

Multiple Access with Collision Avoidance for Wireless (MACAW) is a widely used MAC sub layer protocol. MACAW is useful for mobile ad-hoc networks. It contains new collision avoidance mechanisms. By these mechanisms data transmission is completed in five steps. These five steps are Request-to-Send (RTS), Clear-to- Send (CTS), Data Sending (DS), data packages and Acknowledgement (ACK). RTS is a message, sent from data sender node to receiver node, notifies that a node attempts to transmit data to another node. CTS message is a respond for transmission request. If receiver node available for transmission then sends a CTS message. DS frame informs receiver node about the size of data package. After that, data transmission starts. When it completes properly, receiver node sends an ACK message to sender node. ACK notifies that data transmission completed successfully [13] -[16] .

3. NETWORK SIMULATION

In computer networking field, testing a complete network's behaviors in a real environment is a quite costly process. In this case network simulation techniques provide an opportunity to test network equipment such as routers, servers and cables in an inexpensive way. Besides that, network protocols, networks services and other network features can be tested to see behaviors of nodes. Network simulation actions are performed by network simulators in a virtual environment. A network simulator is a software application that estimates behaviors of nodes, equipment and protocols of a modelled network. Simulators typically support commonly used networking technologies such as Wi-Max, WLAN, and ZigBee. Most of these simulators have a Graphical User Interface (GUI). As well as GUI simulators, Command Line Interface (CLI) simulators are also available. Some network simulation software are open source while some are proprietary software. Commonly used simulators are GNS3, ns, OPNET, NetSim, OMNeT++ [17] [18] .

3.1. Simulated Node Models

In this simulation experiment while evaluating collision effects on network, mobile nodes have been used. These mobile nodes create an ad-hoc network among them. In OPNET simulator these types of nodes are called as "manet_station_adv". While simulating scenario, 50 nodes were used.

3.2. Simulation Model and Experiment Environment

While performing simulation scenarios, OPNET Modeler 14.5 has been used. In this simulation, 2 different scenarios are designed. The simulation was performed in a 1000 × 1000 meters campus area with 50 mobile nodes. These nodes share the common parameter attributes. In table 1, all global simulation parameters are shown in detail.

In this simulation model, MACAW and AODV protocols are used. The performance evaluation and contents of the protocol is exposed by the researchers in the literature before [19] [20] . MACAW as mentioned before, is a powerful collision avoidance protocol and used in this simulation model for its specific purpose. On the other hand Ad hoc On-Demand Distance Vector (AODV) [2] is a routing protocol that is used in mobile ad-hoc networks while nodes determining their destination paths for data transmission. Simulation has been carried out for 1 hour in a 1000 × 1000 meters area, Mobility Model status was stated as Simple Random Waypoint with constant speed of 10 meter/seconds. Network Throughput, Network Load and Delay parameters are taken as Performance Parameters. Data Rate was set as 11 Mbps which is maximum data rate for IEEE 802.11 b. Trajectorywas set as Vector which means mobile nodes change their location unsymmetrically. Finally, Seed value which is number of network events performed in 1 second, was set as 40,000. The successful simulation scenarios have been conducted on simulated different contention-based or contention-less protocols through OPNET in the literature [19] [20] . So it is quite reliable to conduct this simulation scenario through OPNET simulation package.

3.2.1. Simulation Scenario 1

In the first scenario, there are 50 mobile nodes that have an ad-hoc network among them. They move at a constant speed of 10 meters per second. Figure 1 below illustrates these nodes distributed randomly in a 1000 × 1000 meters area.

In this scenario illustrated, Application profile, Profile configuration and Mobility configuration are defined to meet network requirements specified in Table 1. Network model has two scenarios. In first scenario, nodes communicate with each other in a proper way. There is no malicious node and no security attack. One of these nodes acts as an Access Point at the same time. OPNET simulator has evaluated this scenario for 1 hour. Simulation results were measured and evaluated according to network performance metrics. The main purpose for this scenario is to determine status of network under normal conditions. This scenario will be useful while comparing effects of collisions and security attacks to network performance.

Table 1. Simulation scenario parameters.

Parameters	Attributes
Protocols	MACAW-AODV
Simulation Time	1 Hour
Simulation Area	1000 × 1000 (meters)
Mobility Model	Simple Random Waypoint
Mobility m/s	1/10
Performance Parameters	Throughput, Network Load, Delay, Drop Rate
Transmit Power (W)	0.005
RTS Threshold (bytes)	1024
Data Rate (Mbps)	11 Mbps
Pkt. Reception power Threshold	−95 dbm
Buffer Size	1024,000
Pkt. Size (bits)	2000
Pkt. Interarrival time (seconds)	0.03
Trajectory	VECTOR
Start time (seconds)	10
End Time	End of Simulation
No of Seeds	40,000

3.2.2. Simulation Scenario 2

In this scenario again 50 mobile nodes have been used. Unlike Scenario 1, here also 3 mobile jammer nodes have been used. Scenario 2 is shown on the Figure 2.

While these nodes attempting to communicate between each other properly, two jammer nodes violate communication. They constantly sent large size data packages to the network so that it causes less network throughput, collision occurrences and high network traffic. These jammer nodes were specified according to requirements of the project. Jammer nodes transmit data packages in large sizes. It sends constantly 10,000 bits size of data packages. In simulation model this jamming attack will keep being as long as the simulation continue. Therefore network communication is affected adversely.

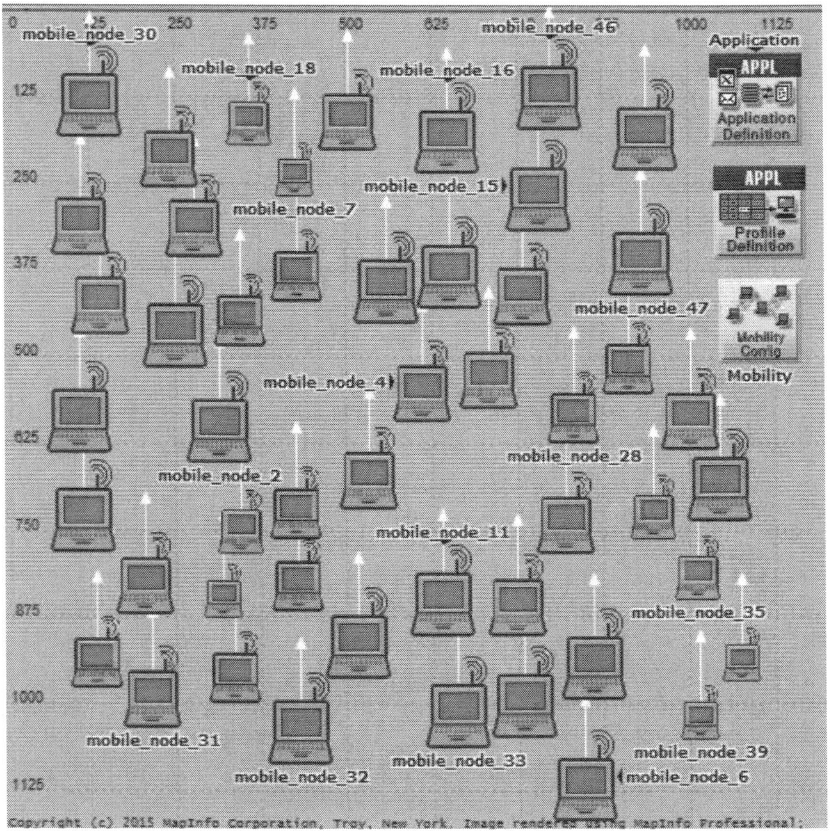

Figure 1. Simulation Scenario 1.

All these circumstances directly affect network throughput. In scenario 2, these conditions have been simulated and evaluated. Comparison results of two scenarios clearly show how jamming attacks cause less throughput and high collision occurrence.

3.3. Performance Metrics

Simulation results are evaluated according to determined network performance criteria. In this experiment four performance metrics are taken. These metrics are Network Throughput, Network Load, WLAN Delay and Data Dropped. The network throughput refers to the amount of bits forwarded successfully from one network layer to another in a given time. Network throughput is typically measured as bits per second (bps), megabits in per second (Mbps) and gigabits per second (Gbps). On the other hand, Network Load is described as measurement of total data traffic on a WLAN Base Station Subsystem (BSS). It shows BSS load statistics of a network separately. Other performance metric which is WLAN Delay, represents latency of packages while they are travelling from one device to another. Finally Data Dropped statistics show total amount of data packages that are discarded by higher network level due to high buffer size of packages.

4. SIMULATION RESULTS

Two scenarios have been subjected to simulation for one hour. In first scenario 50 mobile nodes had a proper communication between each other. There were not any malicious nodes or security attacks. These nodes have used MACAW protocol as collision avoidance protocol as well as they have used AODV protocol as mobile ad-hoc network routing protocol. Likewise scenario 1, scenario 2 had the same protocols, and equal number of mobile nodes. On the other hand unlike scenario 1, scenario 2 had also 3 mobile constant jammer nodes. Network model in scenario 2 was exposed to a powerful and constant jamming attack. These jammer nodes have sent large data packages to the network. In simulation results we have seen the performance of MACAW protocol under jamming attack condition. These 2 scenarios were simulated within a Discrete Event Simulation (DES) environment. Simulation outcomes and statistics were generated by OPNET Modeler 14.5 in graphical charts according to mentioned conditions.

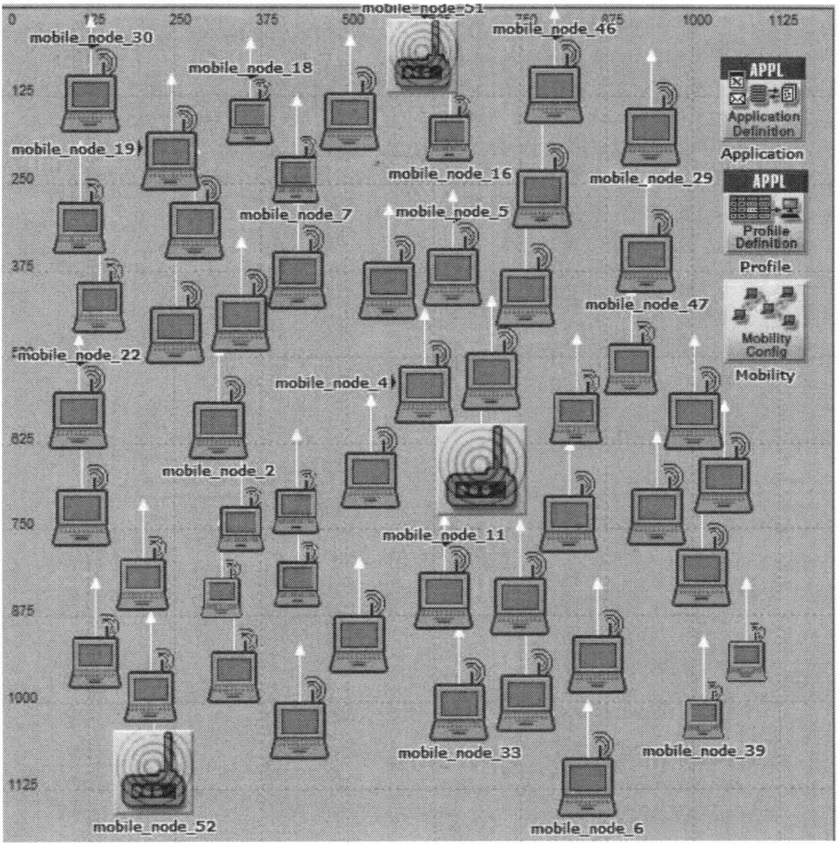

Figure 2. Simulation Scenario 2.

4.1. Average WLAN Throughput Statistics

As stated before, Network Throughput refers to number of bits that are forwarded successfully one layer to another in a given time. Measurement for this statistics is used to be bits per second (bps). In this topic, two scenarios' throughput is compared to each other. It is expected that throughput of scenario 1 would be higher than scenario 2 because as mentioned in previous chapters, malicious nodes and security attacks directly affect overall network performance. OPNET Modeler 14.5 has provided throughput comparison of the two scenarios as a consequence of 1 hour simulation. In the following figure, WLAN Throughput statistics comparison of 2 scenarios is shown.

Figure 3 clearly illustrates average Wireless LAN Throughput comparison of two scenarios. In the first scenario which doesn't have any malicious nodes, it can be easily seen that bit transfer rate is above 8,000,000 bits per second. Under normal network conditions network throughput reaches up to approximately 7.7 Mbit. Second scenario which is represented by a red line in the figure shows that when network is exposed to a jamming attack its overall throughput rapidly decreased below 3000,000 bits per second. It can be clearly seen that jamming attack has a significant impact on overall network performance. It decreases throughput approximately three times.

4.2. Average Wireless LAN Delay Statistics

Wireless LAN Delay statistics represent package latency while they are transferring one layer to another. When network performance is low, package transmission slows down. In this case total network delay becomes high. In figure 4, comparison graphics of scenarios for Wireless LAN Delay statistics can be seen.

Blue line which represents Scenario 1 shows that WLAN Delay rate is close to zero seconds. In normal network state, packages are delivered one layer to another without more delay. However in second scenario it can be seen that package delay have rapidly increased. Jamming attack caused a significant latency of packages.

4.3. Average Wireless Data Dropped Statistics

As discussed previously, data drop rate represents data packages that are discarded by higher level network layer. When buffer size of a data package is higher than determined acceptable value, network automatically drops the data package. As known, in Denial of Service attacks malicious nodes constantly send packages in large sizes to make network resources unavailable. As measure, network administrators adjust server nodes to drop these large size data packages. In simulation scenarios, "Large Packet Processing" option is set as "Drop" in order to protect the network against possible damages of large size packages. Below Figure 5 shows average Wireless LAN Data Dropped statistics.

Figure 5 clearly shows data drop rate comparisons of two scenarios. As seen, red line which represents Scenario 2 is higher than blue line. Because jammer nodes send packages in 10,000 bits size and network directly drops them.

4.4. Average Wireless LAN Network Load Statistics

Network Load represents measurement of total amount of data over entire network. In figure 6 Wireless LAN Network Load statistics comparison of two scenarios is shown.

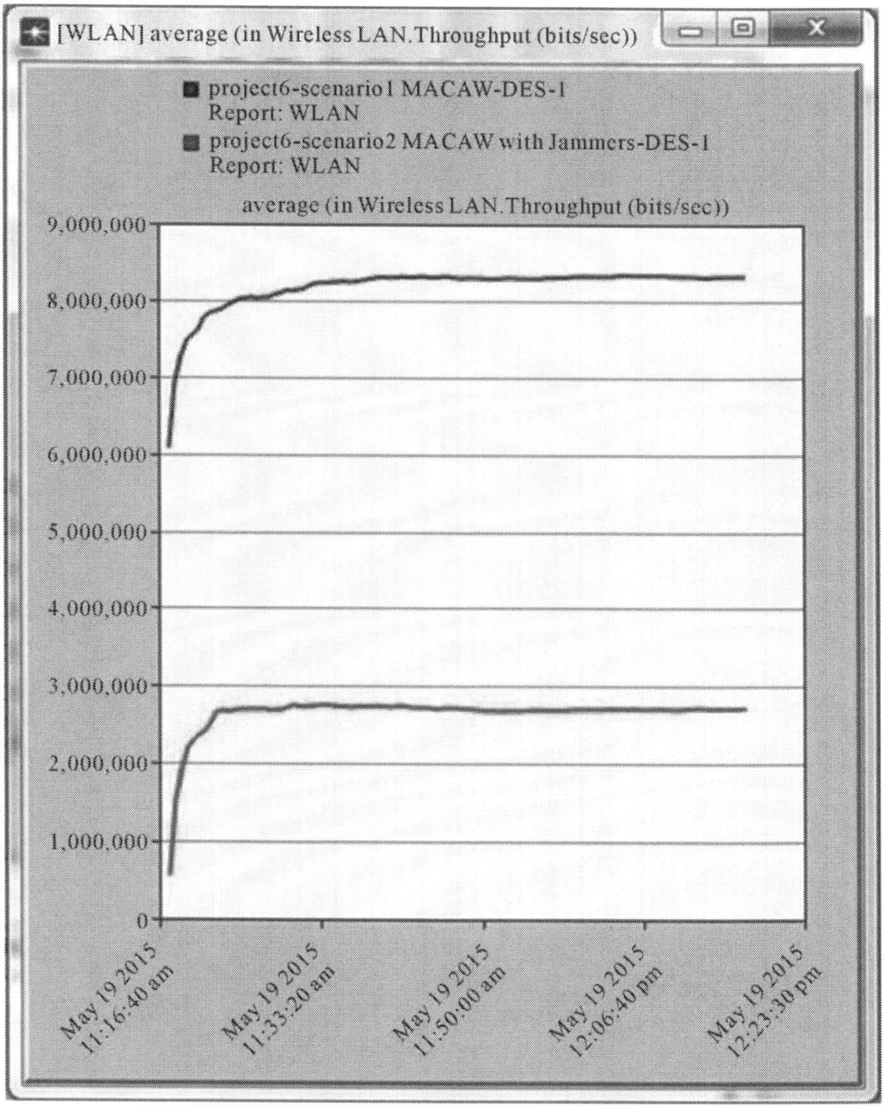

Figure 3. Average WLAN throughput comparison.

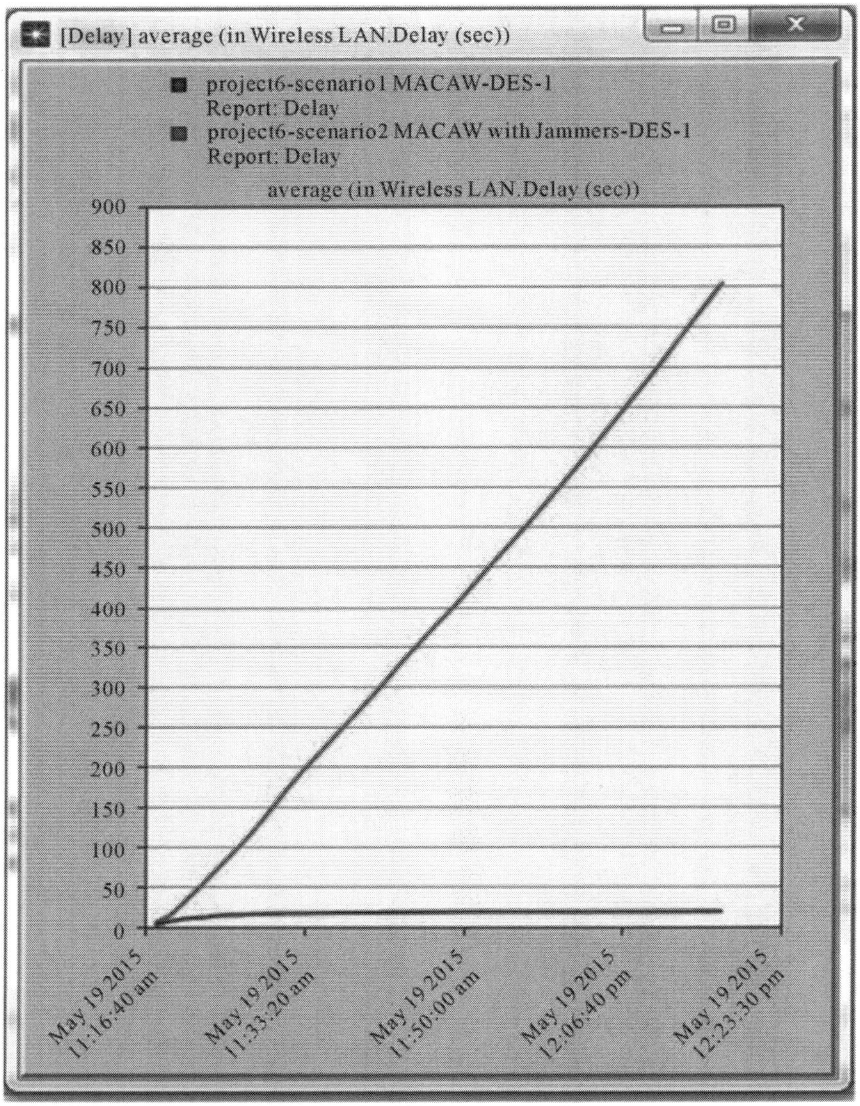

Figure 4. Average WLAN delay statistics.

As it is shown through direct relationship between the average WLAN Data Dropped Rate on Figure 5 and average WLAN Network Load on Figure 6, the scenario 2 had higher data dropped rate due to jamming attack and network load shown on Figure 6 is higher due to injected packages into network through jammers. The huge amount of injected packages dropped from the network that is proven by the Figure 5 with higher data dropped rate of scenario 2 and high network load value ofFigure 6 for scenario 2.

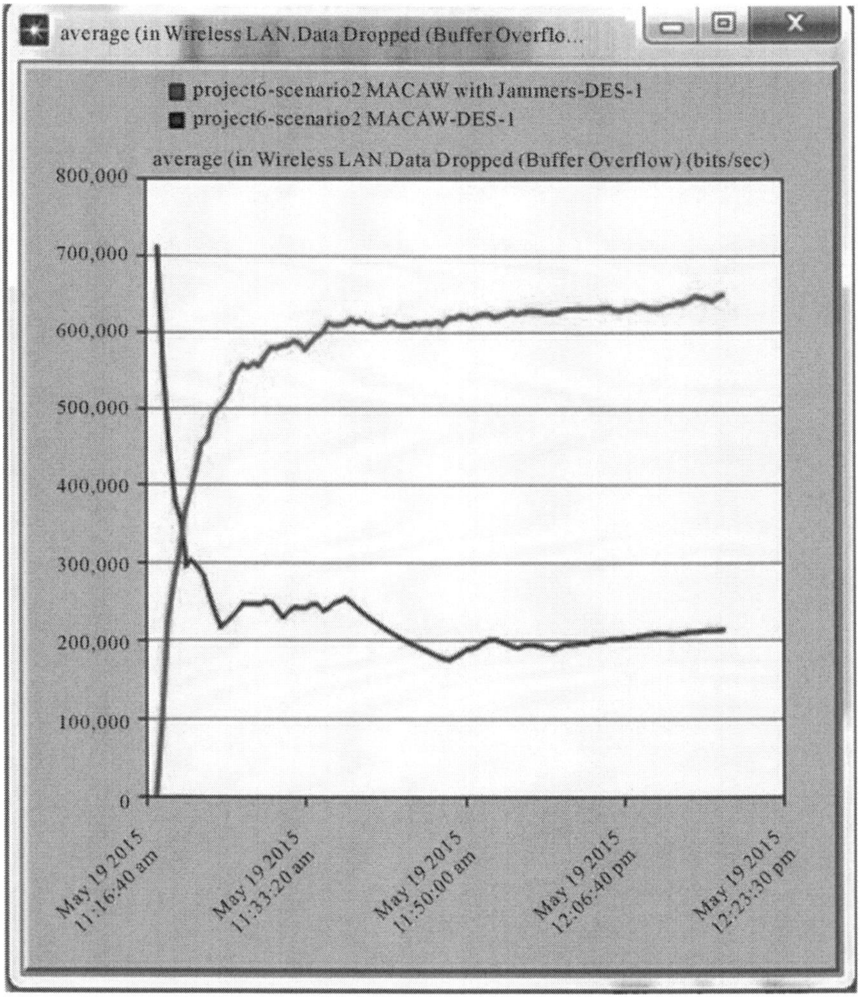

Figure 5. Average WLAN data dropped statistics.

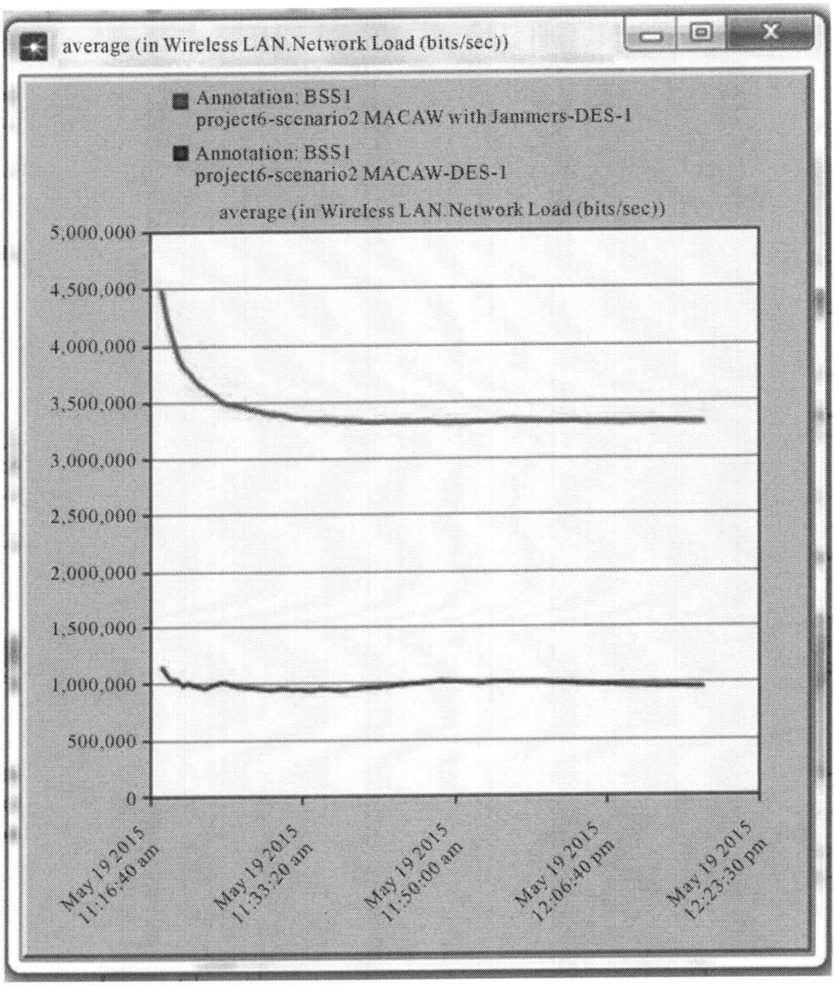

Figure 6. Average WLAN network load.

5. CONCLUSION

In the simulation case of study, the performance of MACAW protocol is evaluated. During this simulation, MACAW protocol has been exposed to a constant Jamming Attack. The main goal of this study is to observe possible impacts of a constant Jamming Attack on MACAW protocol. MACAW has shown a good performance unless it has been exposed to a Jamming Attack. It is seen in the simulation results that, a Jamming Attack in a mobile ad-hoc network leads to loss of performance of MACAW. Based on the simulation results, it can be claimed that Jamming Attacks cause approximately three times loss of network throughput where MACAW protocol is implemented. Delay rate in the network has significantly increased up to 800 seconds during Jamming Attack while it is close to zero second under normal network conditions. On the other hand, Data Dropped statistics show that 600,000 packages are discarded when MACAW is exposed to attack. In normal network conditions, this statistics is stable at the rate of 200,000 dropped data packages. In the jamming scenario, Network Load which is the final performance criteria shows that average load is at the rate of 4500,000 bits per second in the beginning of the simulation whereas it is stable at approximately 3500,000 bits per second at the end of the simulation. However, in the normal scenario Network Load statistics is stable at the rate of 1000,000 bits per second. Jamming Attack causes not only three times decrease in the network throughput but it also causes three times increase in the network load. This simulation experiment is the first study that deals with the performance evaluation of MACAW protocol under a constant Jamming Attack. Depending on results of our simulation experiment, it is strongly recommended other researchers to simulate performance of MACAW protocol under different security attacks such as Man in the Middle, Distributed Denial of Service and Spoof Attack. It is also recommended that precautions against attacks should be taken in MACAW protocol.

REFERENCES

1. Rouse, M. Collision Definition. http://searchnetworking.techtarget.com/definition/collision
2. Obasuyi, G. and Sari, A. (2015) Security Challenges of Virtualization Hypervisors in Virtualized Hardware Environment. International Journal of Communications, Network and System Sciences, 8, 260-273.
3. Sharanappa, P.H. and Mahabaleshwar, S.K. (2014) Performance Analysis of CSMA, MACA and MACAW Protocols for VANETs. International Journal of Future Computer and Communication, 3.
4. Sari, A. and Necat, B. (2012) Impact of RTS Mechanism on TORA and AODV Protocol's Performance in Mobile Ad Hoc Networks. International Journal of Science and Advanced Technology, 2, 188-191.
5. Joa-Ng, M. (1999) Spread Spectrum Medium Access Protocol with Collision Avoidance in Mobile Ad-hoc Wireless Network. INFOCOM'99, Proceedings of the Eighteenth Annual Joint Conference of the IEEE Computer and Communications Societies, 2.

6. Sari, A. and Necat, B. (2012) Securing Mobile Ad Hoc Networks against Jamming Attacks through Unified Security Mechanism. International Journal of Ad Hoc, Sensor & Ubiquitous Computing, 3, 79-94.

7. Zimmermann, H. (1980) OSI Reference Model—The IS0 Model of Architecture for Open Systems Interconnection. IEEE Transactions on Communications, COM-28, 425-432.

8. Sari, A. (2014) Security Approaches in IEEE 802.11 MANET—Performance Evaluation of USM and RAS. International Journal of Communications, Network, and System Sciences, 7, 365-372.

9. Sari, A. (2014) Security Issues in RFID Middleware Systems: A Case of Network Layer Attacks: Proposed EPC Implementation for Network Layer Attacks. Transactions on Networks & Communications, Society for Science and Education, United Kingdom, 2, 1-6.

10. Bharghavan, V., Demers, A., Shenker, S. and Zhang, L. (1994) MACAW: A Media Access Protocol for Wireless LAN's.

11. Sari, A., Rahnama, B. and Caglar, E. (2014) Ultra-Fast Lithium Cell Charging for Mission Critical Applications. Transactions on Machine Learning and Artificial Intelligence, United Kingdom, 2, 11-18.

12. Pan, J. (2008) A Survey of Network Simulation Tools: Current Status and Future Developments. http://www.cse.wustl.edu/~jain/cse567-08/ftp/simtools.pdf

13. Sari, A. (2015) Security Issues in Mobile Wireless Ad Hoc Networks: A Comparative Survey of Methods and Techniques to Provide Security in Wireless Ad Hoc Networks. New Threats and Countermeasures in Digital Crime and Cyber Terrorism, IGI Global, Hershey, 66-94.

14. Sari, A. (2015) Lightweight Robust Forwarding Scheme for Multi-Hop Wireless Networks. International Journal of Communications, Network and System Sciences, 8, 19-28.

15. Sari, A. and Onursal, O. (2013) Role of Information Security in E-Business Operations. International Journal of Information Technology and Business Management, 3, 90-93.

16. Sari, A. (2015) A Review of Anomaly Detection Systems in Cloud Networks and Survey of Cloud Security Measures in Cloud Storage Applications. Journal of Information Security, 6, 142-154.

17. Sari, A. and Rahnama, B. (2013) Addressing Security Challenges in WiMAX Environment. Proceedings of the 6th International Conference on Security of Information and Networks (SIN'13), ACM, New York, 454-456.

18. Sari, A. and Rahnama, B. (2013) Simulation of 802.11 Physical Layer Attacks in MANET. 2013 Fifth International Conference on Computational Intelligence, Communication Systems and Networks (CICSyN), 5-7 June 2013, 334-337.

19. Rahnama, B., Sari, A. and Makvandi, R. (2013) Countering PCIe Gen. 3 Data Transfer Rate Imperfection Using Serial Data Interconnect. 2013 International Conference on Technological Advances in Electrical, Electronics and Computer Engineering (TAEECE), 9-11 May 2013, 579-582.

20. Sari, A. (2015) Two-Tier Hierarchical Cluster Based Topology in Wireless Sensor Networks for Contention Based Protocol Suite. International Journal of Communications, Network and System Sciences, 8, 29-42.

CHAPTER 9

An Empirical Examination of Routing Protocols in Mobile Ad Hoc Networks

Kuncha Sahadevaiah[1], Oruganti Bala Venkata Ramanaiah[2]

[1]Department of Computer Science & Engineering, University College of Engineering,Jawaharlal Nehru Technological University, Kakinada, India

[2]Department of Computer Science & Engineering, University College of Engineering,Jawaharlal Nehru Technological University, Hyderabad, Indi

ABSTRACT

A Mobile Ad hoc NETwork (MANET) is a self-organizing, temporary, infrastructure-free, multi-hop, dynamic topology wireless network that contains collection of cooperative autonomous freely roaming mobile nodes. The nodes communicate with each other by wireless radio links with no human intervention. Each mobile node functions as a specialized router to forward information to other mobile nodes. In order to provide efficient end-to-end communication with the network of nodes, a routing protocol is used to discover the optimal routes between the nodes. The routing protocols meant for wired networks can not be used for MANETs because of the mobility of nodes. Routing in ad hoc networks is nontrivial due to highly dynamic nature of the nodes. Various routing protocols have been proposed and widely evaluated for efficient routing of packets. This research paper presents an overview on classification of wide range of routing protocols for mobile ad hoc wireless networks proposed in the literature and shows the performance evaluation of the routing protocols: DSDV, AODV, FSR, LAR, OLSR, STAR and ZRP using the network simulator QualNet 4.0 to determine which protocols may perform best in large networks. To judge the merit of a routing protocol, one needs performance metrics (throughput, end-to-end delay, jitter, packet delivery ratio, routing overhead) with which to measure its suitability and performance. Our simulation experiments show that the LAR protocol achieves relatively good performance compared to other routing protocols.

KEYWORDS

Mobile Ad Hoc Networks, Routing Protocols, LAR, QualNet 4.0, Performance Metrics, Simulations, Performance Evaluation

1. INTRODUCTION

The advent of ubiquitous computing and the proliferation of portable computing devices have raised the importance of mobile and wireless networking. Wireless networking is an emerging technology that allows users to access information and services electronically, regardless of their geographic position. Ad hoc is a Latin word, which means "for this purpose only". The term "ad hoc" tends to imply "can take different forms" and "can be mobile, stand alone, or networked" [1]. Ad hoc networks have the ability to form "on the fly" and dynamically handle the joining or leaving of nodes in the network. Mobile nodes are autonomous units that are capable of roaming independently. Typical mobile ad hoc wireless nodes are Laptops, Personal Digital Assistants, Pocket PCs, Cellular Phones, Internet Mobile Phones, Palmtops or any other mobile wireless devices. All of these have the capability and need to exchange information over a wireless medium in a network. Mobile ad hoc wireless devices are typically lightweight and battery operated.

A mobile ad hoc network (MANET) is an adaptive, self-configurable, self-organizing, infrastructure-less multi-hop wireless network with unpredictable dynamic topologies [2]. By adaptive, self-configurable and selforganizing, means an ad hoc network can be formed, merged together or partitioned into separated networks on the fly depending on the networking needs. i.e. a formed network can be deformed on the fly without the need for any system administration. By infrastructureless, means an ad hoc network can be promptly deployed without relying on any existing infrastructure such as base stations for wireless cellular networks. By multihop wireless, means, in an ad hoc network the routes between end users may consists of multi-hop wireless links.

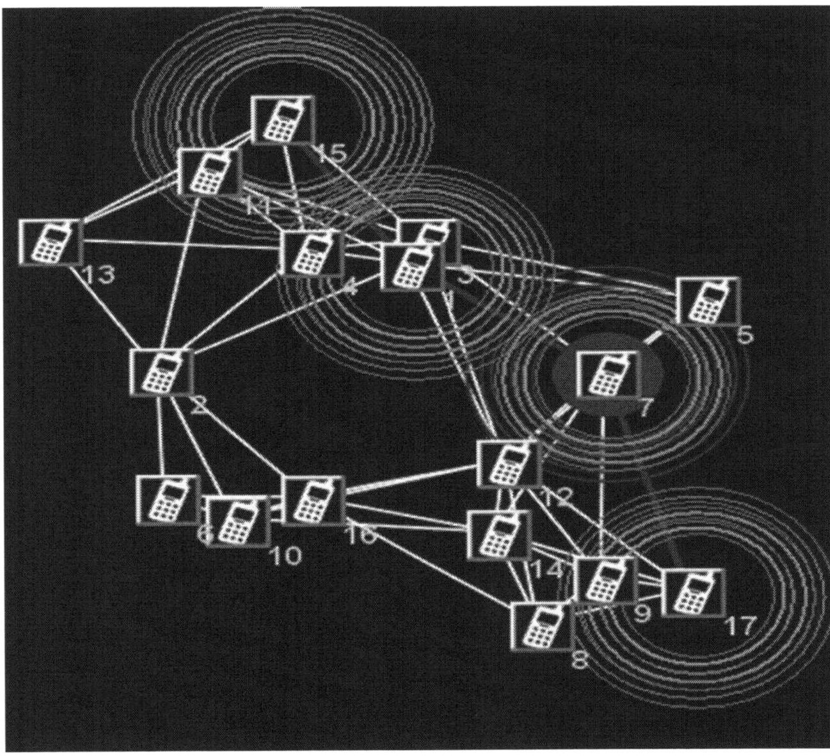

Figure 1. Communication scenario in MANET.

In addition, each node in a mobile ad hoc network is capable of moving independently and forwarding packets to other nodes.

The important characteristics of ad hoc wireless networks [2] are: dynamic topologies, low bandwidth, limited battery power, decentralized control, weak physical protection, etc. Dynamic Topologies: The nodes in ad hoc wireless networks are free to move independently in any direction. The network topology changes randomly at unpredictable times and primarily consists of bidirectional links. Low Bandwidth: These networks have lower capacity and shorter transmission range than fixed infrastructure networks.

The throughput of wireless communication is lesser than wired communication because of the effect of the multiple access, fading, noise, and interference conditions. Limited Battery Power: The nodes or hosts operate on small batteries and other exhaustible means of energy. So, energy conservation is the most important design optimization criteria. Decentralized Control: Due to unreliable links, the working of ad hoc wireless network depends upon cooperation of participating nodes. Thus, implementation of any protocol that involves a centralized authority or administrator becomes difficult. Weak Physical Protection: Nodes in ad hoc wireless networks are usually compact, soft, and hand-held in nature. Today, portable devices like mobile phones or personal digital assistants (PDAs) are getting smaller and smaller. They could get damaged or lost or stolen easily and misused by an adversary.

The domain of applications for ad hoc wireless networks is diverse, ranging from small, static networks that are constrained by power sources, to large-scale, mobile, highly dynamic networks [2,4]. Such networks are frequently viewed as a key communications technology enabler for network-centric warfare and military tactical operations-for fast establishment of military communications and troop deployments in hostile and/or unknown environments, disaster relief operations-for communication in environments where the existing infrastructure is destroyed, search and rescue operations and emergency situations-for communication in areas with no wireless infrastructure support, law enforcement-for secure and fast communication during law enforcement operations, commercial use-for enabling communications in exhibitions, conferences & large gatherings, intelligent transportation systems and fault-tolerant mobile sensor grids. Most of these applications demand a secure and reliable communication.

2. ROUTING IN MOBILE AD HOC NETWORKS

Mobile hoc network (MANET) is built on the fly where a number of mobile nodes work in cooperation without the engagement of any centralized access point or any fixed infrastructure. The nodes in the network are free to move independently in any direction. Node mobility causes route changes. The nodes themselves are responsible for dynamically discovering other nodes to communicate. When a node wants to communicate with a node outside its transmission range, a multi-hop routing strategy is used which involves some intermediate nodes. The network's wireless topology changes frequently and randomly at unpredictable times. Every node in ad hoc wireless network acts as a router that discovers and maintains routes in the network. Hence, the primary challenge is to establish a correct and efficient route between a pair of nodes and to ensure the correct and timely delivery of packets. Route construction should be done with a minimum of overhead and bandwidth consumption. Various protocols-proactive, reactive and hybrid-have been proposed and widely evaluated for efficient routing of packets in the literature [3].

Routing protocols [5] often are very vulnerable to node misbehavior. A node dropping all the packets is considered as malicious node or selfish nodes. A malicious node misbehaves because it intends to damage network functioning. A selfish node does so because it wants to save battery life for its own communication by simply not participating in the routing protocol or by not executing the packet forwarding. A malicious node could falsely advertise very attractive routes and thereby convince other nodes to route their messages via that malicious node.

3. Routing Protocols in Mobile Ad Hoc Networks

The main objective of ad hoc routing protocols is how to deliver data packets among nodes efficiently without predetermined topology or centralized control. Expected properties of MANET routing protocols are [6]: a routing protocol for MANET should be distributed in manner in order to increase its reliability, the routing protocol should assume routes as unidirectional links, the routing protocol should be power-efficient, the routing protocol should consider its security, and a routing protocol should be aware of Quality of Service (QoS). Based on the method of delivery of data packets from the source to destination, classification of the MANET routing protocols could be done as unicast, multicast or geocast routing protocols [6].

Unicast Routing Protocols: The routing protocols that consider sending information packets to a single destination from a single source.

Multicast Routing Protocols: Multicast is the delivery of information to a group of destinations simultaneously. Multicast routing protocols for MANET use both multicast and unicast for data transmission. Multicast routing protocols for MANET can be classified again into two categories: tree-based and mesh-based multicast routing protocols. Mesh-based routing protocols use several routes to reach a destination while the tree-based protocols maintain only one path. Tree-based protocols ensure less end-to-end delay in comparison with the mesh-based protocols.

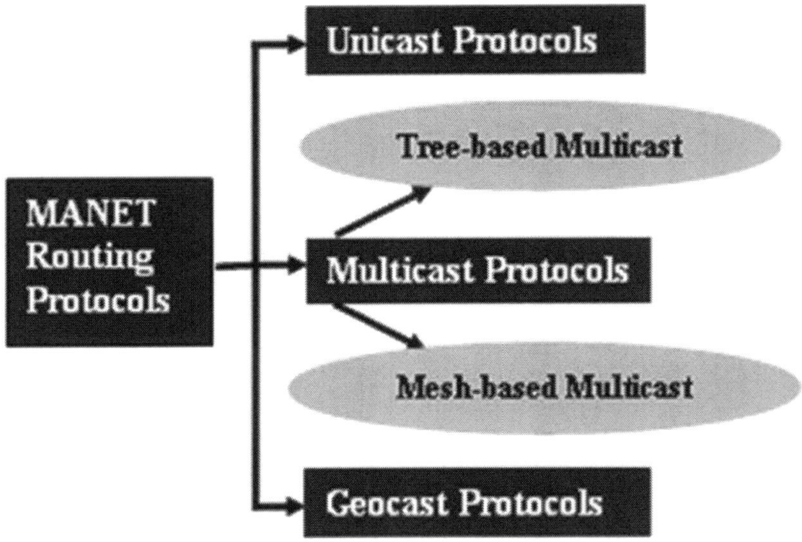

Figure 2. Classification of routing protocols.

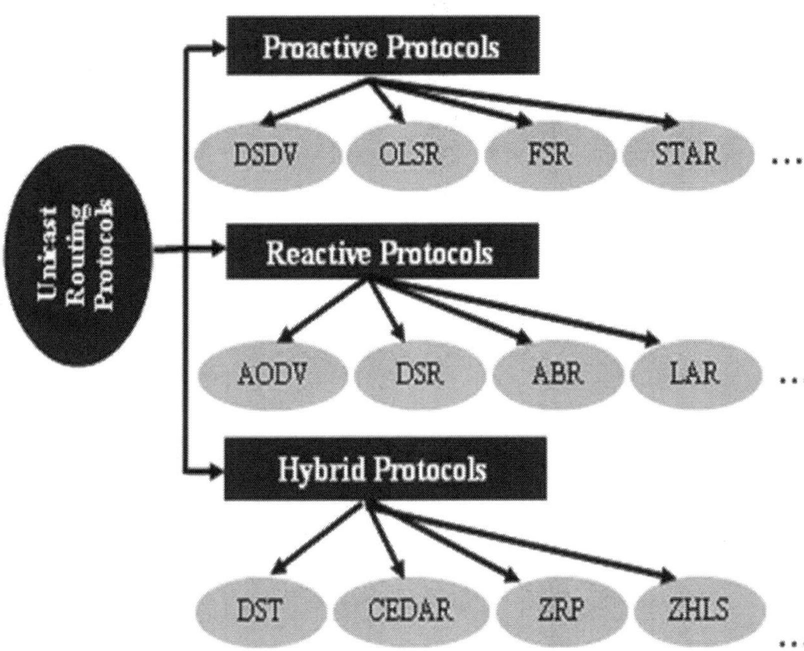

Figure 3. Classification of unicast routing protocols.

Geocast Routing Protocols: The routing protocols aim to send messages to some or all of the wireless nodes within a particular geographic region. Often the nodes know their exact physical positions in a network, and these protocols use that information for transmitting packets from the source to the destination(s).

Ad hoc wireless network unicast routing protocols can be further classified into three major categories based on the routing information update mechanism: proactive or table driven, reactive or on-demand, and hybrid routing protocols.

3.1. Proactive Routing Protocols

In proactive routing protocols, also known as tabledriven routing protocols, each node maintains one or more tables that contain consistent and up-to-date routing information to every other node in the network. The routing information is usually kept in a number of different tables. Proactive protocols continuously learn the global topology of the network by exchanging topological information among the network nodes. When the network topology changes, the nodes propagate update messages and the topology change information is distributed across the network. If the network topology changes too frequently, the cost of maintaining the network might be very high. Each node continuously evaluates routes to all reachable nodes. The overhead to maintain up-to-date network topology information is high.

Some of these protocols are: Destination Sequenced Distance Vector routing protocol (DSDV), Optimized Link State Routing protocol (OLSR), Fisheye State Routing protocol (FSR), Source Tree Adaptive Routing protocol (STAR), Wireless Routing Protocol (WRP), Global State Routing (GSR), Cluster-head Gateway Switch Routing protocol (CGSR), Hierarchical State Routing protocol (HSR).

3.1.1. Destination Sequenced Distance Vector Routing Protocol (DSDV)

The Destination Sequenced Distance Vector (DSDV) [9] is a proactive unicast routing protocol that solves the major problem associated with distance vector routing of wired networks, i.e. count-to-infinity, by using destination sequence numbers. It uses the classical Bellman-Ford routing algorithm with some improvements on routing performance that guarantees loop free routes. Each node maintains a routing table that stores all possible available routes for each destination, the hop counts as routing metrics to reach the destination and the unique sequence numbers to keep up-to-date information about its neighbors. A sequence number created by the destination is used to distinguish stale routes from new one and avoids formation of route loops. The route with higher sequence number is newer. If two routes have the same sequence number then the route with the best metric (i.e. shortest route) is used.

Every node periodically exchange routing table updates to its immediate neighbors. The route updates can be either time-driven or event-driven. Two types of route update packets: full dump and incremental packets are used. The full dump packet carries all the available routing information, i.e., the entire routing table to the neighbors and the incremental packet carries only the information changed since the last full dump. For updating the routing information in a node, the update packet with the highest sequence number is used. The incremental update messages are sent more frequently than the full dump packets. The protocol will not scale in large network since a large portion of the network bandwidth is used in the updating procedures.

3.1.2. Optimized Link State Routing Protocol (OLSR)

The Optimized Link State Routing (OLSR) [11] is a proactive unicast optimized version of a pure link state routing protocol that employs an efficient link state packet forwarding mechanism called multipoint relaying. This protocol performs hop-by-hop routing; that is, each node in the network uses its most recent information to route a packet. The routing optimization is done mainly in two ways. Firstly, OLSR reduces the size of the control packets for a particular node during each route update by declaring only a subset of links with the node's neighbors who are its multipoint relay selectors, instead of all links in the network. Any node which is not in the set can read and process each packet but do not retransmit. Secondly, it minimizes flooding of the control traffic by using only the selected nodes, called multipoint relays to disseminate information in the network. To select the multipoint relaying, each node periodically broadcasts a list of its one hop neighbors using hello messages. From the list of nodes in the hello messages, each node selects a subset of one hop neighbors, which covers all of its two hop neighbors. It provides optimal routes to every destination in terms of number of hops, which are immediately available when needed. As only multipoint relays of a node can retransmit its broadcast messages, this protocol significantly reduces the number of retransmissions in a flooding or broadcast procedure.

Therefore, the protocol works based on the mechanisms of: neighbors-sensing based on periodic exchange of hello messages, efficient flooding of control traffic using the concept of multipoint relays, and computation of an optimal route using the shortest-path algorithm. This protocol does not notify the source immediately after detecting a broken link and source node comes to know that route is broken when the intermediate node broadcasts its next packet. The proposed protocol is best suitable for large and dense ad hoc networks.

3.1.3. Fisheye State Routing Protocol (FSR)

The Fisheye State Routing (FSR) [12] is a proactive unicast routing protocol based on link state routing algorithm with effectively reduced overhead to maintain network topology information. The novelty of FSR is that it uses a special structure of the network called the "fisheye". FSR maintains the accurate distance and path quality information about the immediate neighboring nodes and progressively reduces detail as the distance increases. In link state routing algorithm, used for wired networks, link state updates are generated and flooded through the network whenever a node detects a topology change. However, in FSR nodes exchange link state information periodically only with the neighboring nodes to maintain up-to-date full topology information of the network. To reduce the size of link state update messages, FSR uses different update periods for different entries in the routing table. Link state updates corresponding to the nodes within a smaller scope are propagated with higher frequency.

The FSR protocol is an improvement of Global State Routing (GSR). The large size of update messages in GSR wastes a considerable amount of network bandwidth. In FSR, each update message does not contain information about all nodes. Instead, it reduces the size of the update messages by exchanging information about closer nodes more frequently than it does about farther nodes, which lie outside the fisheye scope. The scope is defined in terms of the nodes that can be reached in a certain number of hops. So, each node gets accurate information about neighbors and accuracy of information decreases as the distance from node increases.

The advantage of FSR is that even though a node does not have accurate information about a destination, as the packet moves closer to the destination, more correct information about the route to the destination becomes available. FSR exhibits a better scalability concerning the network size compared to others as the overhead is controlled in this scheme.

3.1.4. Source Tree Adaptive Routing Protocol (STAR)

The Source Tree Adaptive Routing [13] protocol is based on the link state algorithm. Each node maintains a source routing tree, which is a set of links containing the preferred paths to every destinations and broadcasts its source-tree information to its neighbors and builds a partial graph of the topology. When a node has data packets to send to a destination for which no path exists in its source-tree, it originates an update message to all its neighbors indicating the absence of a path .This update message triggers another update message from a neighbor which has a path. After getting this, the node updates its source-tree and then finds path to all nodes in the network. In addition to path breaks, the intermediate nodes are responsible for handling the routing loops.

STAR will scale well in large networks since it has significantly reduced the amount of routing overhead disseminated into the network by using a least overhead routing approach (LORA) to exchange routing information. However, this protocol may have significant memory and processing overheads in large and highly mobile networks, because each node is required to maintain a partial topology graph of the network (it is determined from the source tree reported by its neighbors), which changes frequently as the neighbors keep reporting different source trees.

3.2. Reactive Routing Protocols

In reactive routing protocols, also known as on-demand routing protocols, a node creates a route in an on-demand fashion, i.e. it computes a route only when needed. When a source wants to send packets to a destination, it invokes the route discovery mechanisms to find the path to the destination. Route discovery usually occurs by flooding a route request packet throughout the network. Route reply is sent back if the destination itself or node with route to the destination is reached. The discovery procedure terminates either when a route has been found or no route available after examination for all route permutations. Reactive routing does not maintain global topological information and, therefore, substantially reduces energy consumption. Some of these protocols are: Ad hoc On-Demand Distance Vector routing protocol (AODV), Dynamic Source Routing protocol (DSR), Associativity Based Routing protocol (ABR), Location Aided Routing protocol (LAR), Light-weight Mobile Routing protocol (LMR), Temporally Ordered Routing Algorithm (TORA), Ant-colony-based Routing Algorithm (ARA), Clusterbased Routing Protocol (CBRP).

3.2.1. Ad Hoc On-Demand Distance Vector Routing Protocol (AODV)

The Ad hoc On-Demand Distance Vector (AODV) [14] routing protocol is a reactive unicast routing protocol. The protocol constructs efficient route on demand with minimal control overhead and minimal route acquisition latency. AODV is essentially a combination of both DSR and DSDV algorithms and it borrows the basic on demand mechanism of route discovery and route maintenance from DSR, plus the use of hop-by-hop routing sequence numbers from DSDV. The destination sequence number can be used to ensure loop-free and to identify which route with the greatest sequence number is newer one.

AODV has bidirectional route from source to destination. To find a path from source to destination, the source broadcasts a route request packet. The neighbors in turn broadcast the packet to their neighbors till it reaches an intermediate node that has recent route information about the destination or till it reaches the destination. A node discards a route request packet that it has already seen. The route request packet uses sequence numbers to ensure that the routes are loop free. When a node forwards a route request packet to its neighbors, it also records in its tables the node from which the first copy of the request came. This information is used to construct the reverse path for the route reply packet. AODV uses only symmetric links because the route reply packet follows the reverse path of route request packet. As the route reply packet traverses back to the source, the nodes along the path enter the forward route into their tables. For route maintenance, when a source node moves, it can reinitiate route discovery to the destination. If one of the intermediate nodes moves, then the moved nodes neighbor realizes the link failure and sends a link failure notification to its upstream neighbors and so on till it reaches the source upon which the source can reinitiate route discovery if needed.

The difference between DSR and AODV is that in DSR, each packet carries full routing information, whereas in AODV, the packets carry the destination address. This means that AODV has potentially less routing overheads than DSR. The other difference is that the route replies in DSR carry the address of every node along the route, whereas in AODV, the route replies only carry the destination IP address and the sequence number.

The advantage of AODV is that it is adaptable to highly dynamic networks. However, node may experience large delays during route construction, and link failure may initiate another route discovery, which introduces extra delays and consumes more bandwidth as the size of the network increases.

3.2.2. Location Aided Routing Protocol (LAR)

The Location Aided Routing (LAR) [15] protocol is a reactive unicast routing scheme. In this, a source node estimates the current location range of the destination based on information of the last reported location and the mobility pattern of the destination. In this, an expected zone is defined as a region that is expected to hold the current location of the destination node. During route discovery procedure, the route request flooding is limited to a request zone, which contains the expected zone and location of the sender node. LAR decreases overhead of the route discovery by using the location information. It limits the search to a smaller request zone, causing significant reduction of the number of routing messages.

This protocol assumes that each node knows its location through a GPS. Two different LAR schemes were proposed in [15], the first scheme calculates a request zone which defines a boundary where the route request packets can travel to reach the required destination. The second scheme stores the coordinates of the destination in the route request packets. These packets can only travel in the direction where the relative distance to the destination becomes smaller as they travel from one hop to another. Both methods limit the control overhead transmitted through the network and hence conserve bandwidth. They will also determine the shortest path to the destination, since the route request packets travel away from the source and towards the destination.

The disadvantage of LAR protocol is that each node is required to carry a GPS. Another disadvantage is, especially for the first method, that protocols may behave similar to flooding protocols (e.g., DSR and AODV) in highly mobile networks.

3.3. Hybrid Routing Protocols

In hybrid routing protocols, some of the characteristics of proactive protocols and some of the characteristics of reactive protocols are combined into one to get better solution for mobile ad hoc networks. These protocols exploit the hierarchical network architecture and allow the nodes with close proximity to work together to form some sort of backbone, thus increasing scalability and reducing route discovery. Nodes within a particular geographical region are said to be within the routing zone of the given node. For routing within this zone, a tabledriven approach is used. For nodes that are located beyond this zone, an on demand approach is used.

Some of the hybrid routing protocols are: Distributed Spanning Tree based Routing Protocol (DST), CoreExtraction Distributed Ad Hoc Routing protocol (CEDAR), Zone Routing Protocol (ZRP), Zone-based Hierarchical Link State Routing Protocol (ZHLS), Distributed Dynamic Routing protocol (DDR), Scalable Location Update Routing Protocol (SLURP), Hybrid Ad hoc Routing Protocol (HARP).

3.3.1. Zone Routing Protocol (ZRP)

The Zone Routing Protocol (ZRP) [16] is a hybrid routing protocol, where the network is divided into routing zones according to the distances between nodes and the routing zone defines a range (in hops) that each node is required to maintain network connectivity proactively. In this, proactive routing approach-Intra Zone Routing Protocol (IARP) is used inside routing zones and reactive routing approach-Inter Zone Routing Protocol (IERP) is used between routing zones. Therefore, for nodes within the routing zone, routes are immediately available. For nodes that lie outside the routing zone, routes are determined on-demand (i.e. reactively), and it can use any on-demand routing protocol to determine a route to the required destination. Route creation is done using a query-reply mechanism. During the forwarding of the query packet, a node identifies whether it is coming from its neighbor or not. If yes, then it marks all of its known neighboring nodes in its same zone as covered. A covered node is a node which belongs to the routing zone of a node that has received a route query. The query is thus relayed till it reaches the destination. The destination in turn sends back a reply message via the reverse path and creates the route.

ZRP is suitable for the networks with large span and diverse mobility patterns. The advantage of this protocol is that it has significantly reduced the amount of communication overhead when compared to pure proactive protocols. It also has reduced the delays associated with pure reactive protocols such as DSR, by allowing routes to be discovered faster. This is because, to determine a route to a node outside the routing zone, the routing only has to travel to a node which lies on the boundaries (edge of the routing zone) of the required destination. Since the boundary node would proactively maintain routes to the destination (i.e. the boundary nodes can complete the route from the source to the destination by sending a reply back to the source with the required routing address).

The disadvantage of ZRP is that for large values of routing zone, the protocol can behave like a pure proactive protocol, while for small values it behaves like a reactive protocol.

4. OVERALL COMPARISON OF ALL UNICAST ROUTING PROTOCOLS

Advantages and disadvantages of proactive, reactive and hybrid approaches are shown in **Table 1**and overall comparison of all unicast routing protocols are shown in **Table 2**.

Table 1. Advantages and disadvantages of proactive, reactive and hybrid routing protocols.

	Advantages	Disadvantages
Proactive	-Up-to-date routing information -Quick establishment of routes -Small delay -A route to every other node in the network is always available	-Slow convergence -Tendency of creating loops -Large amount of resources are needed -Routing information is not fully used
Reactive	-Reduction of routing load -Saving of resources -Loop-free	-Not always up-to-date routes -Large delay -Control traffic and overhead cost
Hybrid	-Scalability -Limited search cost -Up-to-date routing information within zones	-Arbitrary proactive scheme within zones -Inter-zone routing latencies -More resources for large size zones

Table 2. Overall comparison of all unicast routing categories [20].

Routing Property	Proactive	Reactive	Hybrid
Routing Structure	Both flat and hierarchical	Mostly flat, except CBRP	Mostly hierarchical
Route Availability	Always available, if the nodes are reachable	Determined when needed	Depends on the location of the destination
Traffic Control Volume	Usually high	Low	Mostly lower than proactive and reactive
Mobility Handling Effects	Usually updates occur based on mobility at fixed intervals	ABR introduced LBQ, AODV uses local route discovery	Usually more than one path may be available
Storage Requirements	High	Usually lower than Proactive protocols	Usually depends on the size of each cluster
Delay Level	Small routes are predetermined	Higher than proactive	For local destinations small, since Inter-zone may be as large as reactive protocols
Scalability Level to Perform Efficient Routing	Usually up to 100 nodes	Source routing protocols up to few 100 nodes Point-to-point may scale higher	Designed for up to 1000 or more nodes

5. PERFORMANCE EVALUATION AND ANALYSIS

5.1. Simulation Model

The simulations were performed using the network simulator QualNet 4.0 which is a discrete event simulator developed by Scalable Networks. It is extremely scalable accommodating high fidelity models of networks. QualNet makes good use of computational resources and models large-scale networks with heavy traffic and mobility in reasonable simulation times.

The study has been done to compare the efficiency of the various categories of routing protocols: DSDV, AODV, FSR, LAR, OLSR, STAR, and ZRP. The overall goal of our simulation study is to analyze the behavior and performance of the protocols under a range of various scenarios. Simulations have been run using a mobile ad hoc networks composed of 10, 15, 25, 50 and 75 nodes moving over a rectangular 1500 m × 1500 m space and operating over 30 seconds of simulation time. All nodes move according to the random way point mobility model. The traffic sources in our simulation are constant bit rate (CBR) traffic. Each traffic source originates 512 bytes data packets. The simulation parameters are shown in **Table 3**.

Table 3. Simulation parameters.

Parameter	Value
Number of nodes	10, 15, 25, 50, 75
Number of traffic sources	3
Simulation Time	30 Seconds
Traffic Type	CBR
Packet Size	512 bytes
Topology Size	1500m × 1500m
Mobility Pattern	Random way point

5.2. Simulation Metrics

The metrics that are used to evaluate the performance of the routing protocols are: throughput, average end-to-end delay, average jitter, total packets received, packet delivery ratio and routing overhead.

Throughput is the average rate of successful message/ packets delivery over a communication channel. i.e. Throughput is the measure of how fast we can actually send the packets through network. The throughput is usually measured in bits per second (bit/s or bps), and sometimes in data packets per second or data packets per time slot.

Average end-to-end delay is the delay experienced by a packet from the time it was sent by a source till the time it was received successfully at the destination. i.e., the end-to-end delay is the time a data packet is received by the destination minus the time the data packet is generated by the source. Average end-to-end delay includes all possible delays caused by buffering during route discovery latency, queuing at the interface queue, retransmission delays at the MAC, and propagation and transfer times of data packets.

Average jitter measures the packet delay variation. It is calculated as the average of the difference of the inter arrival time between subsequently received packets.

Total packets received is the number of packets received by the TCP sink at the final destination and the number of packets generated by the traffic sources.

Packet delivery ratio is the ratio of the number of data packets successfully delivered to the destinations to those generated by the constant bit rate (CBR) sources. Routing overhead is the number of control packets produced per mobile node. Control packets include route requests, replies and error messages. The routing load specifies the load over communications links for traffic flow.

5.3. Simulation Scenarios

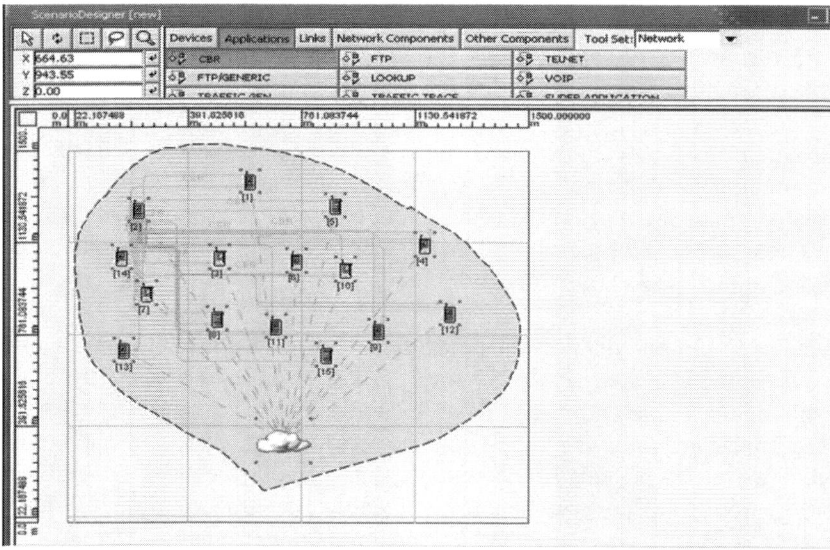

Figure 4. Designer window scenario for 15 nodes.

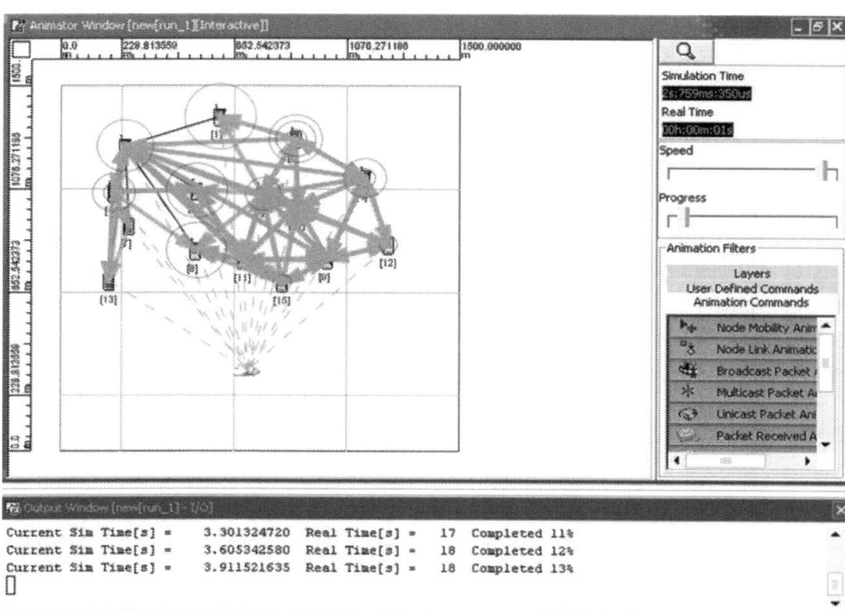

Figure 5. Animator window scenario for 15 nodes.

Table 4. Metric values for 15 nodes.

Protocols/ Parameters	DSDV	AODV	FSR	LAR	OLSR	STAR	ZRP
Throughput(10^4)	5.85	5.85	4.0	6.1	5.7	3.65	4.85
End-To-End Delay	-	-	1.17	3.25	0.08	0.4	1.56
Average Jitter	-	-	3.48	2.5	0.5	0.4	4.68
Total Packets Received (10^2)	3.35	3.35	1.9	3.22	2.97	1.83	2.56

Table 5. Metric values for 25 nodes.

Protocols/ Parameters	DSDV	AODV	FSR	LAR	OLSR	STAR	ZRP
Throughput(10^5)	0.99	1.01	0.63	0.98	0.94	0.51	0.48
End-To-End Delay	-	-	2.8	11.6	0.1	0.6	3.8
Average Jitter	0.1	-	1.2	11.7	0.6	0.6	3.5
Total Packets Received (10^2)	5.6	5.7	2.8	5.4	4.8	2.7	2.4

Table 6. Metric values for 50 nodes.

Protocols/ Parameters	DSDV	AODV	FSR	LAR	OLSR	STAR	ZRP
Throughput(10^5)	2	0.07	1.24	1.17	0.98	1.96	0.75
End-To-End Delay	-	-	7.5	46	0.75	31	40.8
Average Jitter	-	-	20.75	21.3	0.5	36.75	32.5
Total Packets Received(10^3)	1.16	1.16	0.53	1.13	0.08	0.61	0.41

Table 7. Metric values for 75 nodes.

Protocols/ Parameters	DSDV	AODV	FSR	LAR	OLSR	STAR	ZRP
Throughput(10^5)	3.14	3.14	1.87	1.76	3.04	1.28	0.38
End-To-End Delay	-	-	13	78	1	67	42
Average Jitter	-	-	16	96	5	50	25
Total Packets Received (10^3)	1.76	1.76	0.78	0.84	1.54	0.8	0.25

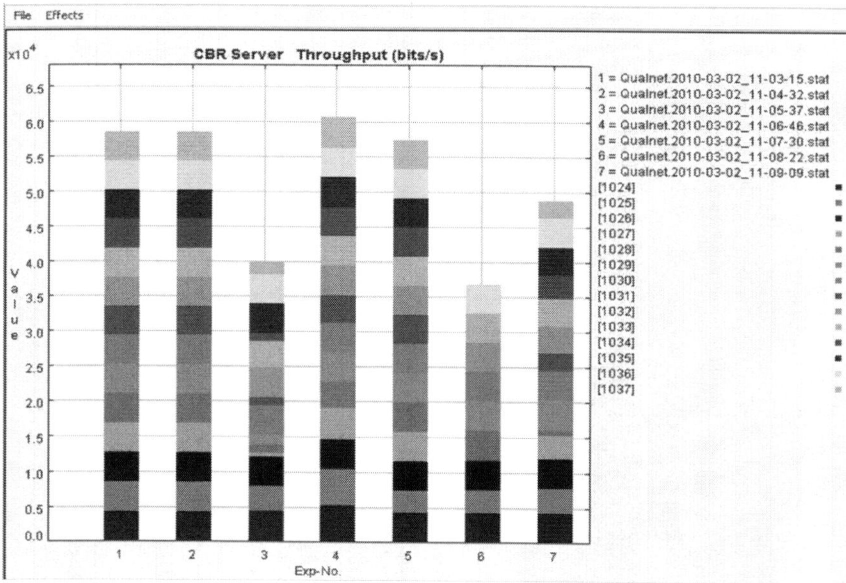

Figure 6. Multi experimental comparison chart (15 nodes) for the metric: throughput.

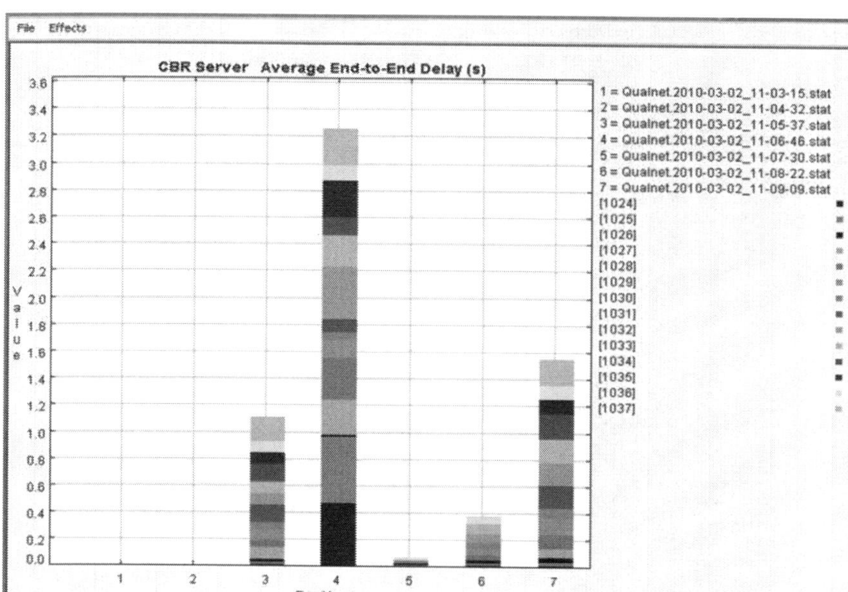

Figure 7. Multi experimental comparison chart (15 nodes) for the metric: Average end-to-end delay.

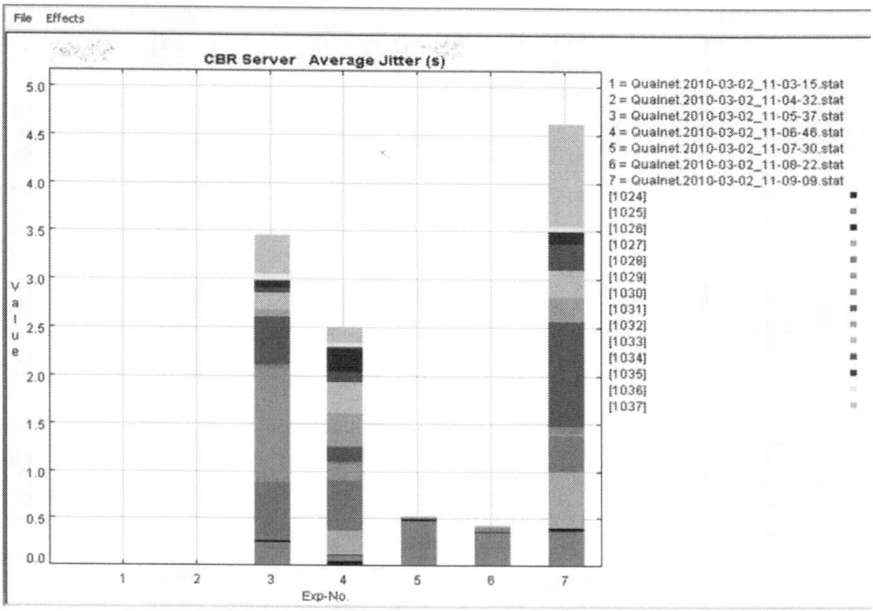

Figure 8. Multi experimental comparison chart (15 nodes) for the metric: Average jitter.

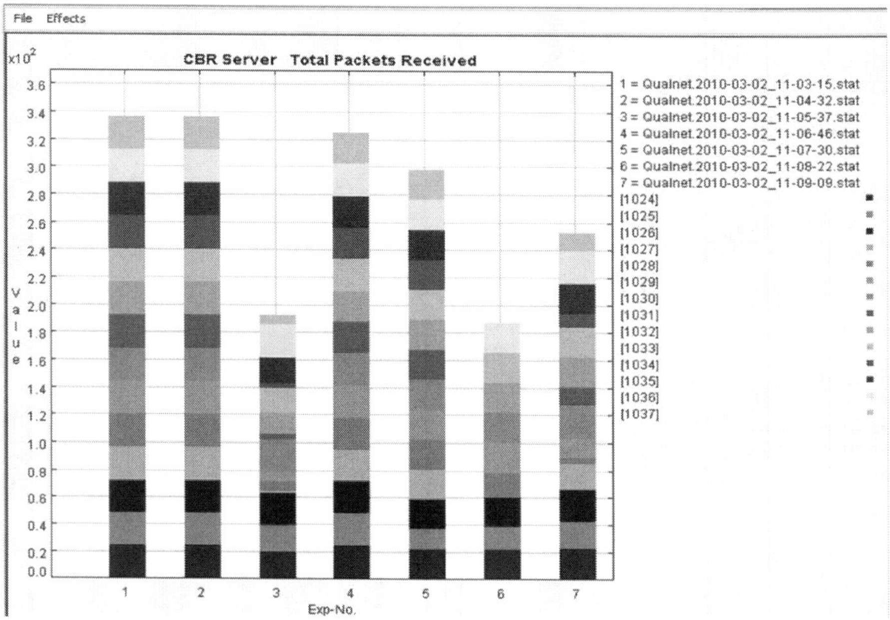

Figure 9. Multi experimental comparison chart (15 nodes) for the metric: Total packets received.

5.4. Simulation Results and Analysis

The simulation study has been done using the network simulator QualNet 4.0 for performance comparison of the protocols: DSDV, AODV, FSR, LAR, OLSR, STAR and ZRP. The all seven routing protocols result in improvements of the performance metrics that include throughput, jitter, end-to-end delay and total packets received.

It was observed from the simulation that DSDV and AODV gives nearly same and maximum throughput in small sized networks. Throughput of FSR, LAR, OLSR, and STAR is increasing as the network size is increasing, but OLSR performs well in large sized networks. Throughput of ZRP is well and it is nearer for small and large networks, but for large sized networks it is decreasing. For end-to-end delay and average jitter, the performance of DSDV and AODV is better than FSR, LAR, OLSR, STAR and ZRP in case of small sized networks. In medium and large sized networks, the end-to-end delay and average jitter of AODV and DSDV protocols are same.

The improvements shown in LAR are gradually increasing than others. Hence, it can be concluded that LAR is the best among the studied routing protocols.

6. CONCLUSIONS

In this article, the classifications of routing protocols for ad hoc wireless networks were discussed. In proactive protocols, each node maintains network connectivity and up-to-date routing information to all the nodes in the network. In reactive protocols, a node finds the route to a destination when it desires to send packets to the destination. In hybrid routing protocols, some of the characteristics of proactive and some of the characteristics of reactive are combined, by maintaining intra-zone information proactively and inter-zone information reactively, into one to get better solution for mobile ad hoc networks.

Generally speaking, reactive protocols require fewer amounts of memory, processing power, and energy than that of the proactive protocols. The mobility and traffic pattern of the network must play the key role for choosing an appropriate routing strategy for a particular network. It is quite natural that one particular solution cannot be applied for all sorts of situations and, even if applied, might not be optimal in all cases. Often it is more appropriate to apply a hybrid protocol rather than a strictly proactive or reactive protocol as hybrid protocols often possess the advantages of both types of protocols.

DSDV and GSR uses destination sequence numbers to keep routes up-to-date and loop-free. HSR and ZHLS are hierarchical routing protocols. FSR reduces the size of tables to be exchanged by maintaining less accurate information about nodes farther away. CGSR and CBRP are cluster-based routing protocol where nodes are grouped into clusters. AODV is an on-demand version of DSDV routing protocol. ABR uses the degree of associativity to select routes and a localized broadcast query is initiated when a link goes down. WRP maintains the best-path information to a destination, avoids routing loops during route discovery process, and converges quickly after a link failure. In LAR, the route request packets propagate in the request zone only. DSR is a source routing protocol where the route is in each packet. DSR had higher routing overhead as compared to AODV. ZHLS and SLURP are highly adaptable to changing topology, since only the node ID and zone ID of the destination is required for routing to occur. They do not use a cluster-head to coordinate data transmission, which means that a single point of failure and performance bottlenecks can be avoided. The ZRP routing protocol is designed to increase the scalability of mobile ad hoc networks. The advantage of this protocol is that it maintains strong network connectivity (proactively) within the routing zones while determining remote route (outside the routing zone) quicker than flooding.

The simulation study has been done using the network simulator QualNet 4.0 for performance comparison of the protocols: DSDV, AODV, FSR, LAR, OLSR, STAR and ZRP. The improvements shown in LAR are gradually increasing than others. Hence, it can be concluded that LAR is the best among the studied routing protocols.

REFERENCES

1. C. K. Tok, "Ad Hoc Mobile Wireless Networks: Protocols and Systems," Pearson Education, Boston, 2002, pp. 28-30.
2. X. Cheng, X. Huang and D. Z. Du, "Ad Hoc Wireless Networking," Kluwer Academic Publishers, Boston, 2006, pp. 319-364.
3. C. S. R. Murthy and B. S Manoj, "Ad Hoc Wireless Networks: Architectures and Protocols," Pearson Education, Boston, 2006.

4. P. Mohaptra and S. V. Krishnamurthy, "Ad Hoc Networks: Technologies and Protocols," Springer International Edition, New Delhi, 2005.

5. F. Anjum and P. Mouchtaris, "Security for Wireless Ad hoc Networks," John Wiley & Sons, Chichester, 2007.

6. S. Misra, I. Woungang and S. C. Misra, "Guide to Wireless Ad Hoc Networks," Springer, Berlin, 2009, pp. 59- 96.

7. S. Basagni, M. Conti, S. Giordono and I. Stojmenovic, "Mobile Ad Hoc Networks," John Wiley & Sons, Chichester, 2003.

8. C. E. Perkins, "Ad Hoc Networks," Addition Wesley, 2001.

9. C. E. Perkins and P. Bhagwat, "Highly Dynamic Destination Sequenced Distance Vector Routing (DSDV) for Mobile Computers," ACM Computer Communication Review, Special Interest Group on Data Communication (ACM SIGCOMM'94), Vol. 24, No. 4, 1994, pp. 234-244.

10. E. M. Royer and C. K. Toh, "A Review of Current Routing Protocols for Ad Hoc Mobile Wireless Networks," IEEE Personal Communications, Vol. 6, No. 2, 1999, pp. 46-55.

11. P. Jacquet, P. Muhlethaler, T. Clausen, A. Laouiti, A. Qayyum and L. Viennot, "Optimized Link State Routing Protocol for Ad Hoc Networks," IEEE International Multi Topic Conference (IEEE INMIC), Islamabad, 2001, pp. 62-68.

12. M. Gerla, X. Hong and G. Pei, "Fisheye State Routing (FSR) Protocol for Ad Hoc Networks," 2002. http://tools. ietf.org/html/draft-ietf-manet-fsr-03

13. J. J. Garcia-Luna-Aceves and M. Spohn, "Source-Tree Routing in Wireless Networks," Proceedings of the Seventh Annual International Conference on Network Protocols, Toronto, October 1999, p. 273.

14. C. E. Perkins, E. M. Belding-Royer and S. R. Das, "Ad hoc On-Demand Distance Vector (AODV) Routing," 2002. http://tools.ietf.org/ html/ draft-ietf-manet-aodv-11

15. Y. B. Ko and N. H. Vaidya, "Location-Aided Routing (LAR) in Mobile Ad Hoc Networks," Wireless Networks, Kluwer Academic Publishers, Vol. 6, No. 4, 2000, pp. 307-321.

16. Z. J. Hass, M. R. Pearlman and P. Samar, "Zone Routing Protocol for Ad Hoc Networks," 2002. http://www.ietf. org/proceedings/55/I-D/draft-ietf-manet-zone-zrp-04.txt

17. M. Abolhasan, T. Wysocki and E. Dutkiewicz, "A Review of Routing Protocols for Mobile Ad Hoc Networks," Ad Hoc Networks, Vol. 2, No. 2, 2004, pp. 1-22.

18. C. Sun, "Design and Implementation of Fisheye Routing Protocol for Mobile Ad Hoc Networks," Massachusetts Institute of Technology, 2000.

19. M. Mauve, J. Widmer and H. Hartenstein, "A Survey on Position Based Routing in Mobile Ad hoc Networks," IEEE Network, Vol. 15, No. 6, 2001, pp. 30-39.

20. M. Abolhasan, T. Wysocki and E. Dutkiewicz, "A Review of Routing Protocols for Mobile Ad Hoc Networks," Ad Hoc Networks, Vol. 2, No. 1, 2004, pp. 1-22.

CHAPTER 10

A Survey of QoS Multicast in Ad Hoc Networks

Viet Thi Minh Do *, Lars Landmark and Øivind Kure

Centre for Quantifiable Quality of Service in Communication Systems (Q2S), Norwegian University of Science and Technology (NTNU), NO-7491 Trondheim, Norway

ABSTRACT

This survey on Quality of Service (QoS) in multicast ad hoc networks uses a framework based on the mechanisms in three important elements: resource estimations, multicast tree/mesh administration, and multicast routing. Our contribution is an exploration of the design space and an identification of areas that have not been fully explored. We discuss the design space of central mechanisms and classify proposed QoS multicast schemes according to the mechanisms they used. In addition, we summarize the scenarios used for evaluating their performance. Furthermore, we identify issues, mechanisms, and scenarios that have not been fully investigated in existing works. The paper provides a coherent understanding of design principles, conceptual operation, and evaluated scenarios of schemes designed for QoS multicast application in mobile ad hoc networks (MANETs). It also outlines new areas for future research in this field.

KEYWORDS

multicast; Quality of Service; ad hoc networks; MANETs

1. INTRODUCTION

Ad hoc networks are self-configuring networks of mobile devices connected by wireless links. The devices are free to move and organize themselves in an arbitrary fashion. Ad hoc networks are suitable for situations where an infrastructure is unavailable or ineffective to deploy. Examples are emergency operations, disaster relief operations, temporary networks, transient vehicle-to-vehicle communication and tactical military networks. In most of these settings multipoint-to-multipoint multimedia communication is a requirement. Multicast is an efficient method to implement multipoint-to-multipoint communication. Multimedia content also requires networks with predictable service or Quality of Service (QoS).

As Internet is making the transition to a ubiquitous network, available anytime and anywhere, more and more of the communication will be over wireless technologies. As already mentioned, not all this can be handled in the context of single hop as in cellular or wireless access. Future Internet will therefore to a larger extent than today also incorporate ad hoc networks. More important, the functionality and the protocols of the future internet must seamlessly handle the challenges of multihop wireless communication.

Our intention is to describe the design space of the protocols for QoS enabled multicast. In addition, we summarize the simulation scenarios used to evaluate these protocols. The end result of the survey is an identification of possible areas and scenarios that could benefit from a more in-depth investigation.

There are several surveys and reviews on the separate topics of QoS and multicast in ad hoc networks. Symeon *et al.* [6], in a paper from 2002, summarized issues and challenges for supporting multicast in ad hoc networks. They classified the multicast protocols as proactive and reactive, tree and non-tree approaches and summarized some of the more typical protocols. The survey is a few years old and does not include QoS multicast in ad hoc networks. In [5], Aaron *et al.*presented a multicast "life cycle" model for fixed networks. They considered three important events happening during a life cycle, namely group dynamics, network dynamics, and traffic dynamics. They also examined some issues and solutions for managing group dynamics and handling failure in QoS multicasting.

Dmitri *et al.* [3] in 2002 and T. Bheemarjuna *et al.* [4] in 2006 both described the issues and challenges in providing QoS for ad hoc networks. They identified a set of required components for all QoS solutions: (1) a QoS routing protocol, (2) a resource reservation scheme, and (3) a QoS capable medium access control (MAC) layer. Lajos *et al.* [7] surveyed various QoS routing solutions for MANETs published in the period 1997–2006. They focused on QoS routing metrics, resources, and factors affecting performance. The protocols were grouped based on their interaction with MAC protocol. Luo *et al.* [1] surveyed multicast routing protocols and classified them into two categories, application independent multicast routing and multicast routing aimed for specific application requirements. The latter group was divided into subcategories based on requirements for QoS, energy efficiency, network coding, and reliable transfer.

However, these surveys only cover some of the subtopics of QoS multicast in ad hoc networks. To our knowledge, there are only two reviews covering the full topic [2,10]. Aisha *et al.* [2] reviewed nine protocols and presented a short description, advantages, and disadvantages of these protocols. Masoudifar [10] reviewed seven QoS multicast routing protocols. The focus was on QoS routing protocols. They were classified based on their dependency on other protocols, whether they could function as a sublayer, as an enhancement of existing protocols, or whether they were completely independent. Both surveys only include a limited subset of the protocols we have analyzed. Their focus is also only on some of the elements we are targeting. Our contribution is an in depth analysis of the design space for more than 30 QoS multicast protocols in ad hoc networks. The end result is an identification of possible mechanisms and scenarios that could benefit from a more detailed investigation.

The remainder of the paper is organized as follows. In the remainder of Section 1 we introduce the challenges and the functionalities required for providing QoS multicast. Section 2 classifies the various protocols based on the mechanisms used to implement the functionalities. In Section 3 we focus on the actual scenario used to evaluate the performance of the various proposed schemes. The limitations of existing scenarios are also described. Most of the existing scenarios are quite limited with the small number of groups and sources. In the conclusion part, Section 4, we identify design mechanisms and usage scenarios that have only been investigated to a limited degree. The 31 protocols surveyed in the paper are listed in Table 1.

Table 1. Description of protocol names.

No.	Protocol	Full Name
1	QAMNet [11]	Quality of service for Multicast in MANETs
2	CQMRP [12]	Cluster-based QoS Multicast Routing Protocol
3	QMRPCAH [13]	QoS Multicast Routing Protocol for Clustering Mobile Ad Hoc Network
4	HVDB [14]	Hypercube-based Virtual Dynamic Backbone
5	QoS-ODMRP [15]	QoS On-Demand Multicast Routing Protocol
6	E-QMR [16]	Cross-layer QoS Multicast Routing Protocol (This protocol is an extenson of protocol QMR[44])
7	Hu* [17]	This protocol was not named by the authors. The first author's name is used instead
8	QMRP [18]	QoS aware Multicast Routing Protocol
9	QoS-AODV [19]	QoS Ad Hoc On-Demand Distance Vector Routing
10	HQMRP [21]	Hybrid QoS Multicast Routing Protocol
11	QoS-MEM [22]	QoS-aware Minimum Energy Multicast
12	LTM* [23]	Lantern-Tree-based QoS Multicast (This protocol was not named by the authors. We call it LTM)
13	MPT* [24]	Multiple paths/trees (This protocol was not named by the authors. We call it MPT)
14	EQMGA [25]	Entropy-based Genetic Algorithm to support QoS Multicast Routing
15	QMOST [26]	QoS-aware Multicast Overlay Spanning Tree
16	LACMQR [28]	Location-based multicast routing for mobile ad hoc networks
17	AQM [29,45]	Ad Hoc QoS Multicasting
18	M-CAMP [30]	Call-Admission Multicast Protocol for MANETs
19	MCEDAR [31]	Multicast Core-Extraction Distributed Ad Hoc Routing
20	QoS-MAODV [32]	QoS–Multicast Ad Hoc On-Demand Distance Vector Routing
21	HQMGA [33]	Hierarchical QoS Multicast routing using GA in MANET
22	QMR [44]	QoS Multicast Routing Protocol
23	EGA [35]	A Genetic Algorithm for Energy-Efficient Based Multicast Routing on MANETs
24	SEQMRAN [36]	Secure Efficient QoS Multicast Route Discovery for MANETs
25	FQM [37]	Framework for QoS Multicast
26	ODQMM [38]	On-Demand QoS Multicast for MANETs
27	MACO [41]	Ant Colony Algorithm Based on Orientation Factor for QoS Multicast
28	AMOMQ [42]	Ad-hoc Mesh-based On-demand Multicast Routing Protocol with Quality of Service Support
29	QoS-MAODV-2Lqos [43]	QoS Constrained Multicast Routing For Mobile Ad Hoc Networks
30	HTQ* [50]	Hexagonal-tree TDMA-based QoS multicast protocol (This protocol was not named by the authors. We call it HTQ)
31	QMMRP [51]	QoS Multilayered Multicast Routing Protocol

1.1. Design Space for QoS Multicast

QoS multicast in ad hoc networks represents specializations of regular data communication. All of these specializations require specific elements in order to address the added requirements. Our main focus is on the QoS aspects, and therefore the elements that are needed to provide QoS in multicast ad hoc environments.

Providing QoS in ad hoc networks has additional challenges due to the wireless medium and the mobility of nodes. The wireless medium itself induces errors and packets are lost as part of the normal operating context. Often the MAC layer offers a shared common channel for nodes in the vicinity of each other. In addition, the interference range of a transmission may be larger than the transmission range. The available resources and the probability of a successful transmission therefore may depend on the details of the topology and the traffic load at neighboring nodes.

1.2. Context

Traditionally, multicast distributions have been classified in terms of structure, either tree or mesh. They were also classified according to how the sources in a multicast group share the multicast distribution; whether it is one per source (source specific) or a common one for all sources (shared tree or mesh). A tree *versus* a mesh is a tradeoff between availability, robustness, and resources consumed. Redundant paths in mesh structure result in higher availability and more robustness. An inherent advantage of shared structures is that no separate mechanism is needed for source discovery. As long as receivers are connected to the common structure, they will receive packets from all sources. With a source specific distribution mechanism, receivers must have some method of discovering the sources within a multicast group. In principle, a directory based solution is possible, ad hoc networks will typically use broadcasting for source announcement. Source specific tree/mesh has the potential for being more efficient (fewer hops between a source and the receivers).

The type of distribution mechanisms affects how resource reservation and admission control is handled. In a shared tree/mesh, without QoS, a new source needs only to find the shortest path to the shared tree. However, in a QoS setting, a source must try to be admitted by all relaying nodes in a shared structure. Shared structures also allow different styles of resource reservation. The reservation can be per source or be shared. The latter is typically exemplified by voice conferences in which participants seldom talk simultaneously. They can therefore share the same reservation, and in this situation a reservation per participant would be a waste of resources. This concept is formalized in the resource usage filter defined in Resource ReSerVation Protocol (RSVP) [55]. Most protocols based on a shared tree use shared reservation style [29,32,43]. Only the protocol ODQMM [38] utilizes both types of reservations, shared and source specific reservation.

1.3. Necessary Elements for QoS Multicast

The functionality of the various protocols can be isolated to a few common elements, namely QoS routing, call admission, resource estimation, resource reservation, and preemption. We will explain in detail these elements in Section 2. Although, the survey describes them sequentially, these elements cannot be organized into a fixed sequence. Different protocols will order them differently or combine several of them into one operation. For example, many of the protocols based on reactive multicast routing combine QoS routing, resource reservation, and call admission.

All the schemes need to identify potential segments of a distribution tree that may have resources or capabilities sufficient to meet the requirements (QoS routing). The segments will be used to search for the best path that can admit the session or admit the combination of session and source. If there is at least one potential segment, admission control determines whether source, relaying node or receiver can be connected to the distribution mechanism. Relaying nodes may occupy part of the resources in neighboring nodes, therefore the impact which relaying nodes make on other relay nodes, sources or groups must be assessed.

Depending on the forwarding model, resources may be reserved on a per source or per multicast group. We make the distinction between admission control and resource reservation although these elements are combined in several protocols; admission control is implicit when resource reservation is successful. However, the resource reservation is not necessary. It is sufficient to assess whether a new source or relay does not have a decremental impact on existing sources and/or relays. Admission control and resource reservation are not alternative elements; the mesh based protocols tend to separate the two [11,15,16,18,37,42]. They will admit sources and relays, but the resource reservation will only be done for a subset of the relay nodes [11,15,16,18,37,42].

Both admission control and resource reservation rely on the estimation of available resources and the estimation of required resources (consumed resource estimation). The complexity of the estimation depends on the capabilities of underlying MAC and physical layer.

The last necessary element is preemption. In a wireless ad hoc network all resources are stochastic entities. Random changes in the conditions of the radio channel or movement and changes in topology may affect the capacity. Earlier admission decisions may therefore result in oversubscription. The oversubscribed traffic must then be rejected or their reserved resources must be released. An explicit part of preemption is monitoring QoS or resource availability. Few protocols have implemented explicit preemption. Instead, preemption is performed as periodic admission control and resource reservation.

1.4. Multicast Model

The original wireline multicast protocols were based on a stringent multicast model. According to this model, a source could send data packets to multicast group without being part of the group, a sender should not need to know the address and identity of the receivers, and any receiver or source could join and leave the group dynamically. The multicast model defines the expectations applications will have to the distribution mechanism and it therefore imposes restrictions on the design space of the QoS multicast protocols. A protocol that does not adhere to the model can have a simpler design and potentially be more efficient. However, the applications may be more complex or costly to develop. The applications must either be tailor-made for the particular protocol, or an additional adaptation layer must be developed.

The QoS requirement for multicast may change the semantics of multicast when there are multiple sources per group. In a non-QoS setting, all receivers in a multicast group receive information from all sources as long as the network is not partitioned. Adding QoS implies that potentially there may not be enough resources on a logical link. The admission to these bottleneck links will depend on the sequence sources and receivers joining the group. If we assume admission control is used, it is then not given that all receivers will get information from the same set of sources. Translated into a video conference setting, there is a risk that the participants do not have the same view of the other participants. A shared distribution mechanism has the same potential problem for inconsistent admission control.

For shared trees, resources can be reserved either as shared or source specific. If the resources are shared by all sources, there is no difference between the semantics for QoS and non-QoS. The admission control is then whether a receiver or source can use the path to the tree. The reservation will not be performed in the rest of the tree. The result is that a source is either connected to all receivers or to none. Likewise, a receiver is connected either to all sources or to none. This is equivalent to whether a path exists in the non-QoS case. However, a shared resource reservation between multiple sources has a limited applicability for offering QoS. The exception is when the application imposes a strict ordering of when the sources use the resources, like voice in a conference.

To preserve the multicast semantics, admission control should be limited to whether a source or receivers should be allowed to join with given QoS requirements or to join without any requirements. To our knowledge the interaction between admission control/resource reservation and the group semantics has been discussed only to a limited degree.

There is a close relationship among the semantics of the admission control, adherence to the multicast model, the type of resource reservation/QoS offered, and the complexity of the protocols. The lack of adherence to the multicast model also indicates the potential need for special design of multicast enabled applications. As shown in Table 2 (see Appendix), many of the protocols do not appear to be designed in accordance with the multicast model.

2. MECHANISMS SPECIFIC TO QOS AND MULTICAST IN AD HOC NETWORKS

2.1. Mechanisms for Multicast Routing

Table 2 summarizes the characteristics of the 31 protocols for QoS multicast in ad hoc networks included in our survey. It provides comparison between protocols in term of routing scheme, multicast distribution type, whether adherence multicast model, tree/mesh initiation, type of admission control, type of reservation according to class and flow, type of reservation according to state, QoS constraints, MAC sublayer, tree maintenance scheme, and resource estimation technique. It also provides comparison between protocols in term of the presence or absence of the resource estimation technique.

2.1.1. Routing Type

The routing decision can be made centrally or distributively among all nodes. In a distributed scheme, all nodes take part in the routing process and determine the multicast tree/mesh structure. Typically, a request-reply process is performed to select multicast routes. The source floods a route request. Intermediate nodes make the decision of whether to forward the route request or discard it. A route reply is sent by the receiver and forwarded to the source. When an intermediate node receives the route reply, it is a confirmation that the node is part of the tree/mesh for the multicast group. Otherwise any state the node is in will time out. Protocols in [15,19,29,32,38] are examples of schemes using the distributed approach.

Table 2

No.	Protocol	Routing Scheme	Multicast Distribution	Adherence Multicast Model	Type of Admission Control	Type of Reservation (class, flow)	Type of Reservation (state)	QoS Constraints	MAC Sublayer	Tree/Mesh Maintenance	Estimating Resource	Resource Estimation Technique	Failure Handling	Group Formation	Group Teardown
1	QAMNet [11]	Reactive	Mesh	Yes	Intermediate	Per class	N/A	B	802.11	Soft	Yes	ConserRate	Soft	Source	Soft
2	CQMRP [12]	Hybrid	SST	No	Intermediate	Per flow	Hard	B,D,J,Buf	Any	Hard	No	–	Local	Source	–
3	QMRPCAH [13]	Hybrid	SST	No	Intermediate	Per flow	Soft	B,D	MACA	Hard	No	–	Global	Reveiver	–
4	HVDB [14]	Hybrid	SST	Yes	Intermediate	–	–	B,D	Any	Hard	No	–	Backup	Source	–
5	QoS-ODMRP [15]	Reactive	Mesh	Yes	Intermediate	Per flow	Soft	B	802.11	Soft	Yes	RateSum	Soft	Source	Soft
6	E-QMR [16]	Reactive	Mesh	Yes	Intermediate	Hybrid	Soft	B	802.11	Soft	Yes	Listening	Soft	Source	Soft
7	Hu [17]	Reactive	SST	No	Source	Per flow	Hard	B	802.11	Hard	Yes	Exchange	Global	Source	–
8	QMRP [18]	Reactive	Mesh	Yes	Intermediate	–	–	B	802.11	Soft+Hard	Yes	Exchange	Soft+Local	Source	Soft
9	QoS-AODV [19]	Reactive	ST	Yes	Intermediate	–	–	D	Any	Soft	Yes	ExBwRE	Soft	Receiver	Soft
10	HQMRP [21]	Hybrid	SST	No	Intermediate	–	–	B	TDMA	Hard	No	–	Local	Source	–
11	QoS-MEM [22]	Reactive	SST	Yes	Source	Per flow	Hard	B	TDMA	Hard	Yes	Timeslot	–	Source	–
12	LTM* [23]	Hybrid	Any	Yes	Intermediate	Per flow	Soft	B	CDMA over TDMA	Soft	Yes	Timeslot	Soft	Source	Soft
13	MPT* [24]	Reactive	SST	No	Source	Per flow	Hard	B	CDMA over TDMA	Hard	Yes	Timeslot	Global	Source	–
14	EQMGA [25]	Proactive	SST	No	Source	–	–	B	Any	Hard	No	–	–	Source	–
15	QMOST [26]	Hybrid	ST	No	Source	Per flow	Soft+hard	B	802.11	Hard	No	–	Global	Source	–
16	LACMQR [28]	Hybrid	SST	Yes	Intermediate	–	–	B	Any	Hard	No	–	–	Source	–
17	AQM [29]	Reactive	ST	Yes	Intermediate	Per flow	Hard	B	Any	Hard	Yes	Exchange	Global	Receiver	SI

18	M-CAMP [30]	Reactive	Any kind	No	Receiver	N/A	N/A	B	Any	Any	Yes	Probing	Local	Any kind	–
19	MCEDAR [31]	Proactive	Hybrid	Yes	Intermediate	–	–	B	MACAW	Soft	No	–	Soft	Common core	Soft
20	QoS-MAODV [32]	Reactive	ST	Yes	Intermediate	Per flow	Soft	B	802.11	Soft	Yes	RateSum	Soft	Receiver	Soft
21	HQMGA [33]	Proactive	SST	Yes	Intermediate	–	–	B,D	802.11	Hard	No	–	–	Source	–
22	QMR [44]	Reactive	Mesh	Yes	Intermediate	Hybrid	Soft	B	802.11	Soft	Yes	–	Soft	Source	Soft
23	EGA [35]	Proactive	SST	Yes	Intermediate	–	–	D,C	Any	Hard	Yes	ExBwRE	–	Source	–
24	SEQMRAN [36]	Reactive	ST	Yes	Intermediate	–	–	B,D,J	802.11	Hard	No	–	–	Source	–
25	FQM [37]	Reactive	Mesh	Yes	Intermediate	Hybrid	Soft	B	802.11	Soft	Yes	Listening	Soft	Source	Soft
26	ODQMM [38]	Reactive	ST	Yes	Intermediate	Per flow	Hard	B	TDMA	Hard	No	–	Local	Receiver	–
27	MACO [41]	Proactive	SST	No	Source	–	–	B,D,J	Any	Hard	No	–	–	Source	–
28	AMOMQ [42]	Reactive	Mesh	Yes	Intermediate	Per flow	Soft	B	802.11	Soft	Yes	RateSum	Soft	Source	Soft
29	QoS-MAODV-2Lqos [43]	Reactive	ST	Yes	Intermediate	Per class	N/A	B,D,Buf,S	802.11	Soft	Yes	ExBwRE	Soft	Receiver	Soft
30	HTQ [50]	Reactive	Any	Yes	Intermediate	Per flow	Hard	B	TDMA	Hard	Yes	Timeslot	Backup	Source	–
31	QMMRP [51]	Reactive	SST	Yes	Source	Per flow	Hard	B	CDMA over TDMA	Hard	Yes	Timeslot	Local	Source	–

Notes:

- Multicast distribution type: ST—Shared tree; SST—Source specific tree; Hybrid (reactive + proactive or geographical + proactive)
- Type of admission control (AC): Source—Source AC, Receiver—Receiver AC, Intermediate—Intermediate node AC
- (–): there is lack of information about the characteristic in simulation of the protocol
- N/A—No Apply
- QoS constraints: B—Bandwidth; D—Delay; J—Jitter; Buf—Buffer capacity level; ST—Stream latency; SR—Stream resolution; SC—Stream continuity; S—Stability
- MAC sublayer: Any—the protocol can be applied to any kind of MAC sublayer
- Resource estimation technique: ConserRate—This technique is based on conservative rate and current traffic rate; RateSum—Rate summaration; Listening—Medium listening; Timeslot—Determining free timeslots and scheduling; Probing—End-to-end probing; Exchange—Bandwidth usage exchanging; ExBwRE—Technique for estimation of other resources than bandwidth
- Failure handling: Soft—soft handling; Local—hard handling and local recovery; Global—hard handling and global recovery; Backup—Backup path switching
- Group formation: Source—source initiation; Receiver—receiver initiation; Common core—common node initiation
- Group teardown: SI—Session is terminated by a session initiato

In the central method, the source (or a dedicated node) collects the topology and resource information from the network and computes the multicast tree/mesh. The next step is to distribute the calculated multicast tree/mesh topology to other nodes.

The central decided routing is used in [17,24,25,41]. The protocol proposed by Hu [17] is designed to correctly estimate interference between different flows. Therefore, all routes satisfying the QoS requirement must concurrently be determined by the source. In MPT [24], the source first discovers the topology, it then uses available bandwidth information of the links in topology to select the multicast routes. The protocol EQMGA [25] uses an entropy-based genetic algorithm to support QoS multicast routing. Here the entropy metric is computed based on the direction and the speed of the nodes and its neighbors. The protocol MACO [41] proposes a biology based ant algorithm where the direction towards the destination is determined by a heuristic method based on location.

In ad hoc networks the topology and resource information changes quite frequently. As a result, the resource information and the calculation of the multicast tree/mesh may be outdated in centralized schemes. The majority of the proposed schemes is therefore based on the distributed approach.

2.1.2. Routing Scheme

The routing scheme reflects the basic ad hoc routing schemes, namely proactive, reactive, geographic routing, and hybrid approach. Among these three types, reactive and hybrid approaches form the majority.

Only two protocols in [31,33] use a proactive approach. In these schemes, the routes to the destinations are maintained in the multicast table of each node. Since the source is aware of the topology (or part of topology) of the network, the multicast routes can be computed immediately. The routing table at each node is updated periodically. MCEDAR [31] is an extension of the CEDAR unicast protocol, where a backbone is established and maintained as the basis for all forwardings. The protocol HQMGA [33] divides the network into clusters and computes a tree for each cluster as well as a tree connecting all clusters. The trees are calculated by a genetic algorithm.

In the reactive approach, the nodes do not collect topology information in advance. Whenever a source or receiver joins a multicast group, join requests are flooded and the possible alternatives are unicast to the initiator from existing member of the multicast group. Reactive routing reduces the overhead at the expense of delay and broadcasting traffic to identify possible paths. There is a close resemblance between the dynamic signaling of joining and leaving groups and the reactive methods used for multicast routing. The two processes can therefore easily be combined. This might be the reason for a fair number of proposals based on reactive routing such as schemes in [11,15,16,18,32].

In geographic routing, packets are routed based on the location of nodes. With only local information, packets can be forwarded to the node that is closest to the destination. Route discovery and maintenance are then not needed. For multicast, geographic routing is used whenever applications require geographic coverage like requesting a target for a specific location. None of the protocols in the survey is solely based on geographic routing. However, two hybrid protocols in [14,28] combine proactive and geographic routing.

The hybrid approach combines the reactive and the proactive approach or combines the geographical and proactive approach. In [12,13,21], the network is divided into clusters. Each cluster has a cluster head which proactively maintains the local cluster topology. Reactive protocols are used to build the multicast tree/mesh between clusters. The clusters can be formed based on the geographical location of nodes, connectivity, signal range, mobility, or relative location between nodes. CQMRP [12] uses a self-terminating algorithm to build clusters. In LTM [23], the local link-state information is collected periodically for each node to identify the lantern which has one or more sub-paths existing between two nodes. The lantern-tree or multicast tree is then constructed reactively. The protocol QMOST [26] relies on a QoS unicast link state protocol (like QOLSR [56]). The overlay multicast tree is built actively after the source has all the necessary topology information. Two hybrid protocols in [14,28] combine proactive and geographic routing. LACMQR [28] is based on a distributed cluster-based QoS multicast routing algorithm. It requires maintaining the local state at each node. The location information provided by the positioning device is used to discover and maintain routes. HVDB [14] also divides the network into clusters and uses the mobility prediction and location-based clustering technique to form stable clusters. The forwarding between logical nodes is done by a location-based unicast routing algorithm.

If the number of receivers is high and the receivers are well distributed, it is not given that separate multicast trees/mesh is needed. It might be more efficient to broadcast the information to all nodes. The overhead could be lower if the broadcast is done efficiently. One example is Simplified Multicast Forwarding (SMF) [34]. SMF may utilize the Multi Point Relay nodes (MPR) of OLSR [49]. If SMF is combined with admission control and preemption, as suggested in [46], it may be considered QoS multicast routing. However, it would only be suited in context where most nodes are receivers.

2.1.3. Multicast Distribution Mechanisms

There are two types of distribution mechanisms, tree and mesh. With a tree structure, each node is associated with one parent that forwards packets. In a mesh, there might be alternative paths and a node can have multiple parents. A relaying node forwards a packet once regardless of who it was received from. A mesh can either be guaranteed or probabilistic. In a guaranteed mesh, a node has multiple nodes that forward packets to it. In a probabilistic mesh, the number of parents depends on the location of the receivers. All of the mesh protocols surveyed are probabilistic. Mesh structures are more robust. However they may consume more resources and the resource reservation mechanism becomes more complex.

2.2. Mechanisms for Providing Multiple QoS Constraints

Common QoS metrics used in the QoS enable multicast protocols include available bandwidth, end-to-end delay, probability of packet loss, delay variance (jitter), life time, and link reliability. Multi-constraints QoS multicast routing can be seen as the problem of solving a multi-constraints Steiner tree. It has been shown to be a NP-Complete problem, and heuristic approaches are usually used to solve the problem. This section outlines the existing proposals dealing with the multiple-constraints QoS problem.

In order to meet requirements (constraints) of applications, routing protocols must use QoS metrics to find QoS satisfied paths. While the number of hops is usually used for selecting routes in none-QoS routing, various metrics reflecting different application requirements are used for QoS routing. Note that QoS metrics used for selecting routes is not necessarily the same as QoS constraints. For example, stability metric can be used for selecting routes to meet the bandwidth requirement of applications. Metrics for selecting QoS paths can be classified into three categories, namely additive, multiplicative, and concave (minimum) properties. With additive metric, QoS of the whole path equals to aggregation QoS metrics of all links along the path. With multiplicative metric, QoS metric of the whole path equals to the product of QoS metrics of all links along the path. With concave metric, QoS metric of the whole path equals to the minimum QoS metrics of all links along the path. Delay, jitter, and cost are examples of additive metrics; packet loss ratio and link reliability are examples of multiplicative metrics; while available bandwidth is an example of concave metric.

The mechanisms for dealing with multiple QoS constraints can be classified into two categories, the constructed metric technique and independent metric technique. Both techniques will be described in detail in the following subsections.

2.2.1. Constructed Metric Technique

With this technique, the protocols use accumulated constructed metric, which is a function of other metrics such as bandwidth and delay, to prioritize the various path segments.

The protocol LACMQR [28] is an example. The constructed metric is a function of several metrics (e.g., delay and cost). When an intermediate node receives a probe packet, it calculates the value of constructed metric of this probe packet. If the value of constructed metric of the new probe is better than that of the previous probe, the node changes its predecessor to the node that forwarded the new probe packet. As a better path has been found, the probe will be forwarded; otherwise, the probe packet is discarded.

2.2.2. Independent Metric Technique

An alternative is to consider multiple metrics independently and only path segments that can satisfy all requirements are considered. Generally, all paths satisfying the QoS constraints are selected first. The next step is to apply an evaluation function, based on the other metrics, to select the best path, for building the multicast tree/mesh. The evaluation function is usually the function of some parameters such as cost of tree, tree stability. The protocols in [12,13,14,26,33,35,41,43] use this type of technique.

In CQMRP [12], the four parameters considered are bandwidth, delay, jitter, and buffer capacity. An intermediate node will forward a request packet (which is sent from source) if the following conditions are satisfied: its available bandwidth is greater than the required bandwidth, the transmission delay and delay variations is less than an allowed delay, and the buffer level is higher than a threshold. This protocol does not use an evaluation function.

QMRPCAH [13] uses delay, bandwidth, jitter, and packet loss metrics. However, the authors mainly considered the delay and bandwidth QoS constraints. In this protocol, the links that violate the bandwidth constraint will first be deleted. Then routing process uses a cost function of link delay to decide the multicast routes.

The protocol HQMGA [33] finds a multicast tree which satisfies the constraints (bandwidth and delay) and maximizes the value of an evaluation function. The evaluation function is a function of tree stability, latency, and the number of nodes that can receive the data stream.

Protocol EGA [35] considers two QoS constraints: propagation delay and residual battery energy. The propagation delay is used for building the multicast tree. The maximum lifetime of the multicast tree is defined based on a function of the total residual battery energy in the multicast tree. The protocol MACO [41] uses a modified biology inspired algorithm for multicast routing. Multiple multicast trees, where the links satisfying bandwidth, delay, and jitter constraints, are found; then the best multicast tree is selected based on the value of cost function of these trees.

In QoS-MAODV-2Lqos [43], QoS constraints are delay, throughput, and cost. Metrics considered for selecting the paths are end-to-end delay, bandwidth, power level, buffer level, stability level, and hop count. The power level is acquired from MAC layer. It indicates the availability of current amount of battery. The buffer level is used to present the available unallocated buffer. Stability level is defined as the connectivity variance of a node with respect to its neighboring nodes over time. The protocol provides services for three classes of applications: the delay sensitive application, throughput constraint application, and best effort application. When receiving the request from source, the receiver selects the path based on QoS class and QoS state, which are included in the request, and sends a reply packet forward to the source. When the source receives the reply packet, the stability metric followed by power level is used to select the path.

2.3. Mechanisms for Admission Control

Admission control is simple mechanism with few design choices. The decision is either to accept or reject connections of a source or a receiver to a distribution tree/mesh. One design choice is the location where admission control is made: at the source, at the receiver, or at intermediate nodes.

With admission control at an intermediate node, each node on a path checks whether it has sufficient resources to accept the multicast flow. Typically, a new source initiates a route request to establish a multicast route to its receivers. Each intermediate node checks if it has sufficient resources to meet the QoS requirements (typically available bandwidth). If so, the node forwards the route request; otherwise, the route request is discarded. The destinations therefore only receive route requests along one or more paths that have sufficient resources. The reply is sent along one of these paths back to the source. The return packets are typically used to confirm the admission control and the associated resource reservation. The actual path to select must then be confirmed in a three way handshake. Most of the protocols use this technique, for instance, protocols in [12,15,16,24,29].

Admission control can also be done at the receivers. M-CAMP [20] performs admission control by end-to-end probing. The source initiates probes, and the receivers can then determine whether to admit the flow. Probe packets are used to measure the quality of the path from the source to the destination. When the destination receives the probe packets, it measures the quality of the probe packet and compares to the known QoS requirements. If the quality of the probe packets is satisfied, the receiver accepts the session; otherwise, the session is rejected. The receiver then sends its decision to the source.

Finally, admission control can be performed at the source. The source calculates the QoS satisfied paths to all the destinations while building a multicast tree. Once a tree with the necessary resources has been identified, all nodes involved are informed of the multicast structure and the source admits itself to the single source tree. Protocols in [17,24,25,26,41,51,22] use this type of admission control.

The advantage and the cost of a particular admission control must be seen in close conjunction with the resource reservation. Admission control at intermediate nodes along potential paths may result in resource reservations that will not be used. Admission control at source or a centralized node may be based on outdated information, but offer more precise resource reservation in terms of nodes involved.

2.4. Mechanisms for Resource Reservation/Release

To achieve QoS, resources must be reserved, either explicitly or implicitly. In implicit resource reservation, the system is viewed as a black box and the number of flows into the system is restricted to those that can achieve the target QoS. There are no resources associated with a particular flow. When a new source or receiver is to be admitted into the system, end-to-end probing is used to determine whether the resulting QoS is acceptable. M-CAMP [30] is an example of a protocol using implicit reservation. With explicit resource reservation, each node associates resources to a particular source or a multicast group. Transmission bandwidth is the limiting resource and therefore the resource reserved. Most of the protocols use explicit reservation.

As mentioned in the description part of the routing methods, many protocols explore alternative paths. If the admission control is performed at intermediate nodes, resource reservation must also be done in conjunction with the admission control. In both cases, there is a likelihood that an allocated reservation is not being used. It may be on a path that is not selected, or a node downstream might reject the join request. Many protocols therefore divide the reservation into stages, like "possible", "likely", and a final commit stage when it is determined that packets will actually flow through the node [15,16,30,42]. This ensures that resources are not unnecessarily blocked. The protocol QoS-ODMPR [15] uses three states (explored, registered, and reserved) for resource reservation. The path discovery process reserves "explored" resources. The response back from the receivers changes the state of the selected forwarding nodes to "registered". Only when traffic actual flows through the node, the reservation state changes to "reserved". Similarly, E-QMR [16] uses three states called free, allocate, and reserved.

It is a policy issue if the sum of the resource reservation in the various stages can be more than the total resources. If most reservations are not committed, oversubscription could be beneficial to avoid unnecessary blocking. The final commit stage ensures that the sum of reserved resources is within acceptable limits. To our knowledge, this policy consideration has not been explored.

The location of the resource reservation is a design choice that depends on the underlying MAC protocol. With a shared access, a node's transmissions will affect the available capacity at neighboring nodes. Two neighboring nodes may not have the same interference patterns and will therefore not necessarily have the same available bandwidth. It is therefore not given that free resources at a node also are free at the neighboring nodes. The protocols only perform reservation at the nodes in the forwarding path. However, the resource estimation may consider the impact of reservation at other nodes, for example in Hu [17]. However, this will not reflect the impact of reserving resources at the node on flows forwarded from other nodes.

As discussed in the Introduction section, there are two types of reservation for shared tree/mesh, namely a shared reservation, which is common for all sources, and a source specific reservation. A shared resource reservation reflects applications where only one source is active. A typical case is voice conferences. One protocol, ODQMM [38], offers both types and with different protocol functions. Reservation for the shared resources only travels to the existing distribution tree, while source specific travels to all nodes in the distribution tree. Several of the protocols do not make this distinction and one must infer the type based on how far the reservation travels in the distribution tree/mesh.

Figure 1(a) illustrates the classification of resource reservation/release mechanisms of QoS enable multicast protocols in ad hoc networks.

Figure 1(b) illustrates the types of reservation/release mechanisms for shared tree/mesh.

If there are multiple sources in a multicast group, source specific resource reservation and thereby admission control may result in that the receivers are not connected to the same set of sources. From an application viewpoint this may not be acceptable. The third alternative is represented by most of the mesh protocols, for example QAMNet [11]. They have source specific reservation along the primary paths, additional forwarders schedule the packets without any guarantees. Thereby they preserve the connection semantics of the non-QoS multicast, all sources will connect to the same subset of receivers. However, the quality may vary. This could be generalized into protocols without admission control, but with resource reservation. All sources and receivers are admitted. If there are enough resources on the selected path, the necessary resources are reserved. Otherwise the source or receivers are connected as best effort [16].

Reservation implies state. Traditionally, state is classified into soft sate and hard state. Hard states is maintained through explicit set up and tear down, while soft state is maintained with explicit and periodic set up and timer based tear down. Most of the protocols in the survey use soft state, since this is well suited for the dynamic topology and the dynamic membership of multicast groups. CQMRP [12] and AQM [29] use hard state for reserving resource. In CQMRP [12], a QoS-error notification message is sent out when the link break occurs. The node will release the reserved resources for the multicast group at the time it receives a QoS-error message. Also, during connection termination, the reserved resources are released by sending explicit resource release message. In AQM [29], a session is started and closed by a session initiator with the initiation message and the termination message, respectively. Additionally, a node informs its forwarders on the multicast graph when leaving a session by sending a leave message. Upon receiving the session termination message sent by the initiator, the forwarder frees the allocated resource.

Reservation mechanisms can also be classified into three types: per-flow reservation (IntServ), per-class reservation (DiffServ), and hybrid reservation (IntServ over DiffServ). In the per-flow reservation method, resources are reserved for certain flows or sources. It follows the IntServ model. Most of protocols use this kind of reservation, e.g., [12,15,16,30,38,42]. The DiffServ model is used by protocols in [11,43]. With this technique, there is no flow reservation and the reservation is implicit. The hybrid reservation used in [16,37] combines some features from both IntServ and DiffServ. In these protocols, the bandwidth is partitioned into fix reservation for accepted sources and shared reservation for other sources. The forwarding node provides IntServ and reserves bandwidth for every source that has been accepted. It provides DiffServ when it receives data packets from rejected sources or best-effort traffic and it has available bandwidth.

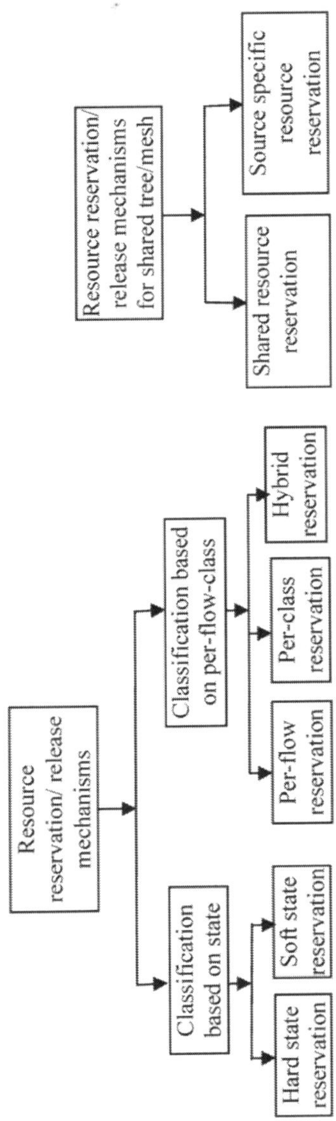

Figure 1. (a, left) Classification of resource reservation/release mechanisms of QoS enable multicast protocols in ad hoc networks; (b, right) Classification of resource reservation/release mechanisms for shared tree/mesh.

2.5. Mechanisms for Resource Estimation

Both admission control and resource reservation depend on resource estimation. The resource estimation for bandwidth depends on the type of MAC layer. In addition, some of the protocols also estimate other resources such as delay, buffer level, and power level. The resource estimation mechanisms are therefore divided into methods for estimation of bandwidth in contention-free MAC, methods for estimation of bandwidth in contention MAC, and methods for estimation of resources other than bandwidth.

2.5.1. Mechanisms for Estimation of Bandwidth in Contention-free MAC Ad Hoc Networks

The protocols in the survey use two types of contention-free MAC sub-layer, TDMA (Time Division Multiple Access) and CDMA-over TDMA. The CDMA (Code Division Multiple Access) system employs spread-spectrum technology and a special coding scheme to allow multiple users to be multiplexed over the same physical channel. CDMA can be overlaid on top of the TDMA infrastructure. In other words, multiple sessions can share the same TDMA slot via CDMA. In CDMA-over TDMA, the use of a time slot on a link only depends on the status of its one-hop neighboring links.

Four protocols in [21,22,38,50] use TDMA while two protocols in [23,24] use CDMA-over TDMA for their sublayer. Protocols in [21,38] assume that the available bandwidth of a link is available from the underlying layers. QoS-MEM [22] uses bandwidth-constrained multicast tree to formulate the QoS-aware Minimum Energy Multicast problem as a Mixed Integer Linear Programming model in a TDMA-based ad hoc network. A suitable scheduling of free slots for each link of the multicast tree can be obtained from this model. In [50], both the hidden-terminal and exposed-terminal problems are taken into consideration in order to possibly exploit the time-slot reuse capability. The hexagonal-based scheme offers a higher success rate for constructing a QoS multicast tree due to the use of the hexagonal-tree structure. A hexagonal-tree is a tree whose sub-path is a hexagonal-path, which is a special two-path structure.

In [23], timeslot reservation is used as a primitive operation for constructing the lantern-path and lantern-tree. The lantern is identified after collecting the local link-state information for all nodes. The lantern-tree then is constructed by the lantern-path search operation and the lantern-tree construction operation. The timeslot assignment algorithm on a path in [24] follows the method proposed in [48]. In this protocol, the available bandwidth of a link is the number of free timeslots over the link. The available bandwidth of a path is the minimum bandwidth of the links along the path. The available bandwidth of a tree is the minimum bandwidth of the paths on the tree.

2.5.2. Mechanisms for Estimation of Bandwidth in Contention-based MAC Ad Hoc Networks

With contention-based MAC, the actual resource can either be direct or indirect of the type "is there enough available resources?". The direct estimation is a hard problem when the wireless channel uses a multiple access scheme. Transmissions from a node may block or interfere with transmissions from other nodes. Correct estimation therefore depends on full topology information and detailed knowledge of interference and transmission range for each node. Indirect estimation is based on end-to-end probing. Here the state of the network is not needed. Instead, the available resources are estimated based on whether the requesting node could be added with acceptable QoS for the information flow.

2.5.2.1. Direct Estimation

The bandwidth estimation in contention-based MAC ad hoc networks must incorporate four factors: available resource estimation, transmission resources consumed by transmitting a flow along a chain of nodes, interference between different branches in the multicast tree/mesh, and interference between different flows.

The bandwidth consumed by a requesting flow at a relaying node is different from the requested minimum bandwidth of the flow, since the relaying will block neighboring nodes from transmitting. Define r as the flow rate measured in Bytes per sec. A relaying node will therefore occupy $h * r$, where h is a function of topology and radio. In unicast, h will typically be between 2 and 7, depending on topology and the ratio between sensing and transmission range [54]. In multicast, the branching at a relaying node may increase the factor even further. In a simplistic case, where the transmission range equals the sensing range, the total capacity consumed at the forwarding node for k branches would be $(2 + k)*r$. A receiving node connecting to an existing relay node does not consume resources. This illustrates that estimation of bandwidth consumed must be different for a source node, a relaying node, and a receiver that is not relaying.

So far, the examples have been formulated as interferences along a path from packets in the same flow. However, transmission of neighboring nodes will affect the available capacity of a node. Hu [17] classified the interference into two groups, interferences from different branches of the same multicast tree/mesh (the hidden multicast route problem) and interference from unicast of another multicast traffic (the hidden route problem).

The available bandwidth needs to be estimated. Three different methods can be identified: information exchange between the nodes, listening on the MAC layer, and summation of rates. The latter neglects any of the effects discussed in the previous paragraphs, and it is therefore not suited for contention based MAC layers.

In addition, 12 protocols do not estimate resource. They assume that the information about resource is available from lower layers. The different methods can be summarized by:

- Bandwidth usage exchanging—In this technique, the information for the metric is gathered by exchanging information of current bandwidth usage of existing session to its neighbor nodes. Protocols in [29,17,18] belong to this category.

In AQM [29], each node sends its current bandwidth usage to its one-hop neighbors. It calculates its available bandwidth based on information received from its one-hop neighbors. The maximum bandwidth capacity of the node is acquired by the MAC layer. The residual bandwidth of the node is computed by subtracting the bandwidth usage of the node and all its neighbors from the maximum bandwidth. Hu [17] also uses this technique to compute available bandwidth.

Each node in QMRP [18] collects bandwidth usage information of its one-hop neighbors and two-hop neighbors by periodically broadcast hello messages. A hello message contains bandwidth usage of the sender and of its one-hop neighbors. When a node receives a hello message, it knows its first and second neighbors and their bandwidth usages. Then the residual bandwidth is computed as the difference between raw channel bandwidth and total bandwidth usage (accumulation of bandwidth usage of the node and its first and second neighbors) divided by a weight factor.

- Medium listening—In this method, a node estimates the available bandwidth by observing the traffic coming in and going out of a node. Each node listens to the channel to determine the channel status (idle or busy) and compute the idle duration for a period of time. In [16,37], the available bandwidth is computed as $T_i/t * BW$, where T_i is the total idle time, t is observation time, BW and is the raw channel bandwidth. However, the above estimation techniques are imprecise because they do not account for packet overhead and coding rates. The advantage is low control overhead. The node, however, cannot release the bandwidth immediately when a route breaks [52] since it does not associate resources with flows.

- Rate summation—In [15,32,42] the capacity is estimated as the difference between the raw rate and the sum of rate of the flows through the nodes. The bandwidth between the node and its neighbor is just obtained by recording the rate through the node.

Figure 2 presents the classification of available resource estimation mechanisms of QoS enable multicast protocols in our survey.

In IEEE 802.11, the carrier sense range is usually more than twice transmission range (the default ratio between these parameters is often 2.2 [47]). Therefore, the transmission of k-hop neighbor nodes (where k is more than two) must be considered. None of protocols in surveyed papers considers the transmission of more than two hop neighbor nodes when estimating available bandwidth. Only one protocol, QMRP [18], considers transmission of two-hop neighbor nodes; two protocols, Hu [17] and AQM [29], take into account transmission of one-hop neighbor nodes.

In networks with a common channel with multiple accesses, the hidden node problem may cause packet collisions. QoS implies stricter boundaries on the packet jitter at each node. The more synchronized multicast is, the higher is the likelihood of packet collision due to hidden node problems. None of the protocols in the survey have investigated this effect.

An additional concern is that available capacity is not the same as usable capacity. If the capacity is utilized to the maximum, the delay might not be acceptable in systems with contention-based MAC. Ideally, protocols should estimate the threshold load that results in a not acceptable delay. This is different from the total capacity. In QAMNet [11], a conservative rate is used instead of the threshold rate. Then the available bandwidth of a node is the difference between the conservative admission control rate and the current rate of the real-time traffic. However, this protocol does not consider any method to obtain this conservative admission control rate, which is still difficult to obtain.

In the previous paragraphs, we have argued that resource estimation requires detailed knowledge of topology and transmission, interference, and carrier sense range. There is a continuous improvement in resource estimation in proposed QoS multicast systems. We also argue that the models are still based on simplified assumptions. The resource estimation will always be an estimate, not only because it is based on modeling assumption. The resource estimation is made when a source or receivers connect. It is therefore a point estimate for a longer period is the future. The accuracy of this point estimate will be a function of movement of all nodes involved and the delays in the information exchange between the nodes. It is therefore not given that more accurate models are the recommended path to follow.

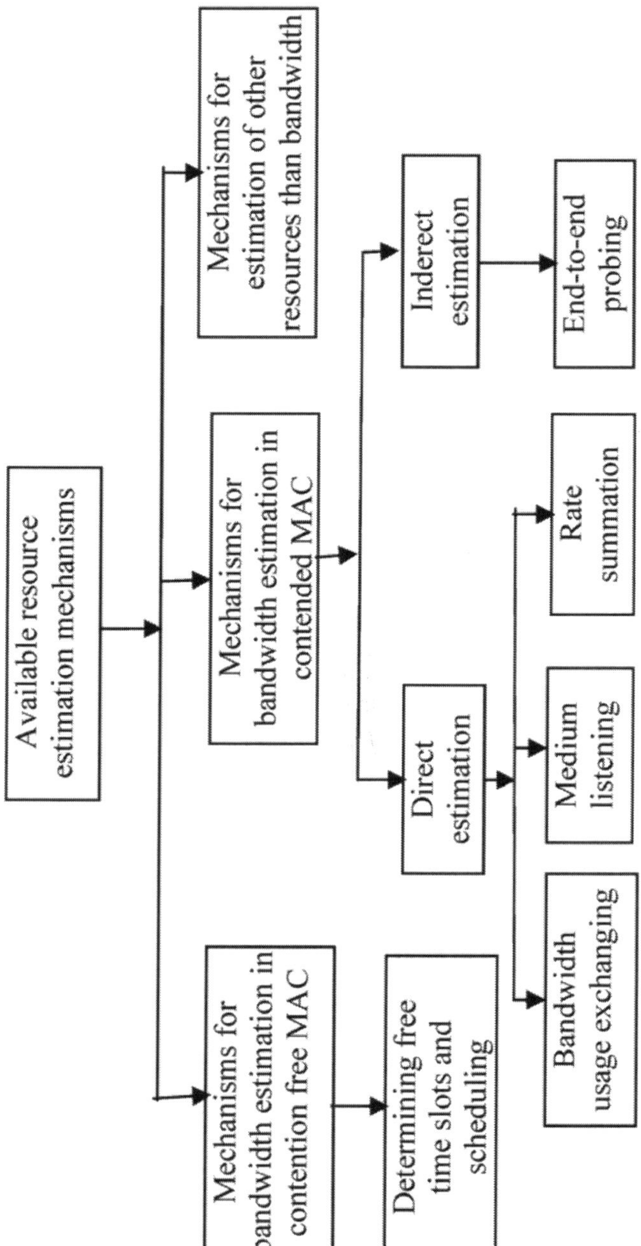

Figure 2. Classification of available resource estimation mechanisms.

2.5.2.2. Indirect Estimation (End-to-end Probing)

The alternative for estimation is to probe the network and measure the end-to-end performance from source to receiver as in [30] or from source to intermediate nodes as in [28]. In the former case, the source sends probes to the destinations. As soon as the destination receives the probe packets, it measures the achieved quality. If the difference between the quality of probe packets and required QoS (known prior) is within an accepted threshold, the receiver accepts the whole transmission; otherwise, it refuses. The method also introduces the priority of packets. The priority of the probe packets is lower than that of QoS multicast packets and higher than that of best effort packets. This priority assignment ensures that the probing traffic does not affect the existing QoS flows. An example of this mechanism is in M-CAMP [30]. In the later case, the sender also sends probe packets to the destinations. When a node receives a probe packet, it checks the QoS constraints and compares the metric (e.g., delay and cost) of the current probe packet with the previous probe packets. If the QoS constraints are satisfied and the metric of the new probe is better than the previous probes metric, the node change its predecessor to the node that the new probe packet came from. This strategy is called "the best predecessor replacement strategy". LACMQR [28] uses this technique for multicast routing.

2.5.3. Mechanisms for Estimation of Resources other than Bandwidth

In these mechanisms, there are no constraints on the kind of MAC layer, since the focus is on parameters at the path level like delay, route stability, power level, buffer level, streaming resolution, streaming continuity, *etc*.

In order to measure delay, the creation time of a route request message is usually included in the route request. When an intermediate node receives this message, delay is computed as the difference between the creation time and the current time. Such one-way measured delay consists of the queuing delay, the transmission time, the collision avoidance time, and the control overhead time. This measured delay is included on each routing table entry corresponding to each destination. QoS-AODV [19] is an example of this technique. The method assumes a synchronized network.

Node stability, called entropy in [25], is calculated based on speed and direction of the node and its neighbors. The end-to-end route stability of a path between two nodes is computed based on the entropy of the nodes along the path and the number of intermediate mobile nodes over the route. The value of end-to-end route stability is used to build the multicast tree. EQMGA [25] uses this technique for QoS multicast routing.

The stability level is defined as the connectivity variance of a node with respect to its neighboring nodes over time. It is obtained by the information of the frequency of the changes in the neighbors of the node. Based on the value of these metrics, protocol establishes the multicast tree. QoS-MAODV-2Lqos [43] considers three metrics (power level, buffer level, stability level) for multicast routing.

2.6. Mechanisms for Tree/Mesh Maintenance

Tree/mesh maintenance mechanisms can be divided into two categories: soft state maintenance and hard state maintenance. For the soft state maintenance technique, the tree/mesh is refreshed periodically by the source or receivers. The period interval is usually several seconds (e.g. six seconds in protocol E-QMR [16]). There is no need to have an additional technique for handling the link break or the leaving/joining of multicast members. When a link is broken, it is repaired automatically at the beginning of the refresh interval. Similarly, as a new node wants to join the multicast group, it waits until the route request is sent again from the source or it sends out a route request in case of receiver initiates tree/mesh structure. A receiver leaves the multicast group by not participating in the tree initiation process. The protocols in [11,13,15,16] use the soft state technique to maintain the tree/mesh.

Figure 3 depicts the classification of tree/mesh maintenance mechanisms in QoS enable multicast protocols.

If the hard state maintenance mechanism is used, an additional technique must be included to handle the link break, the joining of a new node, and the leaving of an existing member node. The main difference between the QoS multicast scheme for wired networks and ad hoc networks is the mobility handling. The nodes usually maintain the information about neighborhood nodes by hello message. The link breakage is detected when no HELLO packet or other control or data packets are received from its neighbors during an interval.

When there is a broken link, the upstream node or the downstream node will initiate an explicit message to recover the route. Similarly, when a node wants to join the multicast group, it initiates an explicit join message. The explicit message in both cases can be sent out locally or globally in the network. In the local maintenance technique, any node which is on the tree/mesh can reply to the message. Then a path from the new node to this member is established and the node joins the tree/mesh. The protocols in [12,29,30] are examples of this technique. In the global maintenance technique, only a source can reply to the explicit message to form a QoS satisfied path from the source to the requested node. This technique is used in [21,24,28].

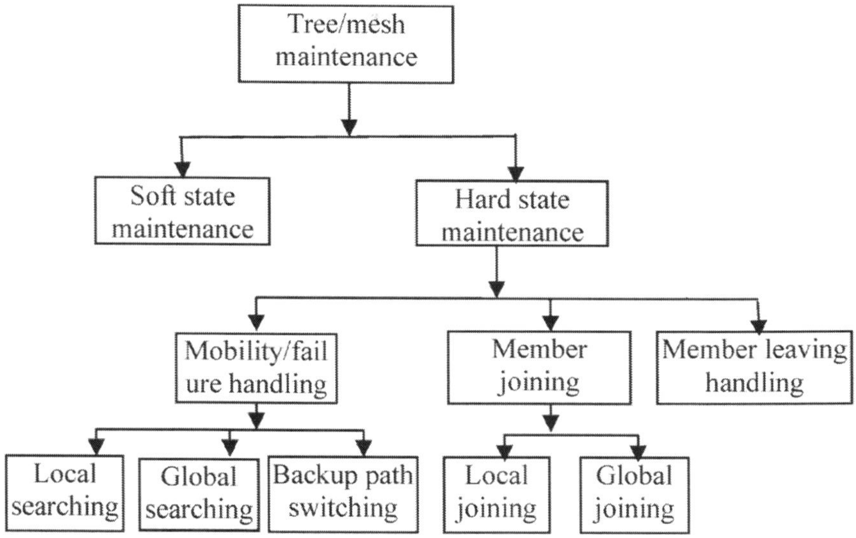

Figure 3. Classification of tree/mesh maintenance mechanisms.

Mesh structures are more robust against link breaks since packets are sent along primary and alternative paths. No separate mechanism is needed until both the primary and alternative paths are broken [11,15,16,18,37,42]. An extension of the mesh structure is to use pre-calculated alternative paths. These are used immediately when a link break is detected. HVDB [14] deals with mobility by using logical hypercube model where there are multiple disjoint local logical routes between each pair of cluster heads. When detecting a link breakage, multiple candidate logical routes become available immediately to sustain the service without QoS being degraded.

When a receiver wants to leave the multicast group, the associated resource must be released and the routing table of involved nodes must be updated. In this case, a prune packet is sent upstream and the upstream nodes will delete the downstream node from its downstream list for the tree in its multicast table. As the upstream node receives the prune packet, it checks whether it has a downstream node other than the receiver. If it has, the node simply deletes the receiver from its routing table. The prune packet is then discarded. If it has not, it deletes the entry for the receiver in its routing table and releases the reserved resource. The node then sends the prune packet to all its upstream nodes before it leaves the multicast tree/mesh and becomes a non-forwarding node. The process is performed until either the prune packet reaches the source or the prune packet is discarded.

2.7. Mechanisms for QoS Preemption

Preemption techniques can be broadly divided into two categories, implicit preemption and explicit preemption. Implicit preemption is the result of performing periodic admission control and resource reservation. Most protocols use this mechanism to maintain QoS condition. Only two protocols [11,17] use explicit preemption mechanism to detect and recover the QoS violation.

In QAMNet [11], each node monitors its real-time traffic class periodically. When QoS violations are detected, a flow is randomly selected and congestion experienced (CE) bit is set in all packets belonging to that flow. This implies that downstream nodes treat the packet as best effort.

In the scheme proposed by Hu [17], a receiver monitors the receiving packets delivered from the source to check whether the bandwidth requirement is obtained. If it detects a QoS violation (the route is unsatisfied), the node will find a new bandwidth-satisfied route to the source.

3. SIMULATION STUDY

The previous chapter mapped the various QoS multicast protocols onto a framework of design choices. A similar commonality does not exist in the performance evaluation of the protocols. In this chapter, we briefly summarize the common features of the evaluation, and identify scenarios that have to a lesser degree been used in the performance evaluation.

Only four of the surveyed protocols do not include a simulation evaluation [14,30,31,38]. Ns-2 [40] is the most popular simulator (9 out of 27) followed by GloMoSim [39] (6 out of 27). The parameters of the simulations vary to a large degree.

In Table 3 and Table 4 (see Appendix), we have tabulated different characteristics of the evaluation. Most of the protocols are evaluated without any common simulation parameter setting. For instance, the simulation area varies from 500 m × 500 m to 300m × 3000m, and transmission range varies from 30 m to up to 2000 m.

As other authors have noted [53], the simulation studies in the ad hoc field do not always give sufficient level of details. As shown in Table 3 and Table 4, for many protocols in the survey there is not sufficient information about parameter settings.

The number of nodes in a scenario varies from 10 nodes to 1500 nodes and reflects the various design goals of the protocols. The number of neighbors is calculated based on transmission range and node density range disregarding any boundary effect. The number is an indicator of whether the protocols are evaluated in topology sparse or dense environments (a number below 10 should be considered sparse).

The risk of network partitioning increases as the expected number of neighbors decreases. A protocol operating in a dense network is more likely to recover from link failure or routing failure compared to operating in more sparse environments. On the other hand, dense networks tend to have more interfering paths making it more difficult to estimate, reserve, or maintain QoS for the ongoing multicast sessions. A fair number of the protocols are evaluated in environments with less than 10 expected neighbors, where there is a risk of partitioned networks.

In Table 3, column 9 (number of nodes/expected number of neighbors) provides an indication of the length of the path from source to receivers. As a group, the protocols are evaluated over a reasonable set of expected path lengths.

Mobility of nodes varies from 0 m/s to 60 m/s. Most of the protocols use Random Waypoint as the mobility model (15/27 schemes). In this model, each node randomly selects the moving direction and move there at a random speed with a uniform distribution. Upon reaching the destination, the node stays there for some pause time. Upon expiration of the pause time, the next destination and speed are again chosen in the same way and the process repeats until the simulation ends. The schemes in [12,18] use the random direction and the random speed for nodes, while the scheme in [13] uses the random direction and the constant speed for nodes. Most scenarios are evaluated over a range of speeds ranging from no movement to vehicle speed (above 10 m/sec). Notable exceptions are [22,33,36], in which [22] evaluates with static nodes, [33] and [36] evaluates at very low mobility with speed ranging from 0 m/s to 1 m/s.

Although the set of protocols span a wide scenario, the multicast aspects of the scenarios were limited. A fair number of the evaluations only have one source per group which reflects a streaming scenario. Protocols in [15,17,21,22,24,25,26,32,36,50] are examples. The number of sources impacts on the efficiency of mechanisms of source specific tree and shared tree/mesh.

Tabe 3

No.	Protocol	Network parameters					Desity & Hops		Speed (m/sec)	Mobility Model	Type of Radio
		Simulator	Area (m × m)	Transmission Range (m)	Capacity (Mbps)	# Nodes	Neighbor Count (Density)	No. of Nodes/Neighbor Count			
1	QAMNet [11]	NS-2	1500 × 300	250	2	50	21.8	2.3	0–20	RWP	802.11 b
2	CQMRP [12]	NS-2	500 × 500	–	–	50	–	–	10–45	RR	–
3	QMRPCAH [13]	NS-2	–	–	1	200	–	–	2-20	CR	–
4	QoS-ODMRP[15]	GloMoSim	1000 × 1000	250	2	50	9.8	5	0.25–5	RWP	802.11
5	E-QMR [16]	GloMoSim	1000 × 1000	250	2	50–100	–	–	0–20	RWP	802.11
6	Hu [17]	NS-2	1000 × 1000	250	-	50	9.8	5	5–20	RWP	802.11
7	QMRP [18]	GloMoSim	1000 × 1000	250	2	50	9.8	5	3–20	RR	–
8	QoS-AODV [19]	NS-2	1500 × 300	250	-	50	21.8	2.3	0.5–20	RWP	–
9	HQMRP [21]	OMNeT++	3500 × 3250–6500 × 6250	2000	0.02	10–45	11–14	1.1–3.2	0–15	–	–
10	QoS-MEM [22]	–	1000 × 1000	50 mW*	–	20	-	-	0	–	–
11	LTM [23]	–	1000 × 1000	100	2	50, 100	1.6; 3.1	31.3–32.3	0–25	–	–
12	MPT [24]	–	100 × 100	30	–	100	28.3	3.5	Low	–	–
13	EQMGA [25]	NS -2	1000 × 1000	250	2	100	19.6	5.1	0–20	RWP	-
14	QMOST [26]	NS-2	1000 × 1000	250	–	100	19.6	5.1	0–10	RWP	802.11
15	LACMQR [28]	Glomosim	1000 × 1000	–	2	300–1500	–	–	–	–	–
16	AQM [29]	OPNET	1000 × 1000	250	10	10–100	2–19.6	5	1–4	RWP	–
17	QoS-MAODV [32]	Qualnet	1000 × 1000	250	2	50	9.8	5	0–42	RWP	802.11
18	HQMGA [33]	GTNetS	3000 × 3000	160	2	1000	8.9	112.4	0–1	RWP	802.11
19	QMR [44]	GloMoSim	1000 × 1000	250	2	50	9.8	5	0.25–5	RWP	802.11
20	EGA [35]	Self-developed	–	–	–	–	–	–	–	–	–
21	SEQMRAN [36]	NS-2	1500 × 300	250	11	50	21.8	2.3	0–1	RWP	802.11 b
22	FQM [37]	Glomosim	1000 × 1000	250	2	100	19.6	5.1	0–20	RWP	802.11

23	MACO [41]	–	–	–	–	20, 100	–	–	–	–	–
24	AMOMQ [42]	GloMosim	1000 × 1000	250	2	50	9.8	5	1–20	RWP	802.11
25	QoS-MAODV-2Lqos [43]	NS-2	1000 × 1000	250	2	60	11.8	5.1	10–60	RWP	802.11
26	HTQ [50]	NCTUns 2.0	1000 × 1000	200	5	20–50	2.5–6.3	8	0.28–11.1	–	–
27	QMMRP [51]	MATLAB	1000 × 1000	250	–	50–100	9.8–19.6	5.1	–	–	–

Notes:

- (–): there is lack of information about the characteristic in simulation of the protocol
- (a–b): the value ranges from a to b
- *: In QoS-MEM [22], transmission range is not provided while maximum transmission power is 50 mW, noise power is –50 dBm, minimum required SINR is 15 dB
- Neighbor count (density) = Π * r * r * N/A where r is transmission range; N is the total number of network nodes; A is area of the simulation area.
- No. of nodes/Neighbor count: Number of nodes/Neighbor count
- RWP: Random Waypoint mobility model

Table 4

No.	Protocol	Multicast group				Traffic type/pattern			Simulating Background Traffic
		# Group	# Sources per Group	# Receivers per Group	% Receivers per Group	Traffic Type	Packet Size (bytes)	Rate (kbps)	
1	QAMNet [11]	1	3	15	30%	CBR	330	118.8	Yes
2	CQMRP [12]	-	-	-	-	CBR	512	-	No
3	QMRPCAH [13]	1	-	10, 20, 50, 60, 100	5%–50%	Message length 5000 bits	-	Maximum 20 Mps	No
4	QoS-ODMRP [15]	3	1	-	-	CBR	512	128, 256, 512	No
5	E-QMR [16]	1	3	15	15%–30%	CBR	512	8	No
6	Hu [17]	10	1	3	6%	CBR	512	-	No
7	QMRP [18]	1	5	20	40%	CBR	512	8	No
8	QoS-AODV [19]	1	10	10–50	20%–100%	CBR	512	16 kbps	No
9	HQMRP [21]	1	1	3–7	15%–30%	1 session per minute	-	-	No
10	QoS-MEM [22]	1	1	5–20	25%–100%	-	-	-	No
11	LTM [23]	-	-	-	-	Message length 1-30Kb	-	-	No
12	MPT [24]	1	1	1-30	30%	-	-	-	Yes

13	EQMGA [25]	1	1	5–30	5%–30%	CBR	512	16–40	No
14	QMOST [26]	1	1	5–50	5%–50%	CBR	–	9.6; 200	Yes
15	LACMQR [28]	2	1–2	–	–	CBR	512	8	No
16	AQM [29]	–	–	–	–	Voice, audio, video	–	–	No
17	QoS-MAODV [32]	3	1	3–30	6%–60%	CBR	1024	128, 256, 512	No
18	HQMGA [33]	–	–	–	–	Stream	–	64	No
19	QMR [44]	1	3	15	15%–30%	CBR	512	8	No
20	EGA [35]	1	2	–	–	–	–	–	–
21	SEQMRAN [36]	9	1	5–50	10%–100%	CBR	256	4	No
22	FQM [37]	1	3	15	15%	CBR	–	118.8	Yes
23	MACO [41]	–	–	–	–	–	–	–	–
24	AMOMQ [42]	1	1–25	50	100%	CBR	512	–	No
25	QoS-MAODV-2Lqos [43]	1	5–25	50	83%	CBR	–	–	Yes
26	HTQ [50]	1	1	2–5	10%	Message length 1–4 Mbits	–	5 Mbps	No
27	QMMRP [51]	1	1	10–30	5%–60%	–	–	–	No

Notes:

- (–): there is lack of information about the characteristic in the simulation evaluated;
- (a–b): the value range from a to b.

Also along the axis of competing traffic the scenarios are limited. Only five schemes consider multiple groups in scenarios: [17] with 10 groups, [36] with nine groups, [15] and [32] with three groups, and [28] with two groups. In addition, only five schemes used background traffic [11,24,26,37,43]. It is not a realistic usage scenario when there is no background traffic in simulation. More important, it is also a limited test of the protocols ability to estimate capacity, interference and needed resource reservation of protocols.

The density of the receivers covers a larger range, but there are a few protocols that have only been evaluated for a limited range of variability. As a group, the protocols seems to have been evaluated for sufficient range of possible receiver densities.

Multicast is usually related to real time applications such as video streaming, audio conference. This is reflected in the universal use of Constant Bit Rate traffic generators (CBR). However, the large packet size more closely reflects packet sizes used in video and not in voice.

The evaluations encompass different metrics. The common ones are PDR (Packet Delivery Ratio), success rate, average latency, packet loss, and routing overhead. These are network centric and do not reflect the group aspect of multicast. Examples of such performance metrics are rate of successful joins and the fraction of groups using overloaded distribution trees [29].

There is no common set of usage scenarios, and therefore also no common performance metrics, topology and traffic scenario. The diversity in the simulation scenarios is therefore to be expected. However, the QoS aspect of the protocols necessitates mechanisms for resource reservation and resource usage. We had therefore expected a larger fraction of the simulation studies to include competing traffic from other groups and unicast traffic.

4. CONCLUSIONS

Our focus has been on discussing the possible alternatives in the design space. There are a large number of proposed protocols, but there are still multiple mechanisms that have not been fully investigated. There are at least three areas that should be investigated further, namely, heterogeneous networks, connectionless multicast and preemption.

- In heterogeneous ad hoc networks, nodes have different transmission ranges, channel capacity and receivers have different QoS requirements. This increases the risk of inconsistent routing tables. Also, performing admission control and resource reservation for different QoS requirements becomes challenging.

- Most of the protocols do not use preemption but utilize periodic admission control. In either case, random choice selects the flows, sources and receivers that are allowed or denied. Multicast packets do not have the same "value". The value of a packet decreases as it traverses the distribution tree or mesh. Its highest value is at the top, since the loss will affect the most receivers. At the same time, a tree with many receivers might have a different value than one with few receivers. None of such considerations are part of the preemption schemes evaluated.

- Connectionless multicast routing or source routing (source computes the route and includes identification of relay nodes in the packet) has only been included in a few protocols. In particular, when there are only a few receivers, and the groups have a limited lifetime, the overhead of maintaining state at all relay nodes might not be optimal.

In the previous section we discussed the evaluation of the proposed protocols. As other authors have clearly identified [53], there is need for a stricter documentation and more common evaluation scenarios. These conclusions also are valid for the subgroup of proposals we have analyzed. QoS in multicast is needed in media distribution, and in an ad hoc network this cannot only be associated with streaming. The protocols should therefore also be evaluated for a larger set of groups and sources. The traffic models should also reflect a wider set of types and background traffic. The latter is important, for it is unlikely, that ad hoc networks are dedicated to only multicast.

A possible lack in most of the proposals is the application viewpoint. For example, few of them discuss the implication of admission control and the application. For some of the proposals, one could risk that participants in video conferences did not have a full mesh view of all the other participants. We believe that future proposals should take an application viewpoint when designing admission control and preemption mechanisms.

REFERENCES

1. Junhai, L.; Danxia, Y.; Liu, X.; Mingyu, F. A survey of multicast routing protocols for mobile Ad-Hoc networks. IEEE Commun. Surv. Tutor. 2009, 11, 78–91.

2. Hashim, A.A.; Qabajeh, M.M.; Khalifa, O.; Qabajeh, L. Review of multicast QoS routing protocols for mobile ad hoc networks. IJCSNS 2008, 8, 108–117.

3. Perkins, D.D; Hughes, H.D. A survey on quality-of-service support for mobile ad hoc networks. WCMC 2002, 2, 503–513.

4. Murthy, C.S.R.; Reddy, T.B.; Karthigeyan, I.; Manoj, B.S. Quality of service provisioning in ad hoc wireless networks: a survey of issues and solutions. Ad Hoc Netw. 2006, 4, 83–124.

5. Striegel, A.; Manimaran, G. A survey of QoS multicasting issues. IEEE Commun. Mag. 2002, 40, 82–87.

6. Papavassiliou, S.; An, B. Supporting multicasting in mobile ad-hoc wireless networks: Issues, challenges, and current protocols. WCMC 2002, 2, 115–130.

7. Hanzo-II, L.; Tafazolli, R. A survey of QoS routing solutions for mobile ad hoc networks. IEEE Commun. Surv. Tutor.2007, 9, 50–70.

8. Badarneh, O.S.; Kadoch, M. Multicast routing protocols in mobile ad hoc networks: A comparative survey and taxonomy. EURASIP J. Wirel. Commun. Netw. 2009, 2009. Article ID 764047.

9. Cordeiro, C.M.; Gossain, H.; Agrawal, D. Multicast over wireless mobile ad hoc networks: Present and future directions. IEEE Netw. 2003, 17, 52–59.

10. Masoudifar, M. A review and performance comparison of QoS multicast routing protocols for MANETs. Ad Hoc Netw.2009, 7, 1150–1155.

11. Tebbe, H.; Kassler, A.J.; Ruiz, P.M. QoS-Aware Mesh Construction to Enhance Multicast Routing in Mobile Ad Hoc Networks. In Proceedings of the First International Conference on Integrated Internet Ad Hoc and Sensor Networks, Nice, France, May 2006.

12. Nargunam, A.S.; Sebastian, M.P. QoS-aware multicast routing for mobile ad hoc networks. Int. J. Bus. Data Commun. Netw. 2008, 4, 1–21.

13. Chunlin, L.; Layuan, L. A QoS multicast routing protocol for clustering mobile ad hoc networks. Comput. Commun.2007, 30, 1641–1654.

14. Wang, G.; Cao, J.; Zhang, L.; Chan, K.C.C.; Wu, J. A Novel QoS Multicast Model in Mobile Ad Hoc Networks. In Proceedings of the

19th IEEE international Parallel and Distributed Processing Symposium (Ipdps'05)—Workshop 8, Denver, CO, USA, April 2005.

15. Darehshoorzadeh, A.; Dehghan, M.; Motlagh, M.R.J. Quality of service support for ODMRP multicast routing in ad hoc networks. Lect. Note. Comput. Sci. 2007, 4686, 237–247.

16. Saghir, M.; Wan, T.; Budiarto, R. QoS Multicast Routing Based on Bandwidth Estimation in Mobile Ad Hoc Networks. In Proceedings of the International Conference on Computer and Communication Engineering, Kuala Lumpur, Malaysia, May 2006; pp. 9–11.

17. Hu, C.; Wu, E.H.-K.; Chen, G. Bandwidth-satisfied multicast trees in MANETs. IEEE Trans. Mob. Comput. 2008, 7, 712–723.

18. Promkotwong, D.; Ohm, S. A Mesh-Based QoS Aware Multicast Routing Protocol. In Proceedings of the 8th ACIS International Conference on Software Engineering, Artificial Intelligence, Networking, and Parallel/Distributed Computing, Qingdao, China, 31 July–1 August 2007; pp. 1046–1051.

19. Brahim, I.B.; Jemaa, M.B. Multicast Routing Protocol for Ad Hoc Networks with a Quality of Service <<Qos-AODV>>. In Proceedings of the IEEE International Conference on Electronics, Circuits, and Systems, Gammarth, Tunisia, December 2005.

20. Manoharan, R.; Thambidurai, P. Hypercube Based Team Multicast Routing Protocol for Mobile Ad Hoc Networks. In Proceedings of the 9th International Conference on Information Technology, Bhubaneswar, India, December 2006; pp. 56–59.

21. Wang, W.; Soong, B.; Chew, J. A Novel Protocol of QoS Multicasting for Large Scale MANET. In Proceedings of the First IEEE Conference on Industrial Electronics and Applications, Singapore, May 2006; pp. 79–84.

22. Guo, S.; Yang, O. QoS-aware minimum energy multicast tree construction in wireless ad hoc networks. Ad Hoc Netw.2004, 2, 217–229.

23. Chen, Y.; Ko, Y. A lantern-tree-based QoS on-demand multicast protocol for a wireless mobile ad hoc network. IEICE Trans. Commun. 2004, E87-B, 717–726.

24. Wu, H.; Jia, X. QoS multicast routing by using multiple paths/trees in wireless ad hoc networks. Ad Hoc Netw. 2007, 5, 600–612.

25. Chen, H.; Sun, B.; Zeng, Y. QoS Multicast Routing Algorithm in MANET: An Entropy-Based GA. In Proceedings of the International Conference on Intelligent Computing, Kunming, China, August 2006; pp. 1279–1289.

26. Hakim, B. A QoS-Aware Multicast Routing Protocol for Multimedia Applications in Mobile Ad Hoc Networks. In Proceedings of the 11th ACM International Conference on Modeling, Analysis, and Simulation of Wireless and Mobile Systems, Vancouver, Canada, October 2008; pp. 244–251.

27. Chen, Y.; Lin, T.; Lin, Y. A hexagonal-tree TDMA-based QoS multicasting protocol for wireless mobile ad hoc networks. Telecommun. Syst. Model. Anal. Des. Manag. 2007, 35, 1–20.

28. Shih, T.; Shih, C.; Chen, C. Location-based multicast routing protocol for mobile ad hoc networks. WSEAS Transac. Comput. 2008, 7, 1270–1279.

29. Bür, K.; Ersoy, C. Ad hoc quality of service multicast routing. Comput. Commun. 2005, 29, 136–148.

30. Pagani, E.; Rossi, G.P. A Framework for the Admission Control of QoS Multicast Traffic in Mobile Ad Hoc Networks. In Proceedings of the 4th ACM international workshop on Wireless mobile multimedia, Rome, Italy, 2001; pp. 2–11.

31. Sinha, P.; Sivakumar, R.; Bharghavan, V. MCEDAR: Multicast Core-Extraction Distributed Ad Hoc Routing. In Proceedings of the IEEE Wireless Communications and Networking Conference, New Orleans, LA, USA, September 1999; pp. 1313–1317.

32. Vida Lashkari, B.O.; Dehghan, M. QoS-aware Multicast Ad Hoc On-Demand Distance Vector Routing. In Proceedings of the World Congress on Engineering, London, UK, July 2007; pp. 1506–1511.

33. Takashima, E.; Murata, Y.; Shibata, N.; Yasumoto, K.; Ito, M. A Method for Distributed Computation of Semi-Optimal Multicast Tree in MANET. In Proceedings of the 8th IEEE Wireless Communications and Networking Conference, Kowloon, China, March 2007.

34. Macker, J.; Dean, J; Chao, W. Simplified Multicast Forwarding in Mobile Ad Hoc Networks. In Proceedings of the 2004 IEEE Military Communications Conference, Monterey, CA, USA, 31 October–3 November 2004; pp. 744–750.

35. Yen, Y.; Chan, Y.; Chao, H.; Park, J.H. A genetic algorithm for energy-efficient based multicast routing on MANETs.Comput. Commun. 2008, 31, 2632–2641.

36. Yang, M.; Layuan, L.; Fang, Y. Secure Efficient QoS Multicast Route Discovery for MANET. In Proceedings of the First International Conference on Communications and Networking in China, Beijing, China, October 2006; pp. 1–5.

37. Saghir, M.; Wan, T.; Budiarto, R. A new cross-layer framework for QoS multicast applications in mobile ad hoc networks. IJCSNS 2006, 6, 142–151.

38. Ng, J.M.; Low, C.P.; Teo, H.S. On-Demand QoS Multicast Routing and Reservation Protocol for MANETs. In Proceedings of the 2004 IEEE 15th International Symposium on Personal, Indoor and Mobile Radio Communications, Barcelona, Spain, September 2004; pp. 2504–2508.

39. Glomosim. Available online: http://pcl.cs.ucla.edu/projects/glomosim/ (accessed on 26 August 2010).

40. Network Simulator (Version 2). 2008. Available online: http://www.isi.edu/nsnam/ns/ (accessed on 26 August 2010).

41. Wang, H.; Shi, Z. An Ant Colony Algorithm Based on Orientation Factor for QoS Multicast Routing in Ad Hoc Networks. In Proceedings of the 2008 Third International Conference on Communications and Networking in China, Hangzhou, China, August 2008; pp. 321–326.

42. Nourazar, S.; Dehghan, M. AMOMQ: Ad-Hoc Mesh-Based On-demand Multicast Routing Protocol with Quality of Service Support. In Proceedings of the 2009 International Association of Computer Science and Information Technology—Spring Conference, Singapore, April 2009; pp. 95–99.

43. Latha, P.; Ramachandran, R. QoS Constrained Multicast Routing for Mobile Ad Hoc Networks. IJCSNS 2009, 9, 66–70.

44. Saghir, M.; Wan, T.C.; Budiarto, R. Load Balancing QoS Multicast Routing Protocol in Mobile Ad Hoc Networks. InLecture Notes in Computer Science; Cho, K., Jacquet, P., Eds.; Springer-Verlag: Berlin, Germany, 2005; Volume 3837/2005, pp. 83–97.

45. Bür, K.; Ersoy, C. Ad hoc quality of service multicast routing with objection queries for admission control. Eur. Trans. Telecommun. 2006, 17, 561–576.

46. Larsen, E.; Landmark, L.; Pham, V.; Engelstady, P.E.; Kure, Ø. Preemption mechanisms for push-to-talk in ad hoc networks. In Proceedings of the 2009 IEEE 34th Conference on Local Computer Networks, Zurich, Switzerland, October 2009; pp. 428–435.

47. Zhao, H.; Garcia-Palacios, E.; Wei, J.; Xi, Y. Accurate available bandwidth estimation in IEEE 802.11-based ad hoc networks. Comput. Commun. 2009, 32, 1050–1057.

48. Lin, C.R. Admission control in time-slotted multihop mobile networks. IEEE J. Sel. Area. Commun. 2001, 19, 1974–1983.

49. Clausen, T.; Jacquet, P. Optimized Link State Routing Protocol (Olsr). RFC Editor 2003. RFC 3626.

50. Chen, Y.; Lin, T.; Lin, Y. A hexagonal-tree TDMA-based QoS multicasting protocol for wireless mobile ad hoc networks. Telecommun. Syst. 2007, 35, 1–20.

51. Badarneh, O.; Kadoch, M.; Elhakeem, A. QoS multilayered multicast routing protocol for video transmission in heterogeneous wireless ad hoc networks. WSEAS Trans. Comput. 2008, 7, 680–693.

52. Chen, L.; Heinzelman, W.B. QoS-aware routing based on bandwidth estimation for mobile ad hoc networks. IEEE J. Sel. Area. Commun. 2005, 23, 561–572.

53. Kurkowski, S.; Camp, T.; Colagrosso, M. MANET Simulation Studies: The Incredibles. MC2R 2005, 9, 50–61.

54. Li, J.; Blake, C.; De Couto, D.S.; Lee, H.I.; Morris, R. Capacity of ad hoc wireless networks. In Proceedings of the 7th Annual international Conference on Mobile Computing and Networking, MobiCom '01, Rome, Italy; 2001; pp. 61–69.

55. Braden, R.; Zhang, L.; Berson, S.; Herzog, S.; Jamin, S. Resource reSerVation Protocol (RSVP)-Version 1 Functional Specification. RFC Editor 1997. RFC 2205.

56. Badis, H.; Al Agha, K. Quality of Service for Ad Hoc Optimized Link State Routing Protocol (QOLSR). Draft IETF2007. draft-badis-manet-qolsr-05.txt.

Index